The Hiker's Guide
to **Wyoming**

by
Bill Hunger

D0232788

FALCON™

Falcon Press® Publishing, Co., Inc.
Helena, Montana

ACKNOWLEDGMENTS

Many people helped this book expand into being, and most of them own names I do not know. The numerous Forest Service, Bureau of Land Management, National Park and Wyoming State Parks personnel who cheerfully answered my ceaseless questions; the many folks met along the way who freely gave me advice or offered me directions or cued me onto a new and exciting adventure; some very special persons who helped extricate me from the seeming disasters that happened along the journey; I can only send a lump thank you to all of you and hope it expresses some of the gratitude I feel.

Special thanks goes to the friends who contributed hike descriptions to this book, whose names you'll meet when you read their hikes. Thanks also to Bruce, who forwarded my name to Mac Bates, and to Mac, the most friendly and helpful editor I know.

Most thanks and the book's dedication goes to you, Jill. Without your multi-level support and love, nothing could have happened.

Unless otherwise indicated, all hike descriptions, photos, and stories are by the author.

Falcon Press Publishing Co., Inc.
P.O. Box 1718, Helena, MT 59624

All text, maps, and photos by the authors except as noted.
Cover Photo: by Peter Cole of Clear Lake and Haystack Peak in the Wind Rivers.

Library of Congress Cataloging-in-Publication Data

Hunger, Bill.
   The hiker's guide to Wyoming / by Bill Hunger.—Helena, MT
: Falcon Press, c1992.
     viii, 222 p. : ill., maps ; 23cm.
   ISBN 1-56044-373-1 :
   1. Hiking—Wyoming—Guidebooks. 2. Wyoming—Guidebooks. I. Title.
GV199.42.W8H86 1992   91787—dc20   91-77718
                                          AACR 2 MARC

♻ Text pages printed on recycled paper

CONTENTS

Pool Hot Springs (handwritten margin note)

Caution

Outdoor recreation activities are by their very nature potentially hazardous. All participants in such activities must assume the responsibility for their own actions and safety. The information contained in this guidebook cannot replace sound judgment and good decision-making skills, which help reduce risk exposure, nor does the scope of this book allow for disclosure of all the potential hazards and risks involved in such activities.

Learn as much as possible about the outdoor recreation activities you participate in, prepare for the unexpected, and be safe and cautious. The reward will be a safer and more enjoyable experience.

LOCATION OF HIKES

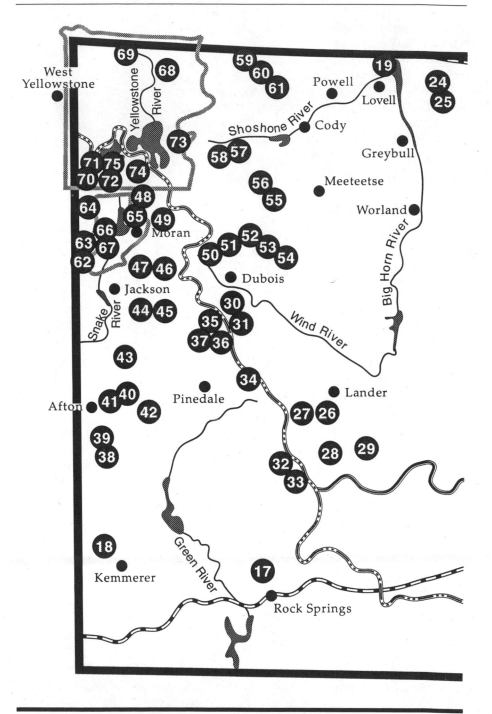

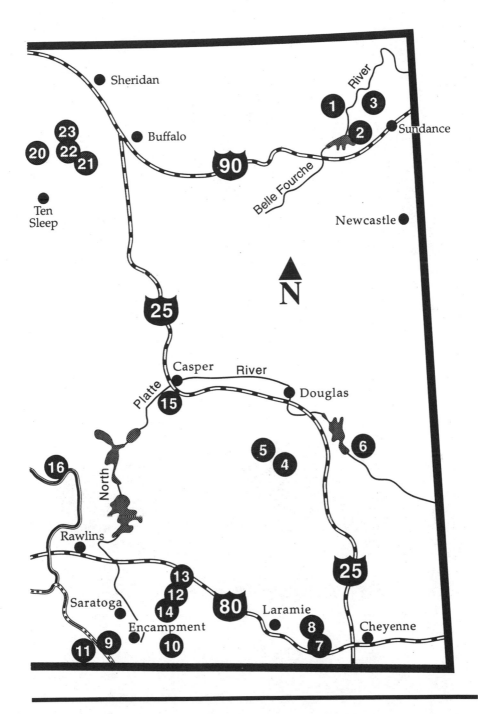

Beauty Lake with Beartooth Butte on the right horizon. JERRY SWAFFORD PHOTO.

HIKING IN WYOMING, AN INTRODUCTION

Welcome to the Rattlesnake Hills! Not exactly the descriptive name you had in mind for this summer's family hiking vacation? Then you probably won't be too interested in visiting the Freezeout Mountains, Hell's Half Acre, or Poison Spider Creek. Tiny towns or former villages like Badwater, Sand Draw, and Smoot may not make the itinerary either.

But look further, deeper into this amazing land that derives its name from a Leni Lenape Indian word that means "undulating plains and mountains." You'll easily find geographic appellations and titles that arouse your curiosity—Devil's Tower and Fossil Butte Monuments for instance, or Soapy Date and Ramshorn Peaks. There are one-time villages named Pitchfork and Goose Egg. Look even further, both on the maps and into your mind, and alluring, almost mystical signatures call. What explorer wouldn't want to hike Two Ocean Pass, Medicine Mountain, Cloud, Sacajawea, and Hallalujah peaks? Diamondville was perhaps quite a town in its time, and by its very name, the Sweetwater River tells a story.

Welcome to Wyoming, an explorer's paradise, a land renowned for both its scenic grandeur and the elements of wild nature that still thrive within that beauty. Wyoming has been labeled "the Alaska of the lower 48 States," but don't let labels precondition your images of the state and thus detract from experiencing it. "Maughwauwama" (that Leni Lenape Indian word), with its vast and unique wild lands, with its remaining large herds of wild animals, defies earmarks and defines itself quite adequately to the persons taking the time to explore and feel it.

This is a hiker's guide to the entire state, and as such it accurately describes hikes and trails and allows you an overview access to information on some of the scenery and adventure to be found. The remarkable history and folklore, the fascinating geological and ecological tales of the state are necessarily excluded except as they may briefly relate to a specific hike. It's my hope that in tasting the picturesque beauty of the state, you'll also be piqued to learn what incident, allegory, or anecdote lies behind the naming of places such as Meeteetse or Bridger or Flaming Gorge.

Actually, a few of the more colorful stories and experiences that illustrate the flavor of Wyoming's trails are presented throughout the book. I was a wilderness ranger for many years in some of the wildest country in the state. The humor and the legends, the vibrations of past events (both wicked and good) that accompany this country are unignorable to any hiker who listens. As you explore the country and trails, you can't help but hear these stories being whispered; you become part of them; you actually help create some of them when you hike Wyoming.

Remember, the hikes presented here are merely introductions. So often, especially in the vast wilderness areas of northwestern Wyoming, the trails can wander for unlimited miles while endless other paths intersect or cross the main trail's course. If I had followed every trail and side trail as far as possible, this would be a guidebook of about seven hikes. Use it as an up-to-date beginning to your own adventures.

Remember too, a state that is wild and beautiful is also a state that is threatened. Natural resources are in constant and greater demand, and Wyoming is a major natural resource supplier. Mineral and timber extraction, along with the developments that surround them, have the potential to irrevocably scar pristine parts of Wyoming. So do enjoy Wyoming's unique beauty and then help protect it by contacting/joining/supporting any of the conservation groups working to protect the state.

More importantly, be a visitor who leaves nary of trace of his visit. Ever-increasing numbers of wildland visitors are yielding greater negative impacts on the lands, which in turn necessitates more restrictions, which tends to knock the wild right out of wilderness. Read the essay on no impact hiking/camping included in this book and then implement its principles into your explorations. Rather than a dry listing of those principles, I've tried to make it and the safety guidelines especially interesting. They reflect my years of wilderness ranger experience in dealing with backcountry cleanup ethics and emergency situations.

The only way you'll be able to extend a true "Welcome to Wyoming" greeting to someone else is if you've both enjoyed the beauty of the state and helped protect it for others.

SAFETY

If you've ever sat near a 12,000-foot Wyoming mountain pass on July 4th, huddled and shivering in a collapsed tent with a drippy sleeping bag around you, watching the landscape and your summer trip die under six inches of raging white blizzard, you know that the high country does not play lightly with the unprepared.

Every Forest Service handout and hiker's guide supplies a safety checklist, and it certainly is a good idea to review something so beneficial before venturing into the backcountry. I've noticed that hikers who read standard, dry checklists often ignore the importance of why certain items are included in these lists. This particular safety list will be presented from an EMT-trained wilderness ranger's perspective and offer you the more common emergencies and blunders that a minimal amount of preparedness would have eliminated or at least mitigated.

In simple terms, there are three principles—all equally important—that should be an automatic part of every hiker's internal repertoire.

• Be trained in, and be able to execute in the field, advanced first aid. In drownings, traumatic shock, and lightning shock situations, in heart attack and other such emergencies, CPR saves lives. To be able to stop bleeding, splint fractures, dress burns properly is to be able to act appropriately and make a difference. No one knowing first aid in a group of six hikers leaves five people capable of running out to get help and no one able to help the accident victim. One person knowing first aid in said group may create the same situation if that one is the person hurt.

• Know, and again be able to execute in the field, survival techniques and tricks. A little knowledge in this field can go a long ways in unexpected circumstances. A vital part of this preparation is to carry proper emergency gear. We can't all be Tom Brown Jr.'s and both endure and thrive in the worst survival situations. But an emergency dry shelter and dry matches, a flashlight, whistle, and signal mirror, some first aid supplies, and high-energy food rations carried at all times in a small survival pack may make a big difference in the wilderness.

• One and two above, and the several safety specifics listed below will blow away with the wind if, in an emergency situation, panic claims the mind. In a minor rock slide, the panicked person freezes and gets hit with flying rocks while the calm person anticipates the stones' pathways and dodges the missiles. A lost hiker who panics usually travels a wayward path that further displaces him (and makes rescue all the more difficult), while someone in the same predicament who calms his mind and thinks through the situation can often backtrack or rationalize his way to safety—or at least remember to stay in one spot until searchers find him. If panic isn't hindering or blocking it, the rational or intuitive mind can usually find or remember a solution to a bad situation.

• Actually, there is an equally important fourth principle. In fact, much of the wilderness country of Wyoming demands that you be astute in the art of map and compass orientation. Included in an appendix to this book is a short course on the subject. But as the treatise author says, be certain you're practiced in the initiation of this necessary skill before venturing into the wilds.

Many seemingly pure mountain lakes may be contaminated with giardia.

Being prepared for wilderness emergencies is an important consideration. But many situations that require such action wouldn't have happened if folks had been more aware of certain dangers and cured the problem via prevention before it began. The following are some of the more common ticklish situations I've seen (for both others and myself) that simply beg for an ounce of prevention.

Altitude sickness.

It's amazing how many people journey to the Wind Rivers from sea level and plan to ascend Gannett Peak, Wyoming's highest. Few guidebook safety lists mention this one, but it's a most common problem. The unacclimated brain and body, deprived of oxygen at higher altitudes, can induce everything from vomiting to total disorientation and confusion. I have practically carried babbling, seemingly mindless persons off peaks and had them not remember a moment of the ordeal when they reached a lower altitude and reclaimed their senses. If you're not acclimated to high elevations, go slow, take several days inuring yourself before bounding to a peak summit. If you feel woozy, sit down and rest and slack off your pace. If you start to get lightheaded and sick, have your friends help you to a lower elevation. Don't be left alone, and don't leave someone alone if altitude sickness is a potential.

A less-serious corollary happens when once-a-year hikers overuse an under-developed body. Fifteen miles in full backpack the first day out can so tie up the muscles in your body that the rest of the trip—if you can stand to hike at all—is absolute agony. Distance isn't as important as enjoying the beauty and preserving yourself while doing it.

Hypothermia and dehydration.

Most safety treatises stress the first condition and ignore the second. The truth is, one of the contributing factors to hypothermia is dehydration. The other, more obvious factors are cold, wind, and wet. Hypothermia can catch the most experienced hiker unawares, and surprisingly, most cases develop when the air temperatures are above freezing in the thirty- to fifty-degree range. Prevention is the easy cure. Stay dry. Keep your energy up with lots of snacks and drinks. Continually adapt the layering of your clothes so you neither sweat too much when exerting nor get chilled when resting. A hypothermic person experiences shivering fits, fumbles things, slurs his speech, stumbles, appears exhausted, and is exceptionally slow to get started after a rest. A hypothermic person will also deny he is hypothermic. Understand that there is virtually no way a hypothermic body can warm itself. Outside heat sources are required. Warm drinks, warm and dry clothes, and a fire help a mildly impaired person. You can wrap a severely hypothermic person in a dozen sleeping bags and his core body temperature will continue to decline. Your bare body next to his bare body, both inside the bags, is the survival key.

Another note on dehydration: When the body is thirsty, it's already slightly dehydrated. Prevention calls for frequent drinks even when not thirsty and "tanking up"—drinking a very large amount of water in one sitting—if the distance to the next drink is far.

Weather

Especially lightning. Lightning striking humans rarely happens in the wilderness. But getting caught in a violent, and perhaps scary, electrical storm in the Wyoming high country is a better-than-average probability. Prevention says to not climb the peak that day if storm clouds are rapidly forming at ten in the morning. But the usual pattern is a perfect day's beginning and a sudden cluster of nasty-looking clouds coming from nowhere when you're a far distance from timberline and shelter. Don't panic. Take this opportunity to witness one of the most spectacular and powerful displays of Nature's might while you crouch on the leeward side of a boulder or rock overhang. And do crouch. Don't sit or lie on the ground. While lightning almost never strikes a person, when it strikes the earth it does create all sorts of erratic electrical currents throughout the ground. Squatting on your rubber-soled boots better insulates you from those charges. Also, it's wisest to seek separate shelters and not cluster your entire group in one setting. If a mishap does result from the storm, not everyone will be hurt, and there will be someone capable of rendering aid.

Winds, violent and erratic, can rise at any moment day and night. Be sure that you've visually checked the trees around your campsite to ascertain that none are precariously leaning toward your tent.

Are you prepared (footgear included) if it rains solidly for three straight days? If it freezes at night? If it snows and freezes during the day? Can your face and nose and ears handle eight days of intense high altitude sun beaming on them? Count on one double negative when it comes to backcountry weather: It will not not surprise you.

Stream crossings

Wyoming was originally designed for horse travel. We who propel ourselves with our own legs for our own enjoyment are a later evolutionary species, and many of the trails haven't adapted to the reality of our foot travel. Bridges over streams and rivers in many areas are often nonexistant. Those waterways, even the smaller ones, are swift and ice cold with slippery, unstable rocks and deep potholes. More than half of the above safety and emergency considerations can suddenly be a reality with one flubbed stream crossing. A solid, long walking stick and a pair of lightweight tennis shoes on the feet greatly aid the wading process. Have your pack waist strap unbuckled so if you slip and go under the water you can extract yourself from your pack and not be weighted by it. Many mountain streams are easily crossable in the cool morning and due to snow melt become raging torrents by evening. Many day hikes have been transformed into impromptu overnighters because of this factor. Ultimately, don't chance crossing a waterway if it looks or feels too treacherous.

Giardia et al.

The moment you decide that the mountain water gods must like you because you've never gotten sick from the water, you may discover that the mountain water gods have a morbid sense of humor. *Giardiasis* is to be considered a potential in every drop of water everywhere in the country. The affliction is absolutely preventable only by boiling water (five minutes) or by purifying it with a specific filter. If you find yourself in sudden fits of diarrhea, fatigue and severe cramps, it's time to leave and seek medical help. If infected, remember to drink copious liquids to combat the dehydrating effects of this invisible protozoan.

Critters.

Little ones, that is. Wyoming's horse flies seem bigger than sea gulls and more persistant than Montana winters. Bites from deer flies form the epitome of a painful experience. Mosquito numbers in certain areas at certain times of the year will give you a new definition of the word "infinite." Long sleeved and legged clothing and adequate bug dope are the sanest preventions. Also know your allergy limits to bee stings and tick bites.

Common sense is the simple prescription for hiking and camping safety. If she hadn't camped right on the trail, she wouldn't have been run over by a herd of horses galloping toward the trailhead at night. If he hadn't stepped so close to the cornice's end, he wouldn't have slipped on the ice and slid out-of-control down several hundred feet of steep snow to ricochet into the boulder field below. If I had positively identified that mushroom, my friend and I wouldn't have spent the night vomiting and being too weak to raise a finger to do anything about it. Planning, preparation, and common sense are the keys to backcountry safety. Make them constant and automatic, and you can enjoy Nature and your presence in Her to the fullest.

MAP LEGEND

MAP LEGEND:

Trail Described	⊖- - - - - - -	Paved Road	▭▭▭▭
Alternate Trail	⊖- - - - - - -	Dirt Road	= = = =:
Cross Country Route	··············	Interstate	⬤ 00
Trail Hiking Directions	▶ ◀	U.S. Highway	00
National Forests	▬▬▬▬	State or Other Principal Road	000
National Monument	▬▬▬▬		
Wilderness Boundary	▬▬▬▬	Forest Road	000
State Park	▬▬▬▬	BLM Road	000
National Park	▬▬▬▬	STATE BOUNDARY	
Continental Divide	▬▬▬▬	Ranger Station	▲
Intermittent Stream	·· ·· ·· ·· ·	Building	■
Falls/Rapids	∿╫	Campground	⋀
Springs	⟋	Picnic Area	⋤
River/Creeks	∿	Mine	⚒
Lakes	⬬	Pass	) (
Glacier	◹	Peak	▲▲
		Ridge	⋀⋀⋀⋀

7

BACKCOUNTRY ETHICS

As a wilderness ranger I was often asked what is the worst situation hikers might encounter on their long trips into the backcountry. Bears? Getting caught in a ferocious lightning storm, or a many-day rainstorm and the resultant flooding creeks? Breaking a leg far from the nearest trailhead?

Actually, it's people. Not you and I, the people searching for Nature's beauty and adventure hiking wildland trails. If people themselves were a trauma to me, I never would have been a wilderness ranger whose job was to contact and communicate with people, and I surely would not be writing a hiker's guide that exposes some of my favorite areas to other persons. But I admit to pain and resentment when I witness the disagreeable results of the actions of unthinking, uncaring, or too many people in the backcountry.

Twenty years ago, managing agencies began promoting no-trace camping and pack-out-what-you-pack-in ethics. They had to. Twenty years ago it was becoming too obvious that multiple campfire rings, stomped-to-death camp-sites, firewood scarcities, and ubiquitous human waste and toilet paper piles were destroying the fragile resource called wilderness. Trails are like rivers. They funnel large groups of persons into singular and specific, often fragile, areas. Thousands of pristine acres can surround the hiker and yet he or she will discover that the immediate setting around a campsite is an absolute mess, because that is where everyone visiting has to hike, camp, and defecate.

Following is a brief listing of the do's and don't's of backcountry keep-it-clean ethics. The principles are a simple mixture of common sense, courtesy for others, and respect for the land. The principles are in every Forest and Park Service handout and hiking book. But in the 1990's—the twenty years later—there's an added factor. "Pack out what you pack in" and "Leave the country as you found it" are mere beginnings. Today these guidelines need to be amended to "Pack out more than you pack in" and "Leave the country in better shape than you found it." This often translates to "Clean up somebody else's mess." If you feel like showing appreciation to the wild country that shows you so much beauty, it's easy to acquire and practice this caring attitude.

Sanitation

The Forest Service recommends you place at least 100 feet between your duty and any water supply, trail, or campsite, but that's not far enough. Twenty years of this advice has left popular campsites surrounded by a septic ring of little troweled pits and displaced rocks that you know what is under—all a mere hundred or so feet away. In this situation, think not in terms of feet, but in terms of yards. Two hundred yards. By traveling that far you'll see views and microenvironments no one else witnesses, and you won't be unearthing someone else's sewage while disposing of your own.

A hole dug six to eight inches deep is the recommended waste burying procedure. A bit shallower, if you can still camouflage the action, is better. More bacteria reside in the soil closer to the surface, and through their action the waste will decompose faster. Burning toilet paper is a good practice, but if your shallow hole is surrounded by dry organic matter, it's safer to pack out the TP in a plastic bag.

Trash

The only thing surer than the fact that aluminum does not burn is the fact that a surprisingly large number of people believe it does. An outfitter guide and I spent an entire night sitting around a blazing campfire, telling Forest Service jokes and kindling a hot fire fueled on the challenge of a bet. He wagered that aluminum did disappear if the fire was hot enough; I maintained that the stuff was elemental and couldn't vanish. The result? Probing the campfire ashes revealed thousands of tiny aluminum blobs sitting beneath the burn pile. From that night on I never saw a trace of aluminum or anything else left in this man's campsites. Such must be the case with all trash—including the ubiquitous candy wrapper. An attitude of packing out what others leave behind goes a long way in helping wilderness remain wild.

Numbers of people

The days of forty people in a single survival class all camping by a lake and fishing it out in three days are mostly gone. It's both illegal in the administrating agency's eyes and undesirable in the school's program, but I still encounter large groups. The resultant noise and impact on meadows and lakes is inevitable no matter how conscientious the group. If your group is large—eight or more people—consider splitting into smaller parties.

Many books and experts warn against hiking alone. If a backcountry emergency or accident arises among a group, it can be serious. Imagine that same emergency happening when the hiker is out alone. It is a potential nightmare. It is important whenever you are heading out on a hike to let someone know where you'll be and when you expect to return. That rule of thumb is especially important for anyone going out alone.

Extended periods of wilderness solitude are not for everyone and especially unwise for beginning hikers. At the same time many of the higher ideals we now express as a civilization have been given to us by sage philosophers who spent time alone in the wilderness: Emerson, Thoreau, Muir. To those who are experienced backpackers and home in the remote wilds without conveniences, many parts of Wyoming still offer the opportunity to get away from the crowds and renew the spirit.

Fires and campsites.

Rarely is anyone going to hike a trail and find a place where many people before have not already camped. Please camp on that same spot. If you build a fire, use a fire ring that's already there. Then, if it's obvious that this is a popular spot, that many more will follow you, leave the site clean and the fire ring intact. That particular spot is receiving use beyond any immediate recovery, and the more that camp on it the better. There's no sense in beginning the use cycle on another pristine site. On the other hand, if you're off the trail on a cross-country adventure and camping in a virgin or near virgin location, make sure that no one who comes by a few hours after you leave will have an inkling someone camped there. Fires built in a shallow pit or on a rock that has been coated with an inch of soil, fires kindled with small squaw wood and allowed to burn down to fine white ashes can be covered or scattered and made to vanish without a trace.

The same is true of campsites. You don't need to dig rain trenches around the tent, and you can scatter pine needles or grass over the flattened area to return to it a natural, undisturbed look. Another aspect of fires is that they need to be put out, completely. Many times I've extinguished smoldering peat five or more feet from a camper's water-drowned fire.

Bathing.

Take it from a ranger who spent weeks at a time in the woods and still had to appear presentable when talking to visitors. You can enjoy all the amenities of cleanliness and never get a drop of soap in a waterway. Jump in, swim, or play in the stream or lake. Soap up away from the water and rinse yourself by pouring pots and/or canteens of water over you.

Other considerations

If a trail gets you to where you're going, stay on it. Just a few people cutting a switchback or blazing a shortcut soon leave ribbons of trails across the landscape. This is especially true in alpine high country, where just a few footprints can began a scarring process on the land.

The only reason a hiker needs a hatchet or an ax on a camping trip is to remove trees that may have fallen across the road leading to the trailhead. Once there, leave them behind. If the country doesn't supply enough downed squaw wood for a fire, better carry a stove.

Avoid the overly popular areas during peak season. When I talked to the Lander District of the Shoshone National Forest about this hiking guide, the recreational forester let me know that I wouldn't be doing them or the land any favors by telling more people about the Cirque of Towers. Areas that are already overrun and restricted won't offer the quality of a place with more solitude.

Check with the local land-controlling agencies for further information and updates, restrictions, and warnings. A little advance knowledge could save you from a trail no longer passable because of a fire, or alert you to an area where wild animals have been a problem.

HIKING IN BEAR COUNTRY

When promised some anecdotes on the uniqueness of Wyoming trails, you can bet that bears will be involved in several of them. All Wyoming mountains and forests harbor bears, and Northwest Wyoming is a last refuge for the endangered grizzly bear. Grizzly habitat includes the Yellowstone and Grand Teton Parks areas, the Targhee, Bridger-Teton, and Shoshone national forests and all private, BLM, and Indian Reservation land immediately surrounding these areas. Admittedly, in twenty-two years of hiking, my most common view of a wild bear has been of its rear side in a full retreat from me. I propose to keep things that way, and here are some precautions that will make it possible. But do remember that there is no generalizing when it comes to bear behavior. Avoiding an encounter is the primary rule.

• Watching for signs of bear on the trail—tracks (believe me, if it's an adult grizzly track, you will know it immediately), fresh scat, bushes that look like a whirlwind has desheveled them, torn up stumps and displaced rocks (indications of a feeding bear)—is a first-step safeguard. Fresh bear signs, especially if some of those signs come from mother and cub bears, form sufficient reason to change directions and trail plans.

• Many people drape themselves with bells or other noisemakers while hiking. The concept is valid. Noise gives the bear notice that you are coming, and since most tooth and claw encounters happen when the bear is surprised by a hiker, lots of noise offers no chance for surprise.

A side effect to this technique is that more crowded trails now echo in a continual jingling cadence that resembles a "parade of the Tinkerbelles." Some veteran hikers who miss the wood's silence, jokingly wonder what would happen if bears ever began associating bell sounds with "lunch." When the brush and undergrowth is thick, and bear images form in your mind, clapping hands, singing, or whistling for a few moments also serve the purpose.

• We love our pets, but leave your dog at home. I once took the neighbor's shepard for a walk. The dog woofed and ran after something in the woods. Something in the woods woofed back and the dog yipped; the dog ran back to me for protection from the boar black bear on his tail. That particular bear was human shy, luckily, and retreated upon seeing me. Don't believe that will always happen.

• There are always stories of a bear attack that happened during a woman's menstration period or after a couple's love making. There's no scientific proof beyond coincidence to confirm a link between an attack and these two events, but they are situations to keep in mind.

• Camping etiquette in bear country dictates practice of the principle of cleanliness. Leave no fish guts, scatter no left-over dinner scraps around the site. Taking this idea a step further, avoiding aromatic foods is a wise idea. If I was a grub- and berry-satiated bear, and the delicious scent of frying bacon or spicy sardines was filling my exceptionally sensitive nose, I might be sorely tempted to investigate.

• Many folks hang their packs, food, and cooking clothes from a tree or from a rope suspended between two trees. Sometime the grizzly bear claw-sharpening marks appear ten feet up the aspen tree which give a good indica-

Much of the Wyoming backcountry is bear country. CHRIS CAUBLE PHOTO.

tion of both how high you need to hang this gear and how large the bear can be.

• If a bear is interested in your camp, not only give him all the room (and gear) he desires but also realize his interest was probably spurred by a previous camper who left garbage behind and allowed the bear to begin an association of food with human camps. For the sake of the person after you, leave a clean camp. Report bear-robber incidents to authorities, for a minor problem bear can be captured and moved before it becomes a major problem bear and has to be killed.

• The next pieces of advice offered in most bear-safety raps are those that sound good on paper but in reality are difficult to follow: "If you do confront a bear, don't panic and don't run," and "if the bear looks aggressive (example: stands up on its hind legs) look for a tree to climb." These are excellent pieces of advice, but try on a hike, when there is no bear around, a spontaneous practice run dropping everything and trying to shinny up or climb a nearby forest tree in 15-30 seconds. Most people attempting this exercise realize that climbing conifer trees—especially pines—takes practice and skills they don't have. It also takes experience and training not to first be overcome by fear when a bear suddenly looms ahead.

• Back to a more earthly reality: most bear maulings usually involve a charging bear and little time for anything but curling the body into a position that protects head and stomach, and playing dead. This non-resistant tactic has yielded many bear attack survivors. Resisting the bear is futile and provokes further attack. The most common denominator in bear maulings is a sow bear with cubs. If you see bear cubs or fresh signs of bear cubs, skedaddle. Mother is nearby.

NOTE: The last several years have heralded an unprecedented number of mountain lion attacks and maulings in Colorado, Idaho, Montana, and

Wyoming. Young cats who haven't learned an instinctive fear of humans while being forced out on their own by their mothers, coupled with an increase in lion population and an increase in humans occupying lion habitat, has created this situation. The latest from a 1991 Mountain Lion-Human Interaction Symposium and Workshop in Denver lists some hints on actions to take if confronted by a mountain lion. The advice is almost opposite that for bear confrontations.

- Face the mountain lion. Most attacks occur from the rear. Make lots of noise. Yell and throw things at them. A cat will generally not attack something larger than itself, so enlarge your image. Hold something over your head to give yourself a bigger appearance. If you're with a child, stand up tall and hold the child high in the air or place him/her on your shoulders.
- If attacked, do not play dead. If knocked down, stand up. Cats are not used to something that fights back.
- Dogs are not a deterrent. In fact, evidence suggests they may be an attraction.

There's a final addition to the other advice: feel and listen. If you see signs of bear, especially cub tracks, if you hear of cat or bear sightings from other hikers and your spine tingles and your hair stands on end, if every radar siren inside you is sounding warnings about the potential, then listen to these warnings. Get out of the area and avoid an encounter.

Encounters with bears and mountain lions are rare, and attacks are even rarer. Fearing their possibility is not enough reason to cancel a backcountry trip. But the potential definitely is enough to advise extra caution and preparedness.

THE HIKES

NORTHEASTERN WYOMING

The broken prairies of the northeastern corner of Wyoming include a small portion of the Black Hills known as the Bear Lodge Mountains. Bear Lodge is a name derived from an Indian description that refers to the vertical furrows creasing the area's most amazing and prominent landmark, the Devils Tower volcanic plug (HIKE 1). Most of the geological remnants from this area's billion-year-old Precambrian schists and granites were pushed and fragmented into mountains in South Dakota's Black Hills. Wyoming's Bear Lodge section of this event was formed more as a side effect of these neighboring activities than as an individual geological undertaking.

The Black Hills name comes from two Sioux words that mean "hills that are black." When seen from a distance, the pine-covered hills rising above the surrounding prairie appear dark colored. The mountains have long been used by plains Indian tribes as a place to purify themselves and seek visions. The 1897 Black Hills Forest Reserve became the Black Hills National Forest in 1905.

For the hiker, these mountains and their surrounding areas offer early season adventures in a state where high elevations keep many trails snowbound until July. It's a unique landscape with open grassland parks and gently forested hills that are pleted by variegated gulches and small canyons. To hike this country also requires some singular planning preparations. Public land in the Wyoming section of the Black Hills National Forest is scattered and minimal. Most of the forestland is heavily logged and densely roaded while recreational trails are non-existant. Hiking opportunities will often originate on or cross private land. (See Wyoming Rules section.)

While not offering hikers the chance for week-long mega-hikes and endless circular loop trails, the Bear Lodge Mountains area of Wyoming is a wonderful arena for the person who sees a small mountain or an unknown creek canyon and blazes his own cross-country day hike into the more open terrain. A wonderous potpourri of unique prairie buttes and winding creek bottomlands surround the forested hills. Permission is usually required to explore those areas on private land. The Bearlodge District of the Black Hills Forest has recently completed their first official hiking trail, the Cliff Swallow Nature Trail (HIKE 3). Another fifteen-mile loop trail, the proposed Sundance Burn Trail is scheduled for construction in 1993-1994. It's a good time to voice opinions to the Black Hills National Forest about converting a bit more of their timber and grazing monies into non-motorized recreation.

HIKE 1

General description: Three separate hiking trails of relative ease and varying distance to the spectacular volcanic neck of a towering natural landmark and the nation's first national monument, created in 1906.

General location: Fifty miles northeast of Gillette and on the western fringe of the Bear Lodge Mountains.

Maps: Black Hills National Forest map and/or USGS Devils Tower quad. Also the Devils Tower National Monument trails pamphlet distributed by the National Park Service.

Special attractions: A captivating and unique example of volcanic/monolithic formation amid original and untouched Wyoming prairie. The area became popular after exposure in the movie "Close Encounters of the Third Kind." A visitor's center explains the history and geology of the region.

For more information: Devils Tower National Monument, National Park Service, U.S. Department of Interior, Devils Tower, WY, 82714, (307) 467-5501.

Finding the trailhead: Twenty-seven miles east of Gillette, exit Interstate 90 to drive north on U.S. highway 14. Twenty-six miles farther, at Devils Tower Junction (Charlie Junction on older maps), turn north on State Highway 24 and drive for six miles. Here follow the national monument signs and State highway 110 west for one-half mile to the entrance station. There is a fee to enter the monument: $1 for a day; $10 for a yearly pass to the monument; and $25 for a Golden Eagle Pass which grants you free entrance for the calander year to every National Park and Momunent in America. It also costs $7 to camp in the park's campground.

Devils Tower from the Joyner Trail

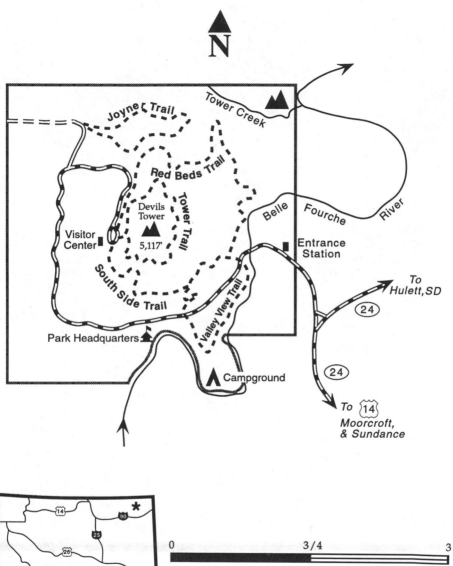

The hike: Three completely different trails offer hikers a chance to explore the many aspects of the looming "Mateo Tepee" or "Bear Lodge," the volcanic plug called Devils Tower. Spend the day in the area and hike all three trails. America's first National Monument holds many faces, and the quick drive to the visitor center and jog around the shorter Tower Trail that most tourists opt for do not reveal the secret moods of this one-time sacred landmark.

Three miles of paved road lead you both to the visitor center and through an open Ponderosa forest that surrounds the 1,000-foot-wide base of the Tower. This creviced rock giant gently tapers to a 275-foot flat summit that sits 1,280 feet above the Belle Fourche River. The monolithic and fluted face of Devils Tower stands 865 feet from base to top, the tallest such formation in the U.S.

South Side, Valley View, and Red Beds Trails

Beginning at the south end of the visitor center parking lot, the nearly four miles of this well-marked and easy-to-follow trail will take you on a grand tour through the many different worlds that immediately surround the Devils Tower. Ponderosa forests, open meadows, cactused badlands, and river-carved sedimentary layers make appearances. All the while, the awesome faces of Devils Tower loom over the various landscapes.

Hike .8 mile along this trail. The signed Valley View Trail intersects and journeys downhill toward the Belle Fourche (pronounced "bell foosh") River. A swing along this trail loop introduces you to the peaceful meadows and cottonwoods that surround the prairie river, and it offers remarkable views of the tower from a flatland perspective. An active prairie dog town thrives within this trail's boundaries. Looping back across the road to rejoin the Red Beds Trail, the path continues into many astounding vistas. It also reveals a perspective of what Wyoming countryside looked like before cattle and grazing claimed the state.

The trail is moderate in rating due to the quite noticeable elevation loss and gain. Incredible views of the river and the redland moonscape it has cut through friable sedimentary layers forms an added attraction to this hike. The trail circles around the Tower and ends at the north end of the visitor center parking lot. There is no water along the trail.

The Tower Trail

Although it always feels unnatural to have pavement instead of pine needles beneath the hiking boots, the 1.25-mile paved Tower Trail that surrounds the base of Devils Tower is well worth the hour it takes to hike. Neck-craning views of the 800-foot rock columns that rise directly above you engender amazement and respect. Viewing some of the rock climbing parties inching their way up shear walls and little cracks adds a sense of proportion to the scene. (All rock climbers must register with the rangers.) Interpretive plaques along the way point out the Tower's natural processes.

The trail is well marked and begins at the east end of the visitor center parking lot. Rattlesnakes have been seen along these trails, and interestingly, they also live on the rocky football field top of the Tower.

Joyner Ridge Trail

Devils Tower can become quite crowded with visitors during the peak tourist season. 0.6 mile before the visitor center, an unmarked, hard-surfaced road leaves the main thoroughfare and journeys north for .3 mile to the Joyner

Ridge Trailhead. This unpopulated section of the park offers the most glorious views of the Tower imaginable, the best in the park.

The 1.5-mile-long trail is as sweet and serene a hike as one could wish for. It first traces the lands where meadow and forest merge. Then it drops past sandstone cliffs, cuts through secluded meadows, and wanders into ravines with groves of deciduous trees and shrubs. The trail loops back through the open prairie and ends where it began. Photographic opportunities exist every step of the way. The trail is presently unmarked by the Park Service.

Spring, early summer, and fall are optimal times to visit this park. Its margins are small, but some wonderful opportunities for cross-country wandering exist, especially along the northern and western boundaries of the park.

HIKE 2 *KEYHOLE STATE PARK*

General description: An easy day hike beneath and atop the sandstone cliffs that help create the Keyhole Reservoir on the Belle Fourche River.

General location: Approximately twelve miles west and eight miles north of Moorcroft, on the western fringe of the Bear Lodge Mountains.

Maps: USGS Carlile and Grasshopper Butte quads, and the park map distributed by Keyhole State Park.

Special attractions: Unique sandstone butte formations, water sport activities including fishing and swimming, and the best, most diverse and abundant bird watching in the state of Wyoming.

For more information: Superintendent, Keyhole State Park, Moorcroft, WY, 82721, (307) 756-3596.

Finding the trailhead: To reach the Keyhole State Park Volksmarch area, leave Interstate 90 thirteen miles east of Moorcroft at exit 165, the Pine Ridge Road exit. Follow this aptly named road to the north for approximately seven miles and into the Keyhole Park—named after a keyhole-shaped brand used by some local ranchers. Turn left or west at the information booth, drive past the park headquarters for approximately 1.7 miles toward the marina and park near the trailer court, where the trailhead begins at southern shores of the mouth of Cottonwood Bay.

The hike: The Wyoming State Parks & Historic Sites organization deserves a collective handshake and thanks from every one who feels hiking forms a special part of his or her life. They've implemented a program called "Volksmarch" in ten of their state parks. Volksmarch is a ten kilometer (six mile) excursion that is designed to help people discover the beauty, uniqueness, and diversity of an area through the wonderful means of walking. The term "Volksmarch" literally means "a walk of the people."

Everything from new trails to old roads to waterfront shores comprise parts of the walks. Many of Wyoming's state parks revolve around developed reservoirs. Volksmarch offers a welcome focus on hiking amid the standard motorized recreations. Information is available from the Wyoming Recreation Commission, 2301 Central Ave., Barrett Bldg., Cheyenne, WY, 82002, (307) 777-7695, and from the American Volkssport Association, 1001 Pat Booker Road, Suite 101, Universal City, TX, 78148, (210) 659-2112.

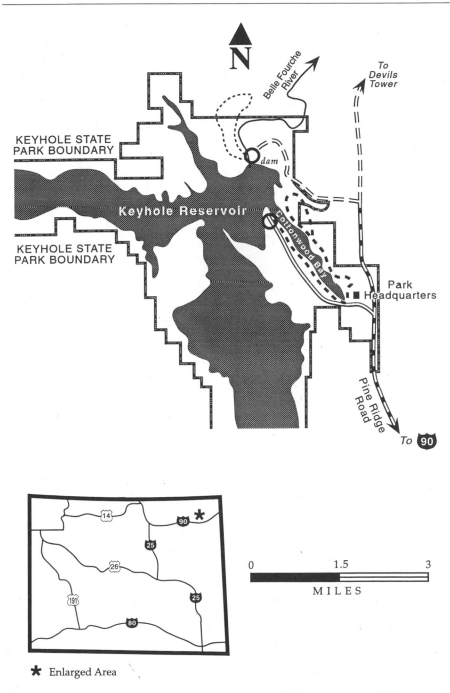

The path follows the waterline of Cottonwood Bay. It passes below the trailers and a campground before gaining some solitude by circling the bay and traversing a series of wooded sandstone buttes. The complete walk traces the northern Cottonwood Bay shoreline, makes a large loop among the buttes, and follows the original shoreline pathway back to the trailhead. Brown and yellow IVV signs mark the trail's pathway.

When I visited the park (May, 1991), many years of drought had left the reservoir thirty-six feet below normal water level. Cottonwood Bay was an exposed mudhole, and the Volksmarch hike could hardly be called an exciting or pretty undertaking. But the rolling country around the lake is quite intriguing. Exploration did lead to an alluring section of land that offered an excellent couple hour to half-day hiking adventure amid a splendid and secretive setting.

Instead of turning left at the park information sign, continue northward for another 1.5 miles to the end of the pavement. Here a gravel road jogs to the left or west and leads to the reservoir's dam structure. One half mile later this road forks; turn right or north and follow a windy narrow road 1.2 miles to the parking lot beside and below the reservoir dam. Across the Belle Fourche river and directing its course, a crescent of sandstone buttes and cliffs sweep to the north. This escarpment offers a wonderland of hiking and exploration excitement.

The exceptional quality of the Keyhole area is its feathered life. Two hundred and twenty-five different species of birds have been sighted at or near the lake. By spending the morning in this second area, by hiking up the dam and then following the game trails that travel near the edges of these butte tops, I must have spotted a third of these birds. By descending the cliffs via various ravines and tracking other game trails back along the western shores of the river, I probably saw another third. The final third remained hidden, but they were singing a chorus of songs that was almost deafening. This cross-country wandering above and along the rather tiny Belle Fourche River offered privacy, silence and peace, glorious scenery, great wildlife, escape from the development that accompanies such resevoirs, and a small chance to touch a tiny section of pristine Wyoming.

Special note . . . private lands do surround the butte just described, and permission is needed to explore the woodlands and prairies they contain. Also, Keyhole Park does charge a $4 per night camping fee. And the summer of 1991, especially June, drenched Wyoming with record rains. The reservoir has regained some of its capacity.

HIKE 3 *CLIFF SWALLOW LOOP TRAIL*

General description: A moderately easy and exceptionally diverse hiking and mountain biking trail beginning and ending near the only natural lake found in the Bear Lodge Mountains.

General location: Fourteen miles (as the raven flies) north of Sundance, in the heart of the Bear Lodge Mountains.

Maps: Black Hills National Forest Map and/or USGS Black Hills quad. USGS Alva quad is optional. This is a brand new trail and maps do not locate it.

The Black Hills. Beaver Creek during high runoff.

Special attractions: Beautiful, deciduous riparian habitat complete with beaver workings. Also great views of an exceptional valley.

For more information: Bearlodge Ranger District, Hwy 14 East; P.O. Box 680, Sundance, WY, 82729, (307) 283-1361.

The hike: Don't envy the raven who can cover the long and winding road to Cook Lake in fourteen miles. Forest Service Road 838, the Warren Peak Lookout Road, allows you a wonderful chance to seek out the nontrailed and cross-country exploration opportunities available in the Bear Lodge Mountains. This north-south "thoroughfare" travels through wooded canyons and ravines, beside peaks, over divides, across flats, and along streams, and offers many chances for one to park the car and wander to an unnamed summit or into a remnant wild creek beginning. Drive two miles west of Sundance on U.S. Highway 14 and turn right where the brown Forest Service sign directs you north to the Cook Lake Recreation Area via road 838. The pavement survives for 7.5 miles where another Cook Lake sign directs you to turn right on to a dirt road. Approximately 5.6 miles of this graded gravel road passes you over splendid divides and through thick aspen forests to a stop-signed intersection with Forest Service road 843. Turn right here, following the Cook Lake sign. One and seven tenths miles later, turn left at another intersection where the sign says you're five miles from Cook Lake. Almost four miles later road 842 cuts to the left and leads you the last mile to the Cook Lake Recreation Area. If a major rainstorm pummels the area, the last four miles of this route will need some drying time before a low clearance vehicle can navigate it.

The Cliff Swallow trail is newly completed. I was one of the first to hike its length this spring (1991). Trailhead access requires that you follow the road along the east shore of Cook Lake, drive across the north end outlet of the

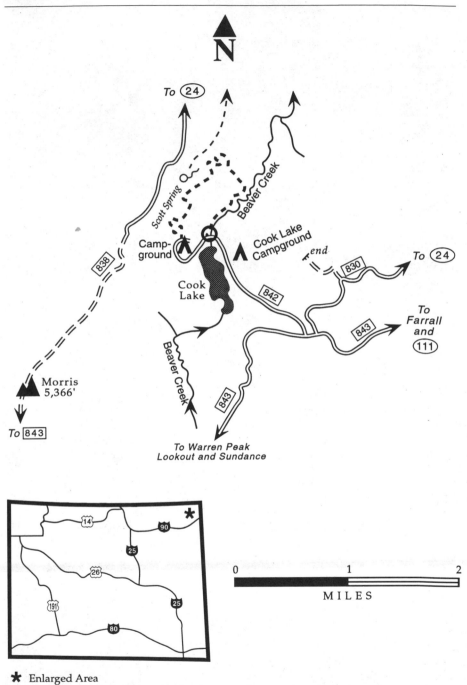

lake and park your vehicle in a marked parking area just to the northwest of the lake. Walk back east toward the dam and cut down the dam's banks north to the creek, staying on the west side of Beaver Creek. The trail shortly manifests where it cuts through a wooden cattle gate. There were no trailhead signs when I trekked here, but the recreational forester says they will soon be in place.

I can't imagine a sweeter or more diverse day hiking experience than this three-and-a-half-mile loop trail. For over a mile it follows a vibrant and quite "alive-with-beaver-activity" creek bottom. Some excellent campsites exist in the various riparian settings, for those who wish to escape the tumult of a developed recreation area. (A fee is charged to camp at the Cook Lake Recreation Area). Please notice that little sign of camping activity exists along Beaver Creek, and do your part to keep that no-use look healthy. After about 1.2 miles, the trail crosses a barbed wire fence (a good fence, one that keeps cattle out of the watershed environment) and begins a long wind up the north side of a pine covered mountain. Easy to follow, the trail tops out and skims a high ridge for the next mile and a half. This section climaxes at an impressive overview of the Beaver Creek valley you just hiked. Gently switchbacking back down the mountain, the trail ends at the upper section of the Cook Lake Campground. This excellent hiking trail is moderately hard due to the 400 feet of elevation gained and then lost again, but proper switchbacking greatly eases that difficulty.

Please note. . . This is the Bearlodge Ranger District's first trail, and they've really created a gem. The district has traditionally been all timber and cattle in its orientation, and I hope readers will write the district and both compliment the fine trail creation and encourage an expansion of this needed resource.

SOUTHEASTERN WYOMING
The Laramie Range

Wyoming's geological connection to Colorado's impressive Front Range mountains is a long and erratic cluster of granite named the Laramie Range. Extending from south of Casper to north and west of Laramie, these rugged-sloped mountains afford a drainage system unique to mountain ranges. Many of the creek drainages flow from west to east across and through the entire range. These waterways originate in the high valleys west of the mountains and refuse to allow the granite-cored peaks to hinder their eastward trek.

Streams and peaks survive as best they can amidst a hodgepodge of land ownership designation, but roads (many, many roads in this country) and trails cross and recross so many boundaries that one cannot guess how many private property permissions one must acquire to hike an area. Checking with the Forest Service districts or the BLM offices in Casper and Rawlings may help in your information search.

One also needs to be advised that the Medicine Bow National Forest visitor map and most topography maps are extremely outdated concerning this range of mountains. The dashed lines, keyed as trails by the map symbol explanations, are in reality two-track jeep roads. Land swaps have occured, and more are in the planning. The Douglas Ranger District that oversees this area presently lists two hiking trails in the Laramie Mountains. Two or three others are on the planning board.

The range is exceptional in its ruggedness and beauty, but you do need to know where you are if you venture cross-country (see Wyoming rules and Appendix I.)

HIKE 4 *LARAMIE PEAK*

General description: A moderate and fairly steep day hike to the highest summit in the Laramie Range.

General location: Forty-five miles directly south of Douglas.

Maps: Medicine Bow National Forest map and/or USGS Laramie Peak quad.

Special attractions: Rugged and unique lands that are a bold cross between mountains and high prairie. Laramie Peak, 10,272 feet above sea level, is the highest peak in the Laramie Range.

For more information: Douglas Ranger District, 809 South 9th Street, Douglas, WY, 82633, (307) 358-4690.

Finding the trailhead: Two roads carry you to Esterbrook, which is not really a town but a Forest Service work station. My favorite leaves Interstate 25 at Glendo (exit 111) and wanders westward for twenty-two miles on what's called the Esterbrook Road. A second route, Wyoming Highway 94, leaves the interstate directly south of Douglas. Seventeen miles of it is paved before it becomes graded Converse County Road 5. Eleven more miles places you in Esterbrook—The road has the potential to be difficult in a two-wheel-drive vehicle during or just after a rainstorm. Here a signed intersection guides you west along Converse County Road 5 the eighteen miles to the Friend Park Campground and Laramie Peak trailhead.

The hike: The scattered mountains of the Laramie Range are generally forested to their summits and are quite rugged due to the rocky landscaping of the granite-cored anticlinal uplift that formed them. Laramie Peak, the area's highest, sports a newly constructed 5.15 mile (one way) trail leading to its summit from the Friend Park Campground. The long and rough drive to Friend Park takes you through some of the finest prairie-merging-into-mountain vistas imaginable.

The trail follows beautiful Friend Creek for a mile before crossing the water (via a bridge) and beginning a steep ascent that never relaxes its grade for the next four miles. This is a rather deluxe trail, wide and well maintained, but also one on which you know you're hiking uphill. The mountainside that it traverses is a never-ending slope of behemoth granite boulders. Lodgepole pines poke through the rock where they can and create a quite thick and sterile forest.

A trail sign at two miles notes Friend Creek Falls, which looks more like a steep cascade than a waterfall. This will be the last water available along the trail in later summer. In late May water flowed everywhere and the last thousand feet of elevation gain required some intense snow stomping.

There are also glorious panoramas from the summit of the spreading prairies that this mountain rises above. The rest of the Laramie Range forms a fascinating rock hodgepodge below. Give yourself an entire day to hike this trail.

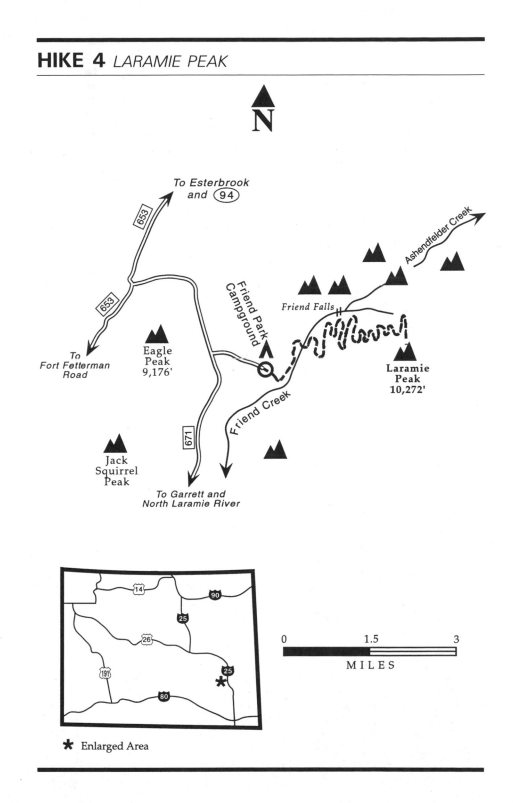

HIKE 5 *LA BONTE CANYON*

General description: A fun, easy, and especially beautiful day hike that follows a major creek into a deepening mountain canyon.

General location: Approximately thirty-five miles south and west of Douglas, in the Medicine Bow National Forest.

Maps: Medicine Bow National Forest and/or USGS Saddleback Mountain quad.

Special attractions: Some of the best wildlife habitat in this section of Wyoming. Wonderful meadows and deciduous forests.

For more information: Douglas Ranger District, 809 South 9th Street, Douglas, WY, 82633, (307) 358-4690.

Finding the trailhead: Leave Interstate 25 at exit 146 and drive southeast on Wyoming highway 96 for 3.2 miles to the intersection of Wyoming highway 91. Or, find your way to downtown Douglas and head south on Wyoming Highway 94. Less than one mile beyond Interstate 25, (you pass under the Interstate) State Highway 96 intersects with a westward or right turn. Three miles along 96 you again turn south or left onto highway 91. After 12.8 miles of southward driving, the pavement ends, state maintenance ends and Converse County Road 24 comes into being. Three miles farther the road forks. Turn left onto Converse County Road 16, the Fort Fetterman Road, and drive approximately fifteen miles until you intersect the well-signed La Bonte Canyon/Curtis Gulch Campground Road. This road journeys eastward and parallels La Bonte Creek for five miles and ends at the Curtis Gulch Campground, where the trail begins.

The hike: The La Bonte drainage is a prime example of a creek that begins west of the Laramie Range yet travels uninterruptedly eastward through the mountains. This area contains a large proportion of contiguous Forest Service land. The hiker can freely explore adjacent creek drainages and surrounding hills. And exploration is what the La Bonte area is all about. La Bonte, by the way, was a French trader and trapper who frequented the region in the 1830's. Here he should have remained. The Ute Indians killed him in Utah in 1840.

The trail criss-crosses the creek for almost the first two miles, but the canyon is easily hikable by simply skirting the north side of the creek. This is a south-facing slope and therefore quite open. Game trails usually follow the untrailed side of the creek, and where rocky structures do descend into the stream's side, it's not difficult to switchback a short way up the mountainside and pick a route around them.

By the time you follow both the regular trail and the impromptu trails the three miles to the end, you will have been amazed by this spectacular and generally unknown hiking paradise. Be prepared for lush meadows, gallant cottonwood and pine forests, picturesque rock cliffs, flowers beyond description (especially in May and June) and wildlife everywhere. The creek bottom is classified as the La Bonte Big Game Range, so livestock grazing is not allowed here. Beyond the trail's end, the canyon becomes especially rugged and narrow. Private land soon claims the area.

The Douglas Ranger District currently claims but two hiking trails in its landscape. La Bonte is one. And it is open to ATVs and ORVs. Three- and four-

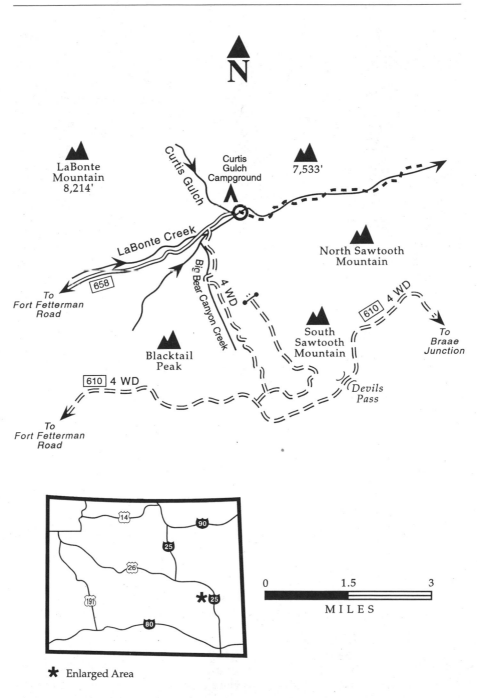

North

N

LaBonte
Mountain
8,214'

Curtis Gulch

Curtis
Gulch
Campground

7,533'

LaBonte Creek

North Sawtooth
Mountain

658

To
Fort Fetterman
Road

Big Bear Canyon Creek

4 WD

610 4 WD

To
Braae
Junction

Blacktail
Peak

South
Sawtooth
Mountain

610 4 WD

Devils
Pass

To
Fort Fetterman
Road

14

90

25

26

191

★ 25

80

0   1.5   3

MILES

★ Enlarged Area

Guernsey State Park.

wheeled machines do use the La Bonte road/trail. The Douglas district appears to be at a point of realizing that it has little to offer in the way of non-motorized recreation. Now is the time to send a letter, both to the district and to the Medicine Bow National Forest Supervisor, (605 Skyline Drive, Laramie, WY, 82070) supporting a La Bonte road closure and encouraging the two or three new hiking trails they have in the works.

HIKE 6 *GUERNSEY STATE PARK*

General description: An easy to moderate day hike amid the animated canyons, prairies, and buttes that surround the North Platte River.

General location: Approximately thirteen miles north and fifteen miles east of Wheatland, along the North Platte River.

Maps: USGS Guernsey Reservoir and Guernsey quads, and especially the Guernsey State Park Volksmarch map handout.

Special attractions: Fascinating CCC (Civilian Conservation Corps of the 1930's) historic buildings and artifacts, great views, good birding, and some interesting prairie hiking.

For more information: Superintendent, Guernsey State Park, Guernsey, WY, 82214, (307) 836-2334.

Finding the trailhead: Exit 92 on Interstate 25 sends you eastward on U.S. Highway 26 toward the small river town of Guernsey. Fifteen miles from the interstate and just west of the town, a sign directs you northward to Guernsey

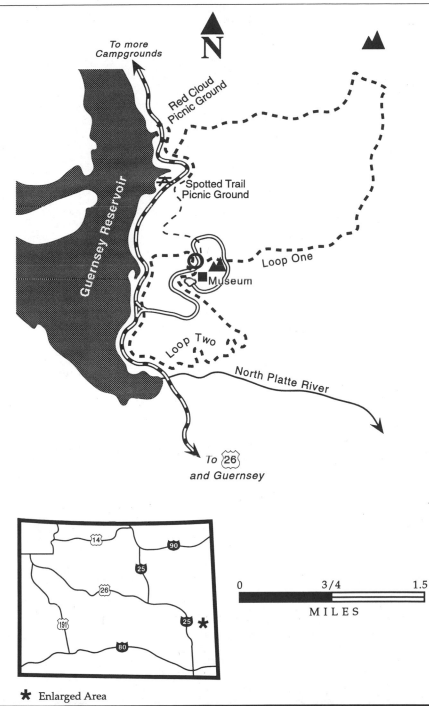

To more
Campgrounds

N

Red Cloud
Picnic Ground

Guernsey Reservoir

Spotted Trail
Picnic Ground

Loop One

Museum

Loop Two

North Platte River

To 26
and Guernsey

14

90

25

26

191

25 *

80

* Enlarged Area

0   3/4   1.5

MILES

State Park. In 1991 the Wyoming Parks System was experimenting with a fee charging system, using the Guernsey park as a prototype. It cost $3 to enter, and an additional $4 to camp inside the park boundaries. After passing the fee collection building, follow the main paved road 1.5 miles. Shortly after you cross the dam, a gravel road—well signed—turns right and winds its way to the park's museum. Here the hiking begins.

The hike: A small and geologically unimportant thrust named the Hartville Uplift, aided by the cutting powers of the North Platte River, has created a most scenic land in the southeastern area of Wyoming. In 1927, after Charles A. Guernsey kidnapped a group of Denver-bound U.S. Senators by detouring their train to Hartville so he could show them his proposed dam site, the Bureau of Reclamation completed a 105-foot earthen dam, changing river canyons to lake shorelines. Guernesy State Park was created when the CCC estabilshed itself in the area from 1933 to 1936. If you enjoy adding historical fact finding to your hiking adventure, the Guernsey State Park museum and other remnants of CCC activities in Guernsey Park are worth the seeking.

The park's 6.2 mile Volksmarch trail consists of two seperate loops. The trick to following these sometimes confusing trails, besides acquiring a free copy of the Volksmarch trail map, is to look for the International Volksmarch trail sign. These brown and yellow beacons consist of an "I" sitting atop a "V" sitting atop another "V".

Loop one leaves the museum parking lot and retraces a half mile of the gravel road which brought you to the museum. IVV signs will first direct you westward for a short jaunt to a small butte and back, and then send you northeast through eastern Wyoming prairie and open forests. The walk wanders northward to the foot of some high sandstone escarpments and then traces a way westward, down and along a dry ravine to the lake. Here it follows a main paved road for half a mile before again going cross-country through the juniper and ponderosa hills and back to the museum. This first loop is about four miles in length. There is some fine cross-country hiking along prairie hilltops if you leave the northern-most point of the trail.

The second loop of this walk, about two miles in length, begins at the northwestern side of the museum, again marked well by the IVV signs. It winds quickly down to the paved road where it follows the highway south for nearly a mile. At the dam, the trail then cuts eastward along the cliffs overlooking the North Platte River. Quite spectacular views and old CCC structures add to the trail's story. The last .5 mile of the trail climbs some old and newer road beds back to the museum.

A park ranger noted that some exciting CCC trails exist on the west side of the reservoir, and that the park service would begin maintainence work on them in 1991. It should also be noted that in late summer, every year, the reservoir is completely drained so nearby irrigation ditches will be lined with the lake's accumulated silt and become more waterproof. That may or may not be an exciting time to visit the park.

The Sherman Mountains

A dozen miles east of where the city of Laramie would one day rise, nature—forty million years ago—flipped a few handfuls of leftover Rocky Mountain granite on to the Laramie Plains. These rocks eventually formed the Sherman Mountains, a limited group of small hills skirted by Interstate 80 on the south and west sides. Time weathered many of the prominent, massive boulder formations into fascinating glens of piled and balanced rock structures.

A small, section of this boulder-mountain country is owned by the Medicine Bow National Forest. Although hiking opportunities are limited in this tiny, over-roaded section of forest, a couple of unique walking experiences do exist.

HIKE 7 VEDAUWOO

General description: Long known as a rock climber's paradise, Vedauwoo offers hikers many chances for small and easy explorations through the unique blocks and towers of weathered Sherman granite.

General location: Seventeen miles east of Laramie, just north of Interstate 80 in the southern section of the Sherman Mountains.

Maps: Medicine Bow National Forest map and/or USGS Sherman Mountains West quad. (NOTE: These maps are fairly outdated on the road patterns in this section.)

Special attractions: Awesome and intriguing rock formations and structures.

For more information: Medicine Bow National Forest, Laramie Ranger District, 2468 Jackson St., Laramie, WY, 82070, (307) 745-8971.

Finding the trailhead: Leaving Interstate 80 seventeen miles east of Laramie and following graveled Forest Service road 700 east for one mile, you'll intersect a lightly paved road—Forest Service road 720—and a sign directing you north to the Vedauwoo Campground. Continue along this road as far as it goes to the north end of a parking lot.

The hike: The Vedauwoo area (pronounced VAY-da-voo), an Arapaho word meaning "Earth Born," has been used through the ages by Indians as a site of ancient religious rites. In more modern times it became a little-known and highly challenging rock climbing area. Recently, a picnic- and camp-ground have transformed the area into a popular day and overnight recreation site.

Just past the wooden parking barriers and to the left, a nature trail begins a winding ascent up and through the amazing green and pink, lichen-covered rock mountains. Smooth granite boulders display the gamut of various shapes and sizes. The trail zigs and zags for about three quarters of a mile before it ends at a lofty and picturesque overview of the Crow Creek valley and the jagged Sherman Mountains to the north.

Although this is a short trail, the opportunity for play and exploration in this area is unlimited. A person can easily log five or more miles by simply exploring around the rock bases and by scrambling up any alluring ravines

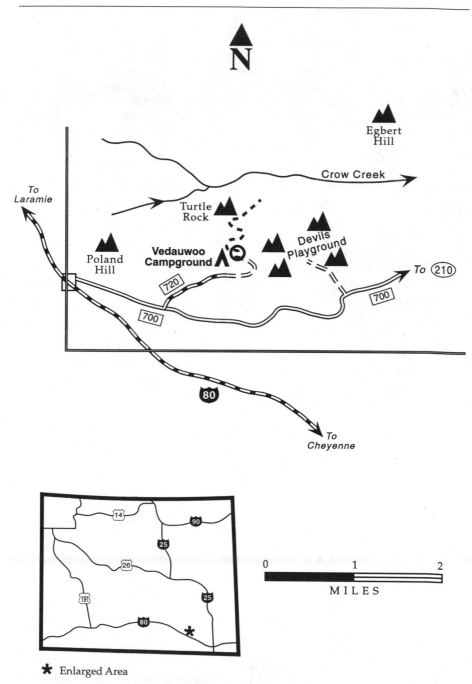

Fascinating Vedauwoo rock formations.

that pleat the rock structures. This becomes especially true if you continue eastward along Forest Service road 700. For six miles past the campground road there are endless places to park the car and wander into unique and exciting rocky, high mountain prairie and woodland settings. In fact, the campground area is popular and can be quite crowded. As is so often the case, isolation and unappreciated beauty await but a mile away from the crowds. The land is gentle, open, and conducive to cross-country hiking.

Water should be carried, as most of the streams dry up as summer progresses.

HIKE 8 *HEADQUARTERS NATIONAL RECREATION TRAIL*

General description: A moderately easy, four- to eight-mile day hike taking you through an amazing variety of mountain habitat. This is a fun trail because it offers so many unexpected scenic treasures along its route.

General location: Thirteen miles east of Laramie in the Sherman Mountains.

Maps: Medicine Bow National Forest map and USGS Sherman Mountains West quad.

Special attractions: Rugged and wild mountains amid gentle and peaceful settings.

For more information: Medicine Bow National Forest, Laramie Ranger District, 2468 Jackson St., Laramie, WY, 82070, (307) 745-8971.

Finding the trailhead: Turning south after leaving Interstate 80 via exit 323, the Happy Jack Road exit, takes you to the Summit rest area. Instead of turning into the rest area, continue south on Forest Service road 705. There is a trailhead to this trail one half mile down this road, where the pavement ends.

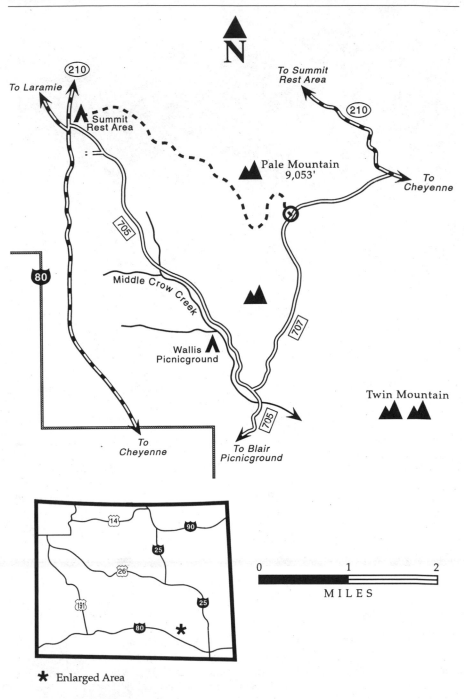

Being next to the rest area, it was fairly crowded, and I opted to seek out the "other side of the mountain." The views were well worth driving 4.3 miles along gravel road 705 to a well-signed intersection where Forest Service road 707 jogs to the north. Another 2.2 miles along this gravel road brought me to a sign announcing the Headquarters Trail. No other cars were at this trailhead.

The hike: The Sherman Mountains, viewed from Interstate 80, appear to be bland little blips of rock sitting atop an uninteresting prairie. The Headquarters Trail again proves that books should not be judged by their covers, especially when read at seventy miles per hour. The mountains are named for Civil War General W. T. Sherman by a surveyor, Grenville Dodge who discovered them when he was chased this way by Indians in 1855. Sherman Pass at 8,235 feet elevation, was the highest point on the Union Pacific's turn-of-the-century railroad.

This well-maintained and easy-to-follow National Recreation Trail can be hiked as a four-mile round trip to a scenic overlook, an eight-mile round trip to the Summit rest area and back, or a four-mile one-way (two-car or thumbing back) jaunt to the rest area. Whatever you choose, its the kind of trail that urges you to take your time and enjoy the variegated scenery. It passes through a gamut of environments, from sage and grassland meadows to aspen, ponderosa, lodgepole, and limber pine forests, from moist north-sloping climates to south-sloping dry and rocky biotas. At any point one can leave the trail and climb the pinkish granite rock outcroppings for exceptional views of the endless prairies below. The first 1.5 miles sport a fair uphill grade. The last .5 mile of the trail, before it reaches the rest area, crosses a high and treeless plateau. In between, the country and plant life constantly change. A surprising feeling of wildness holds the entire area.

Water will probably be nonexistant both on the trail and in the forest should you decide to camp in the country. Both Vedauwoo and these mountains, with all the exposed rock, really cook in July and August. Spring, especially, and fall are ideal times to hike here.

SOUTH CENTRAL WYOMING
The Sierra Madre Range

Wyomingites have created a poignant economic history of cyclic booms and decimating busts that center around natural resources, especially minerals. An exceptional, lower-altitude Continental Divide Range named the Sierra Madres has been the site of this oft-repeated story. When a simple sheepherder's red clay turned out to be seventy percent pure copper in 1896, the path was paved for the, then, world's largest copper mine to spring into being. A dozen years passed before the owners went bankrupt. The Encampment area's glorious precursor to the state's future uranium and oil booms and busts slipped into ghost town ruins and forsaken human ambitions.

Today the mining is a memory, but the friendly town of Encampment survives as a take-off point for excellent hiking. Approximately forty-five miles of the Continental Divide National Scenic Trail cross through the Hayden

Ranger District of the Medicine Bow National Forest. Three smaller wilderness areas thrive in these mountains, offering the hiker everything from rugged, narrow river canyons to high-elevation grandeur. If history is a hobby you pursue, nowhere is it more vividly presented than at the Grand Encampment Museum located in the town of Encampment. A few hours spent touring this no-cost and incredible re-enactment of historic buildings and settings will add much depth to the sights (or sites) you might discover when hiking this area. (Grand Encampment Museum, P.O. Box 395, Encampment, WY, 82325, (307) 327-5308).

HIKE 9 *ENCAMPMENT RIVER AND WILDERNESS AREA*

General description: A gentle to moderate, two- to three-day hike beside the rushing rapids and calm, smooth stretches of a unique wilderness river.

General location: Approximately six miles south of the town of Encampment, on Bureau of Land Management lands and in the Medicine Bow National Forest.

Maps: Medicine Bow National Forest map and/or USGS Encampment and Dudley Creek quads. (Wilderness boundaries are not shown on these maps.)

Special attractions: This is a very rugged, unpopulated, and scenic canyon. Many untrailed side creeks enter into the Encampment River. Brook, brown, and native trout call the river home.

For more information: Hayden Ranger District, Medicine Bow National Forest, P.O. Box 187, Encampment, WY, 82325, (307) 327-5481. Bureau of Land Management, Rawlins District Office, P.O. Box 670, Rawlins, WY, 82302, (307) 324-7171.

The hike: Local history—not to be confused with official history—tells a story of Thomas Edison fishing in the Encampment area. He shattered his bamboo pole beyond repair, and that night he threw the splintered rod into the camp fire. The stringy bamboo filaments glowed in the heat and supposedly inspired Edison to try a filament for the lighting element in his bulbs. Personally, if Edison had discovered and was fishing the beautiful Encampment River when this event occurred, I'm surprised he ever made it back to his laboratory.

Wyoming Highway 70 forms the main drag through Encampment. Two-tenths of a mile west of the town, a BLM sign points left or south to the Encampment River Trail and Campground. This gravel/dirt road is easy to follow for its two-mile length. A second road skirts a wooden fence surrounding the campground and leads to an obvious parking lot. Walking through a gate and a short distance up river places you on an arched bridge spanning the river and at the trailhead.

The Encampment River is a surprisingly large and swift moving stream. Hiking its shores in May and June can reveal a powerful white water cascade. The first four miles of the trail is a BLM production. The surrounding hills are sage covered and rather bald while the river is lined with cottonwoods. Scenery-wise, the country is awesome. It's a real treat to watch the conifer trees slowly invade and predominate the habitat as you walk the miles up the river. If you plan to hike this trip as a day hike, a delightful view of the river canyon setting occurs in the first mile beyond the forest service boundary (four miles up the trail). Here the trail climbs a hillside and cuts back

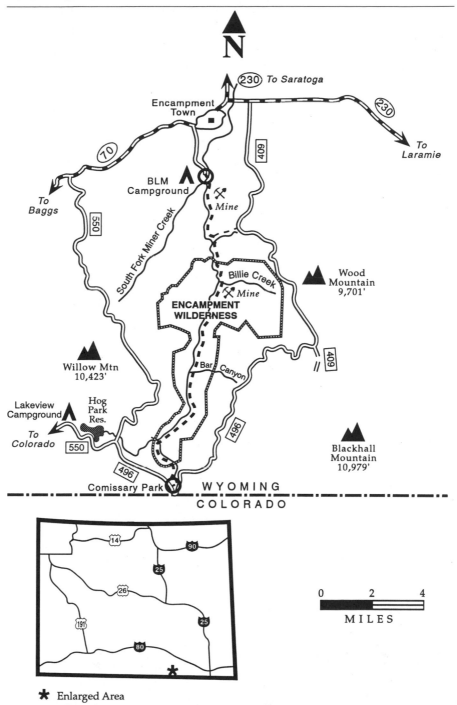

into Purgatory Gulch, as aspen-lined creek that marks the wilderness boundary.

The first few miles after entering the wilderness, the trail peacefully meanders through various woodland settings. Several campsites are found here, and the river seems to sing a more mellow song. Seven miles up canyon, the trail again climbs high onto the hillside. The water now carves its way through a narrow and rocky gorge, and the river churns powerfully. A few miles later the trail does return to the river bottom, but the forest is now thick lodgepole and spruce and campsites are scarce to find in the rocky and narrow channel.

This sixteen-mile-long trail exits the river at a trailhead named Commissary Park. A great one-way, two-vehicle trip would be to park one car at the BLM campground and the other at Commissary Park. To reach this second trailhead, drive west from Encampment on Wyoming Highway 70 to the forest boundary. Turn south on well-signed Forest Road 550 and follow it for 15.5 miles. Turn left or southeast onto Forest Service 496 (the Rim Road) and drive three miles to the trailhead parking lot next to the Encampment River in Commissary Park.

Encampment River is a blue-ribbon fishing area. Be advised that the first mile of the river from the BLM campground has no public access. Other than one private holding near the Forest Service boundary, the rest of the river is open and calling. The lower trail loses snow and is hikable early, but you should plan on conducting a thorough tick inspection afterwards. Of the several side streams that cross the trail, I only had to wade Billie Creek, and it was no more than knee deep and quite short.

It is interesting to experience the deep wilderness feeling that accompanies hiking in this small wilderness area. Few people hike the trail's length, and few signs of their passing exist.

HIKE 10 PLATTE RIVER WILDERNESS/ NORTHGATE CANYON

General description: A rugged, long day hike or enjoyable overnighter beside the shores of an exceptional wild and scenic river.

General location: Approximately twenty-five miles south and east of Encampment in the southwestern corner of the Medicine Bow Range.

Maps: Medicine Bow National Forest map and USGS Elkhorn Point and Overlook Hill quads. (Wilderness boundaries not shown on these maps.)

Special attractions: Isolation, scenery, blue-ribbon trout fishing, abundant and varied wildlife and waterfowl, and the many changing faces of a powerful river.

For more information: Hayden Ranger District, Medicine Bow National Forest, 204 West 9th St., Encampment, WY, 82325, (307) 327-5481.

Finding the trailhead: Wyoming highway 230 begins its roundabout journey to Laramie one mile north of Encampment. A most scenic route to drive, there is a green road sign twenty-four miles east of Encampment pointing east to what's called the Six Mile Road. This is also Forest Service road 412 and leads to the Six Mile Gap Campground. Road 412's two mile distance is graveled and quite narrow, and dead ends just east of the campground at the Platte River trailhead. Here an information sign maps and explains the Platte River Wilderness and introduces Platte River Trail Number 473.

The hike: The Encampment River, despite its size, radiates the lively spirit

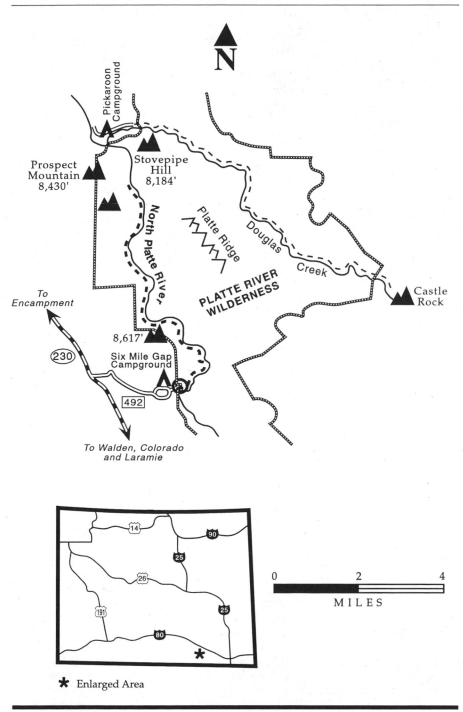

The Platte River Wilderness Area.

of a swift mountain stream and feels like an instrument playing a higher alto string. The neighboring North Platte River vibrates in bass tones. Its water moves more surely and with a deeper, more powerful rhythm.

I hiked this canyon in late May, and the water volume and hydraulics were awesome to behold. The Hayden district ranger feels that fall is the best time to experience this canyon when peaceful waters offer more fishing, swimming, and bald eagle observation opportunities. He may be right in one sense. Traveling that trail in the spring yielded more ticks per mile than any other trail I've hiked.

This is a fairly rugged trail that traverses just as rugged a country. The first miles are not thickly forested but do contain many great and towering grandfather conifer trees. Every half mile or so, flat land benches overlook the river and afford good camping spots. After 3.5 miles, the canyon narrows while the trail climbs to high and rocky overviews of the area. It's another 1.5 mile before the trail rejoins the river bottom. These last miles offer an entirely different face of easy-going river and cottonwood/aspen covered land benches that gently slope toward the water. These open slopes afford great cross-country journeying. After six miles of hiking, the trail grows dim, and one mile later it ceases existence. The district ranger notes that during late August and September it is sometimes possible to ford the river and follow a fisherman's trail along the eastern shore two miles north to Pickaroon Campground.

If you are a bird watcher, waterfowl and raptors are ubiquitous and abundant in this area. Be aware that the only source of water is the river; there are no real side canyon streams along this trail. The Northgate Canyon is a river runner's paradise. Often the trailhead parking lot will appear crowded, but most of the vehicles belong to water buffs. Most of the fisherpersons who frequent the trail never travel more than the first few miles.

HIKE 11 *BABY LAKE TRAIL*

General description: A generally secluded trail traveling six miles through forests and mountain meadows. Total elevation gain of this hike is 2,600 feet.

General location: Approximately twenty miles west of Encampment, in the northern section of the Huston Park Wilderness Area.

Maps: Medicine Bow National Forest visitor's map and USGS Bridger Peak and Red Mountain quads.

Special attractions: A fun trail that is half deep timber and half high mountain meadows. Exceptional scenic vistas.

For more information: Hayden Ranger District, Medicine Bow National Forest, P.O. Box 187, Encampment, WY, 82325, (307) 327-5481.

Finding the trailhead: To reach the trailhead, drive west from Encampment on Wyoming Highway 70 for approximately twenty miles. On the way, you'll cross the Continental Divide at Battle Pass (9,916 feet). This spot and a location one mile south at the Huston Park trailhead are good places to park one vehicle if you want to make a nine-mile one-way hike with the Baby Lake Trail. Approximately six miles farther, a few hundred feet before the Lost Creek Campground, turn left (south) onto Forest Road 811. After 300 feet make another left turn onto a more primitive road. The Forest Service is planning to upgrade this road in the future so sedans can drive to the trailhead parking area located about three-quarters of a mile south. Meanwhile, if you're driving a low-clearance vehicle, you should park along the gravel just off the highway. Either way, follow the road south for three-quarters of a mile to an area designated "Trailhead Parking."

The hike: The Baby Lake Trail is a scenic hike through lodgepole forests and high mountain meadows. Although easily completed in one day, there are numerous campsites along the way. The trail gets its name from the fact that it follows Baby Lake Creek. It does not specifically go to Baby Lake.

On foot from the parking lot continue south and downhill on a primitive road to the Huston Park Wilderness Boundary. The road pre-dates the area's wilderness designation. In .5 mile it descends 400 feet to an old sheep bridge across Battle Creek.

The bridge and the Baby Lake Trail are legacies of sheep grazing on national forest lands. Reconstructed in 1962 to provide access for sheep grazing, it now provides access for hikers and backpackers. Sheep use of the Baby Lake area was discontinued in 1986. While hiking this area, notice that most of the trees are relatively young. Huge fires, on the scale of the recent Yellowstone conflagration, killed many of the trees in the Sierra Madre Mountains between 120 to 140 years ago. For about 100 years after these fires, the area was relatively open, meaning the trees were small and there was room between them for grass and shrubs to grow. Over the past several decades, as the trees have grown larger, they have shaded more of the ground. This shading has gradually decreased the amount of grass and forbs for livestock and wildlife.

After crossing the bridge, bear left up a short hill. Blazes and cairns (refurbished in 1991) mark the trail from this point on. For the next hour or so, your hike will be through lodgepole pine forests. In about two miles the trail begins to parallel Baby Lake Creek. Out of sight of the trail, the creek is evident

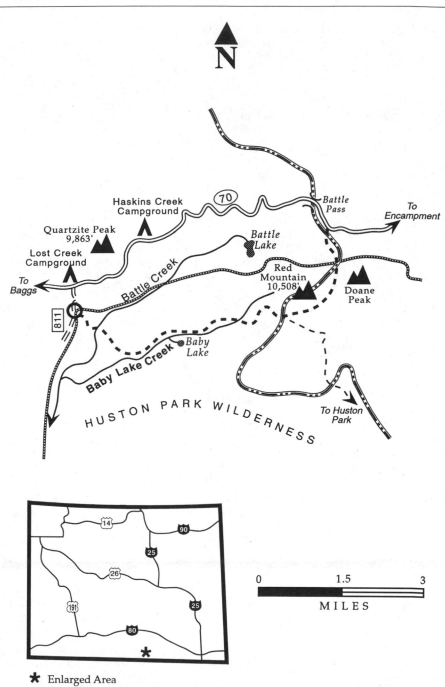

by the murmur it makes behind a screen of alder and willows. Baby Lake is located about .8 mile south of the trail in a large meadow. The term lake is generous.

In a short time the vegetation begins the transition from heavy forest to an area of mixed forest and mountain meadows. The trail across these meadows is often overgrown with lush grass. Be alert for blazes on trees at the far end of the meadow. Cairns and posts also mark the route. These meadows are a favorite bedding ground for the many deer and elk in the area. Both their beds in the grass and their tracks are commonly seen in the area.

After traveling through several meadows, the trail gradually steepens until it reaches the Continental Divide at the low saddle just south of Red Mountain. This can be a turn-around point or one can continue and turn southward onto the Continental Divide National Scenic Trail and into alpine Huston Park. Looking back, one gets a great view of the Snake River Valley. Ahead are the lush meadows at the head of Long Park.

For those who left a vehicle near Battle Pass, continue on and slightly downhill for another quarter mile to the junction with the Huston Park Trail. Turning north, it's a short three miles to the highway at Battle Pass.

In 1968 the National Trails System Act was passed and included authorization for the study of the Continental Divide National Scenic Trail. The CDNST proposes to be a continuous trail from Canada to Mexico, totaling 3,100 miles, spanning twenty-five national forests, three national parks, four BLM districts, endless private land, and five basic life zones as it traverses the Rocky Mountains. This trail does not yet exist in completed form, but forty-five miles do exist in the Hayden District of the Medicine Bow National Forest. Almost eleven miles of the CDNST follow the Continental Divide in the 31,300 acre Huston Park Wilderness.—*Mike Murphy*

MEDICINE BOW MOUNTAINS
The Snowy Range

Directly west of the flat, dry, high prairie surrounding Laramie, Wyoming State Highway 130, in a few miles, climbs to above timberline elevations and into a gorgeous display of alpine beauty. The Snowy Range and its high altitude flora and fauna sit atop the northern end of the Medicine Bow Mountains. This unique range, with its quartzite cliff faces and many-laked basins, reflects the ancient glacial activity that carved its present physical features and stark beauty. It is so named because snow exists perpetually on some of the mountain slopes, and they appear white most of the year.

Lorraine Bonney, author of numerous Wyoming guides and narratives, notes: "The Medicine Bows may be one of the most abused mountain ranges in the country." The entire mountain range—except for the Snowy Range—looks like a checkers game where the surviving forest has had most of its pieces jumped by clearcuts. The Forest Service's forest plan allows future logging, oil, gas, and mineral developments in the few remaining roadless areas, which happen to be the most popular area on the forest, for hikers and elk.

Except for climbing Medicine Bow Peak, the Snowy Range trails presented in this book mention alternative approaches to the creek bottoms, ridgetops,

Snowy Range high lake country. MIKE GOSSI PHOTO

and open alpine lake country of this range by less popular trailheads. As is the case everywhere, a little cross-country trekking in this glorious mountain land soon separates you from almost everyone else.

HIKE 12 *SHEEP LAKE TRAIL*

General description: An easy day, overnighter, or three-day packing trip on a relatively untraveled trail with good fishing and camping spots.

General location: Forty miles west of Laramie in the middle of the Snowy Range.

Maps: Medicine Bow National Forest visitor map and/or USGS Sand Lake quad.

Special attractions: Deer, elk, coyote, subalpine parks, and wildflowers.

For more information: Brush Creek Ranger District, 212 S. 1st, P.O. Box 249, Saratoga, WY, 82331, (307) 326-5258.

Finding the trailhead: The southern trailhead begins at Brooklyn Lake near the Brooklyn Lake Campground. Signs direct you to this area 4.5 miles east of Snowy Range Pass on Wyoming State Highway 130. Here Forest Service Road 317 exits the highway north at the Nash Fork Campground and winds northward just over two miles to the Brooklyn Lake Campground.

The northern trailhead begins 100 yards east of Sand Lake. Sand Lake is accessible from Interstate 80 by taking exit 287 north of Arlington and driving west along the frontage road for 1.2 miles. Here a sign directs you south onto what becomes Forest Service Road 111. Follow it for thirteen

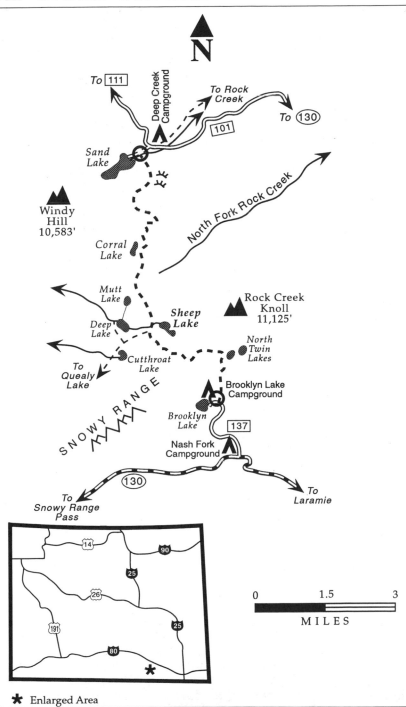

N

To 111

Deep Creek Campground

To Rock Creek

101

To 130

Sand Lake

North Fork Rock Creek

Windy Hill 10,583'

Corral Lake

Mutt Lake

Rock Creek Knoll 11,125'

Sheep Lake

Deep Lake

North Twin Lakes

Cutthroat Lake

To Quealy Lake

Brooklyn Lake Campground

SNOWY RANGE

Brooklyn Lake

137

Nash Fork Campground

130

To Snowy Range Pass

To Laramie

14

90

25

26

191

25

80

★

0   1.5   3

MILES

★ Enlarged Area

miles to the intersection of Forest Service Road 101. Turn left or east here, and one mile later you come to the Deep Creek Campground. A road turns south off of this campground and leads to the trailhead. These roads, being well-maintained logging roads, are fine for the smallest compact car. Sand Lake is also accessible from Wyoming State Highway 130 by turning 2.5 miles west of the tiny town of Centennial onto Forest Service Road 101. It's a twenty-mile northward drive along this gravel road to the Deep Creek Campground.

The hike: Beginning at Brooklyn Lake Campground and traveling north, the hiker finds a rocky, well-traveled trail rising 300 feet over the 2.5 miles to Sheep Lake. Don't be surprised to find several hundred sheep grazing along the way The land is leased from the Forest Service. Sheep Lake and neighboring Deep Lake are popular day and overnight hikes.

North of Sheep Lake, hiker traffic thins considerably and so does the trail. The countryside here is formed from high glacial plains and contains few trees. Jeff Lake provides cover, campsites, and fair fishing. Farther north at Corral Lake the remnants of old horse pens can be found. Here the trail is relatively flat, traveling slightly downhill through lush grass meadows that alternate with forested settings. The final mile before Sand Lake turns into old jeep tracks through the timber.

Late season travel is advised in this country if you want to avoid mosquitos and experience the abundant wildflowers. Spring comes exceptionally late to this high land. This trail can be combined with Hike 13 (the Deep Creek Trail) and continue north past Sand Lake for those wishing to travel longer distances or to view the entirety of descending Snowy Range ecosystems.—*Mike and Mary Gossi*

HIKE 13 *DEEP CREEK/ROCK CREEK*

General description: A gentle day, overnight, or longer stroll (all downhill one way) on an excellent trail through timbered settings. Total distance is eleven miles one way.

General location: Thirty five miles west of Laramie, in the northern section of the Snowy Range.

Maps: Medicine Bow National Forest map and/or USGS Sand Lake, Arlington, and White Rock Canyon quads.

Special attractions: A wonderful chance to follow a mountain stream from high glacial plains to the high desert floor.

For more information: Brush Creek Ranger District, 212 S. 1st., P.O. Box 249, Saratoga, WY, 82331, (307) 326-5258.

Finding the trailhead: Follow the access directions to the Deep Creek Campground (HIKE 12) for the southern trailhead and a downhill hike. Leave Interstate 80 at exit 287, the Arlington exit, and travel south along the frontage road .25 mile. Where the sign notes the Rock Creek Trailhead, turn left or east on the rougher road and travel 1.5 miles through private land to the northern, Rock Creek trailhead and an uphill beginning.

The hike: Deep Creek, which merges with and becomes Rock Creek, can be a point-to-point eleven-mile hike. Rock Creek and nearby Rock Mountain

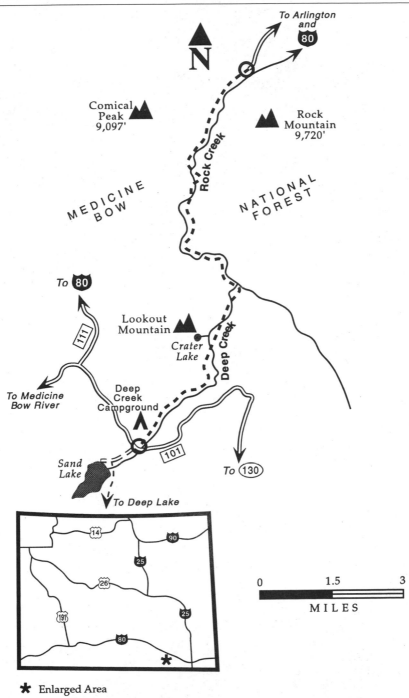

A view from Medicine Bow Peak MIKE GOSSI PHOTO

are obviously named. In 1883 this area contained a major Union Pacific railroad cattle shipping center. Hundreds of carloads of cattle were shipped every day from here to northern Wyoming. Now the area plays a major role in Wyoming's bentonite production.

Beginning at the Deep Creek Campground, the trail leads down from open glacial plains into forested canyons. Downstream 3.5 miles an unofficial trail cuts to the west and heads to Crater Lake. Here the hiker enjoys some nice campsites and good fishing. Despite its name, Crater Lake is glacially formed and spring fed.

Slightly over a mile farther, the trail crosses Deep Creek and joins the western side of larger Rock Creek. Now it travels first through fir and spurce forests and then into thinner pine forests as the canyon bottom nears the forest boundary. The rocky scenery is impressive here. The northern end of the trail is heavily used by joggers and day hikers.—*Mike and Mary Gossi*

HIKE 14 *MEDICINE BOW PEAK*

General description: A short, scenic peak climb with moderate elevation gain that can be hiked as a loop hike.
General location: Thirty-five miles west of Laramie, near the Snowy Range Pass crest, in the Medicine Bow Mountains.
Maps: Medicine Bow National Forest map and/or USGS Medicine Bow Peak quad.

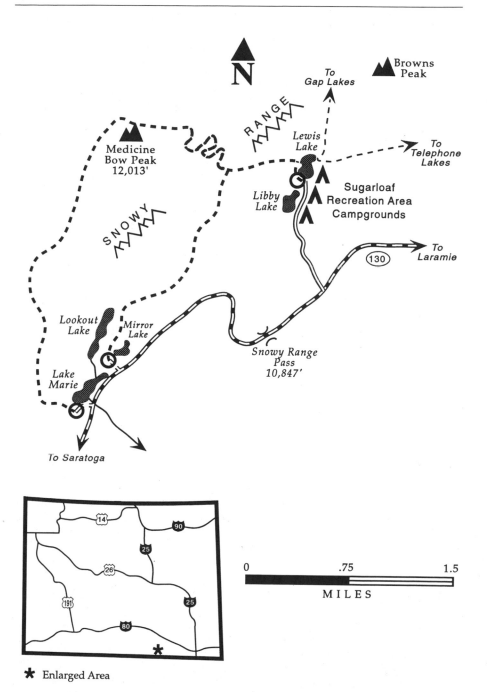

Special attractions: Ready access plus fairly short and easy hiking for such unparalleled views and alpine peak grandeur.

For more information: Brush Creek Ranger District, 212 S. 1st., P.O. Box 249, Saratoga, WY, 82331, (307) 326-5258.

Finding the trailhead: The peak can be accessed from three locations. Sugarloaf Recreation area, .5 mile east of Snowy Range Pass on Wyoming Highway 130, provides the shortest route. Beginning from the trailhead at Lewis Lake, which is reached by following the signs and driving one mile north of the main highway into the Sugarloaf Recreation Area.

The hike: Medicine Bow Peak, at 12,013 feet is the highest summit in the Snowys. One of the area's first fire lookouts used to be atop this lofty mountain, but it was eventually abandoned and dismantled because it was in the clouds much of the time. The well-marked and well-used path rises 1,300 feet to the summit in less than two miles.

The Lake Marie Trailhead, located one-and-a-half miles west of the highway pass, adds an extra 300 feet elevation gain to the climb. This trail is not quite as steep as the Lewis Lake access and follows the gentle back side of the Snowy Range, providing great views to the north and west.

Mirror Lake Campground forms the third access point. It's located about one mile west of Snowy Range Pass. Starting at this point, the hiker passes beside many small lakes of a glacial moraine and beneath the cliffy face of Medicine Bow Peak's eastern side. This Mirror Lake Trail joins the Lewis Lake Trail after a couple of miles, and it's about a mile to the top from this point. At the summit one witnesses spectacular views, south to Rocky Mountain National Park in Colorado and north to Gap, Telephone, Deep, and Sheep lakes.—*Mike and Mary Gossi*

CENTRAL AND SOUTHERN WYOMING

This vast and somewhat barren-appearing section of high plateau desert comprises much of Wyoming. Here the roads are long and the trails, if they exist at all, are short. The mountain ranges that rise in these areas haven't gained notice that a national forest might bring to them. The extensive flats, rolling hills and intermittent ravines creating much of this country are known mostly to local ranchers and more recently by developers and ATVers.

But occasional hiking treasures do exist here for the people who both know how to seek them out and how to appreciate them for what they are. A large-scale topographical map of the area reveals endless hills and mountain ranges and washes, many with quite alluring contours and names. A BLM surface map of the area shows who owns what and reveals that a majority of the land boasts federal or state government ownership. A trustworthy vehicle and an adventuresome spirit can place you in the middle of, or on top of, some of the wildest, most spectacular, most unknown scenery in Wyoming.

The Bureau of Land Management (BLM) is the majority stockholder on these lands, controlling nearly one eighth of this country's land area. The 1976 Federal Land Policy and Management Act (FLPMA) authorized the agency to pursue multiple use management directions, and lately the BLM appears to be taking a more balanced management approach. Recreation, habitat preservation, endangered species protection and wilderness find themselves in the BLM's active vocabulary. Trails and wilderness study areas and riparian rehabilitation on these "lands that no one else wanted" are now being put together.

HIKE 15 GARDEN CREEK FALLS

General description: A spectacular but steep day hike to an impressive waterfall.

General location: A few miles directly south of Casper, on Casper Mountain.

Maps: Bureau of Land Management CASPER surface land management map or USGS Casper topographic quad.

Special attractions: Great photographic opportunities around a lofty waterfall. Also some nice cross-country ridge hiking with good viewing areas.

For more information: Bureau of Land Management, 1701 East E St., Casper, Wyoming, 82601, (307) 261-7600 or 261-7650. Also, Casper Chamber of Commerce, 500 N. Center, Casper, WY, 82601, (307) 234-5311.

Finding the trailhead: Turn south after leaving Interstate 25 exit 185, near the east end of Casper, onto State Highway 258 or Wyoming Boulevard. Circle the southern end of Casper for 6.5 miles on this road. Here a stoplight and a Casper Mountain Road sign and a Wyoming Highway 251 sign point the direction southward. Two miles of uphill driving takes you to the Wyoming Highway 252 junction where you turn right or west and follow paved 252 for .3 mile. A blue Rotary Park sign labels a paved road that veers off to the left. After .7 mile on this road you arrive at a graveled parking lot and the beginning of the Garden Falls trailheads.

The hike: Anyone who has driven Interstate 25 south through Wyoming has noticed this alluring, timbered mountain rising above the prairie and south of the city of Casper. Although most of Casper Mountain is privately owned and inaccessable, this small Rotary Club park affords the opportunity to explore a small part of the steep topography overlooking the city. Garden Creek Falls, especially in the spring, is a sensational waterfall for this part of the world.

There are two ways to view these falls. Southwest of and before crossing the bridge over Garden Creek, a maintained trail wanders up the creek a short distance to the best overall vista of the waterfall. Across the bridge and along the eastern shores of Garden Creek, a second trail follows the waters and soon climbs the steep cliffs surrounding the falls. This trail branches into many pathways and routes across the cliffs, but a main course does exist. The trails on this side are unofficial. These trails climb beside and above the 120-foot waterfall and offer some interesting views. A nice picnic area sits near the stream above the falls.

These "trails" that lead to the head of the falls are exceptionally steep and quite exposed. If you've a fear of heights, they're not advised. Also note that the area, being so near a larger city, is kind of a party hotspot. This makes early morning a great time to visit the country and the view the falls.

An exciting addition to this short hike are the human "game" trails that break away from the paths on the east side of the creek and lead to a nice, less steep ridge walk that overlooks Casper and the prairie beyond. They are steep, but

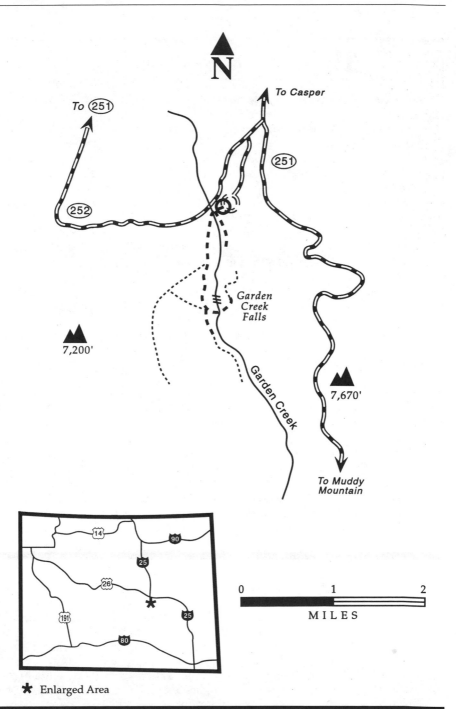

Garden Creek Falls.

the ridge is unpopulated and worthy of exploration. Another opportunity to cross-country exists above the falls. Most folks quit hiking just beyond where the falls begin. But a sweet little path does trace its way up the canyon and through a varigated woodland along the eastern side of the creek.

Be aware that cross-country paths leading to the top of the falls do exist on the western side of the creek, but they are beyond exceptionally steep and slippery, to the point of being dangerous. Map aficionados will notice that something labeled "Asbestos Spring" lives near the headwaters of this creek. Perhaps you should carry your own drinking water to the park.

HIKE 16 *FERRIS MOUNTAINS*

General description: A trackless, virtually unknown range of mountains with elevations topping 10,000 feet.

General location: Approximately forty-five miles north of Rawlins, near a high desert pass and small settlement called Muddy Gap.

Maps: Bureau of Land Managment BAIROIL surface management map and USGS Spanish Mine, Youngs Pass and Muddy Gap quads.

Special attractions: Unpopulated and unknown deep canyons, steep slopes and high mountain ridges and peaks.

For more information: BLM Rawlins District, 1300 Third Street, P.O. Box 670, Rawlins, WY, 82301, (307) 324-7171.

Finding the trailhead: Driving north from Rawlins on U.S. Highway 287 for forty-five miles places you at the one gas station town named Three Forks or Muddy Gap. South and east of this highway junction area lies an unknown range labled the Ferris Mountains.

Currently it takes a real bloodhound to nose out the legal byways into this range. According to the recreation director at the Rawlins BLM office, the only legal access into the Ferris Mountains at this time is via county and offshoot BLM roads on the north side of the range. The BLM hopes to gain more access to the area and mark the roads in the future. As it stands now, even the county roads sometimes have no signing; they seem to be the more gravelly ones that intersect the main highways with stop signs. It's oftentimes anybody's guess which are the BLM legal access roads. The map accompanying this area describes road access as it stands in 1991, but the recreation director's major recommendation is that persons contact the Rawlins office before heading into the Ferris Mountains area.

The hike: The absolute hardest chore a guidebook author faces is deciding whether or not to reveal to the hiking crowd the biggest secret he has discovered. The Ferris Mountains form a BLM wilderness study area of 22,245 acres, one of the largest as-yet untouched areas the BLM owns. Nine- to ten-thousand-foot forested peaks hide from view the shrub-covered and unforested slopes, the grassy meadows and riparian zones that occur in the many open parks of this range. The mountains are rugged, quite steep and essentially roadless. Wildlife abounds here, as does unusual geology.

The greatest joy of the Ferris Mountains is that they exemplify wilderness as wilderness used to be. They not only are unscathed by roads, they also contain no trails. The hiking experience of the Ferris Mountains is one of driving to the area, parking near the scenery or landscape that attracts you the most, and just wandering anywhere the calling takes you. I can't draw a map of a specific hike because there is none. This area is a vast playground without any of the confines (i.e., trails) we've allowed to dominate most other hiking playgrounds. Variety and surprising beauty rule this country. I wandered aimlessly for a day in the northeastern corner of the range and experienced vast, untrammeled valleys, crystal creeks, sandstone hogback ridges, flowers beyond comparison, juniper/pinion forests and snow-dappled forested mountaintops sporting incomparable views in all directions.

A trip into the Ferris mountains is recommended for those who have strong

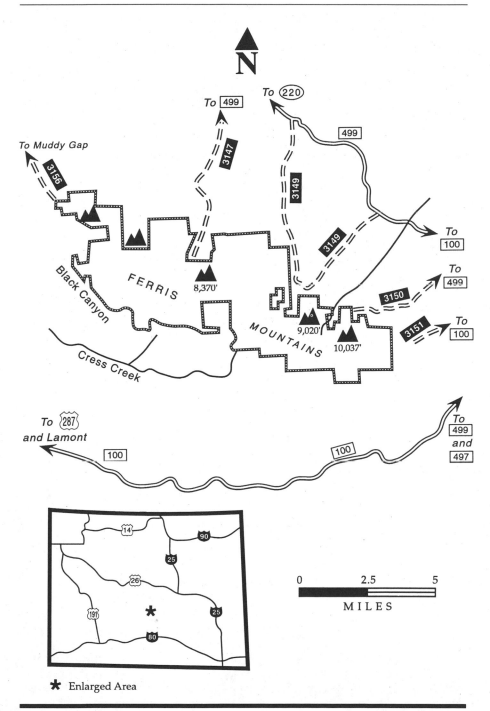

map and compass skills. It is not for the novice hiker. The place offers you both the chance to grab a topo and test your map and compass skills and the chance to test your luck at wandering into something new and surprising.

The water in these mountains is good, which is to say that it's not alkali, as most of the water in this section of Wyoming is. Be aware though that lots of cattle roam this country. Be also aware that if it rains and your rig is off the county road, where you are will be home until the sun shines for a few hours.

The Ferris Mountains area has been recommended for wilderness classification by the BLM. It now must gain similar approval from the President and Congress. Letters and loud voices are needed if this wild land is to remain that way.

HIKE 17 *FOURTEEN MILE RESERVOIR*

General description: A short and easy adventure into a lush microenvironment in the middle of harsh high plateau desert country.
General location: Fourteen miles due north of Rock Springs.
Maps: A map is not necessary for this short hike, but the landscape is portrayed on the Bureau of Land Management Rock Springs surface management map and on the USGS Pilot Butte quad.
Special attractions: A peaceful water and lush plant setting in the middle of dry and open country. A nice walking break in the middle of long drives.
For more information: Bureau of Land Management, Rock Springs District, P.O. Box 1869, Rock Springs, WY, 82901-1869, (307) 382-5350.
Finding the trailhead: This BLM rest stop is located fourteen miles north of Rock Springs along U.S. Highway 191 (on the way to the Wind Rivers). A blue and white highway sign points to the rest area.

The hike: This little trail will never be your great escape in hiking. In fact, the drone of the highway and a few towering powerlines a mile away are constant companions here. But there are some excellent reasons for including this area in the hiker's guide.

Sweetwater County, Wyoming's largest, seems to be part of the travel in getting to most anywhere else in the state. Long miles of driving through geographic names like Red Desert Flat, Alkali Flat, Greasewood Flat, and Bad Lands Hills leave the traveler aching in the joints and convinced that nothing viable exists in this section of Wyoming. Tiny Fourteen Mile Reservoir offers one the chance to stretch the legs with a decent walk and to witness firsthand how much life does hide in the nooks and crannies of the Red Desert.

Someone dammed a tiny spring and created a small lake in the middle of sage-dominated slate and bentonite lands. The trail begins north of the picnic tables and is easy to follow as it wanders back to a feeder spring that is situated at the base of some badland-type hills. Suddenly you find yourself amid a world of thick bushes and thicker water-loving plants, where bird songs resound and the alkali scent of the country is moist instead of dry and dusty. After the trail crosses the trickle of a waterway, it cuts up a steep slope. Atop this little hill you can turn left and follow a circular trail back to the car with great overviews of the reservoir and surrounding country. Turning right above the

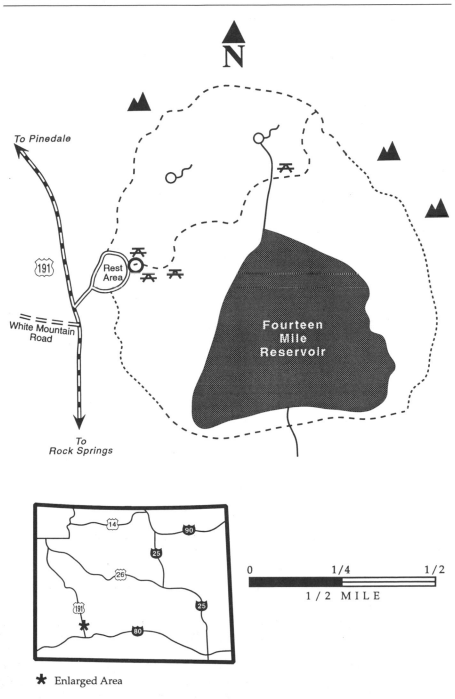

Fourteen Mile Reservoir

To Pinedale

Rest Area

White Mountain Road

To Rock Springs

0   1/4   1/2

1/2 MILE

★ Enlarged Area

spring and following the faint trail cross-country leads you across hilltops, into a ragged ravine, and finally across the dam itself. The first loop is about a half mile long; the second closer to a mile.

Morning is the finest time to hike Fourteen Mile, being soft with colors and noisy with birds. If you arrive in the heat of the afternoon, I didn't see any "no swimming" signs when I was there.

HIKE 18 *FOSSIL BUTTE NATIONAL MONUMENT*

General description: A historic, geologically fascinating and amazingly beautiful place to spend a day hiking two separate trails and reliving ancient land formation stories.

General location: Approximately twelve miles west of Kemmerer along US Highway 30.

Maps: Fossil Butte National Monument Quarry Trail and Activities handouts and/or USGS The Rock Slide, Nugget and Fossil quads. Kemmerer Reservoir quad is optional.

Special attractions: Fossil beds amid limestone cliffs, all deposited from an ancient sea bed. Great hiking in open prairie and atop picturesque buttes with far-reaching views.

For more information: Fossil Butte National Monument, P.O. Box 592, Kemmerer, WY, 83101, (307) 877-4455.

Finding the trailhead: Fossil Lake Trail-From Kemmerer, drive west on U.S. Highway 30 for 10.5 miles. A sign here directs you north toward the monument on paved Lincoln County Road 300. After two and a half miles of westward driving, another sign points north and a paved road takes you the mile to the visitor center.

Quarry Trail-About one mile along Lincoln County road 300, after you've turned off the main highway, a sign notes the location of the historic quarry trail, and a short gravel road leads to a parking lot by the now-deserted old contact station.

The hike: The Wyoming prairie assumes a new and exciting countenance in the state's southwestern corner. Here, white limestone and reddish shale buttes rise and fall like land-locked waves. Actually, waves is an apt description, because this entire area, 50 million years ago, was a vast subtropical lake teaming with multiple varieties of fish, insects and plants. The ancient flora and fauna en masse were perfectly preserved by the calcium carbonate particles that covered them with a protective blanket. The site is now preserved by National Monument classification, and here paleontologists still seek answers to questions about the past.

Highly recommended is a tour of the visitor center. The monument has two separate hiking trails, and they serve as a nice introduction to the area. But a real joy for the hiker is to cross-country it to a high butte top and bask in the spacious and rolling prairie-scapes. The Park Service permits and encourages cross-country hiking.

NOTE: Within the National Monument everything, from fossils to flowers, is protected. It is illegal to remove any fossils. I did listen to stories of people spending time in jail for removing fossils they found lying on the ground.

Limestone buttes contain fossilized flora and fauna, Fossil Butte National Monument.

Fossil Lake Trail

Beyond the visitor center, continue following the paved road north and uphill for two more miles. A picnic ground is situated among a grove of aspen trees, and .3 mile beyond this point a small parking lot marks the Fossil Lake Trailhead.

Be sure and look to the north, once you've hiked .3 mile up this trail, for a superb beaver dam constructed above a trickling spring amid a splendid aspen grove. This 1.5-mile-long loop trail travels through some of the best views in the park while leading you uphill to the one active quarry in the monu-

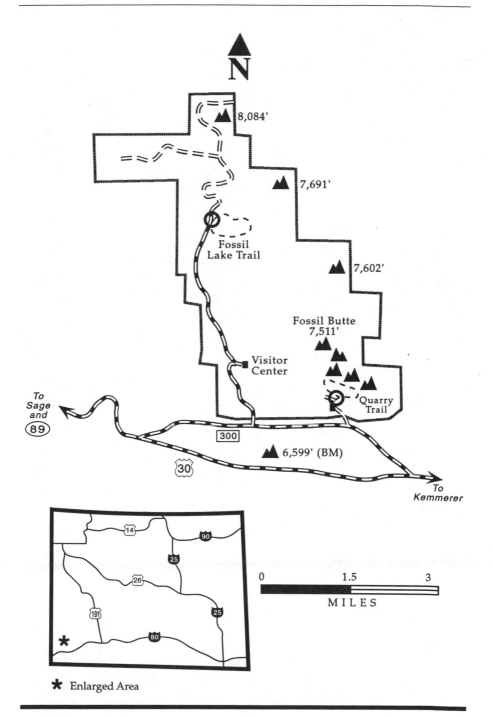

ment. The final version of the trail was scheduled for completion in the summer of 1991. When I was there much of the trail was orange-ribboned primitive pathway. The trail circles beneath the quarry cliffs and then decends the steep hills through a thick and mature aspen grove. It ends at the picnic ground.

While hiking this area, you'll probably find yourself looking eastward and up to the ridgetop above you. It's called Cundick Ridge and is a glorious cross-country wander.

Quarry Trail

This 2.5-mile loop trail climbs to a historic fossil quarry on the face of Fossil Butte. Remnants of the "fishermen", as the turn of the century fossil collectors were called, are evident along the route. This is an interpretive trail, and several unobtrusive markers explain the history, geology and wildlife highlights of the area. The trail gains over 600 feet elevation in a short distance. If the loop part of the trail is traveled clockwise, the uphill slope is not as steep. If it rains while you're hiking, count on sliding through some honest gumbo.

At the high northwest corner of the trail's loop, a short side trail switchbacks up the butte's face to the old quarry site. West of this trail is the best place to cross-country hike to the top of Fossil Butte and into the scenic high prairie. Bring a bottle of water, especially during summer, Also carry some binoculars, for wildlife and raptors are abundant.

NORTH-CENTRAL WYOMING
The Big Horn Mountains

Wyoming owns fifty peaks that tower more than 13,000 feet above sea level. But three of these giants reside outside the Wind River Range, one of them being 13,167-foot Cloud Peak in the Big Horn Range. These impressive mountains sweep in a crescent arc from southern Montana toward the center of Wyoming where they nominally merge with the Owl Creek Mountains. The Big Horns offer granite summits, timbered slopes, crystaline water sources, and valuable wilderness habitat in the midst of the monotonous sagebrush prairies of the Powder River Basin to the east and the dry plains of the Bighorn Basin to the west. These basins, rich in uranium, oil and coal, propose to devour much of the precious water supplied by the Big Horns.

Three indian tribes, the Cheyenne, Sioux and Crow, journeyed into these mountains for solitude and spiritual inspiration. The Crow Indians especially defended the Big Horns as religious and hunting grounds. Today's Big Horn battles focus on the remaining pieces of the range's original structure, as industry, roads and people all vie for a share of what's left of the mountain pie.

One hundred and twenty miles long, and at the widest point fifty miles wide, these mountains are dazzling in their recorded history, wilderness grandeur, spectacular alpine lakes, hiking and exploration possibilities.

HIKE 19 *SYKES MOUNTAIN*

General description: A half day's exploration into some uniquely harsh and seldom visited Wyoming landscape.

General location: Approximately twelve miles north of Lovell, by the western shores of Yellowtail Reservoir in the Bighorn National Recreation Area.

Maps: USGS Sykes Spring quad.

Special attractions: Untrammeled, almost mysterious desert sandstone country; great views of the Bighorn Basin, the Big Horn and the Pryor mountains extending into Montana.

For more information: Bighorn Canyon National Recreation Area, South District, 20 Highway 14A East, Lovell, WY, 82413, (307) 548-2251. (Be advised, it's highly unlikely the above visitor's center knows much about this untrailed and unvisited area.)

Finding the trailhead: Three miles east of Lovell on U.S. highway Alternative 14, Wyoming State Highway 37 ventures northward and into the recreation area. Follow this paved road about ten miles to the well-signed Horseshoe Bend turnoff. For the last couple of miles, a mound of reddish rock has been visible to the east. This unimpressive (from the road) hunk of nothing is Sykes Mountain. The best access parking is at an old and abandoned bar on the west side of the state highway, just before (south) of the Horseshoe Bend Road.

The hike: The Sykes Mountain cross-country adventure is certainly not a hike for everybody. It is geared, rather, for backpackers well-versed in cross-country travel. Those who love to wander for wandering's sake will probably enjoy this bizarre piece of landscape. As far as I can tell, it is the only viable piece of hiking exploration the Bighorn Canyon National Recreation Area Wyoming side affords.

I guarantee your first thought after parking will be "What on earth do I want to hike this dismal pile of rock rubble for?" I also guarantee that appearances are deceiving.

Easiest and most exciting access to this desert mountain follows the first dry, unnamed little north-south drainage that intersects the Horseshoe Bend Road. Hike about .1 mile east of the Highway 37/Horseshoe Bend Road intersection and turn south and into this first canyon. If you cut up the second north-south drainage to the east, you'll soon be against an impassable cliff. A great game trail exists on the west side of this first drainage, and you can follow it into the canyon. Where a rockslide heaps into the canyon bottom, the game trail crosses to the east side of the drainage and continues its upward climb. This is the last game trail clue I can offer, for the canyon and climb now become a fascinating piece of cross-country work in finding your way upward through a maze of miniature canyons, scrub juniper and ragged rock formations. The journey is never too difficult, but it is always rugged and climbs a series of rocky stepping stones.

After a mile weaving upward, you face a gaping canyon whose ridge forces the journey eastward. Traveling east as far as possible, you come to a steep escarpment that overlooks the Big Horn Canyon, Yellowtail Reservoir, and the Pryor Mountains to the North. From here the highest point of the mountain, Crooked Point, is visible. It's worth it to wander across the rock and

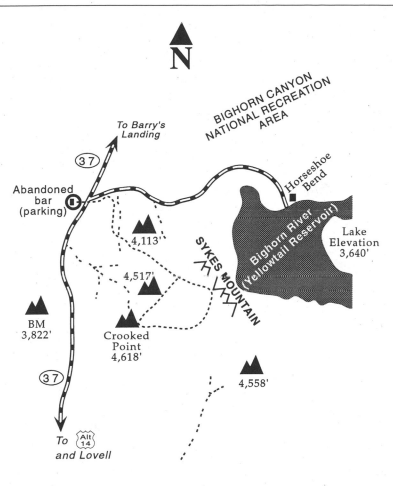

N

BIGHORN CANYON NATIONAL RECREATION AREA

To Barry's Landing

37

Abandoned bar (parking)

Horseshoe Bend

4,113'

SYKES MOUNTAIN

Bighorn River (Yellowtail Reservoir)

Lake Elevation 3,640'

4,517'

BM 3,822'

Crooked Point 4,618'

37

4,558'

To Alt 14 and Lovell

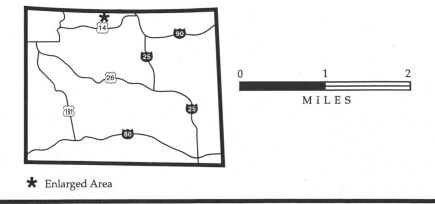

14

90

25

26

191

25

80

0 1 2

MILES

★ Enlarged Area

sand flats and up the hillside to this summit. Unusual weathered sandstone formations live atop that point, and the 360-degree view of the Bighorn Basin is astounding.

This land is harsh and stark. First appearances dictate that nothing could live up here. But after a few hours and several miles of wandering, I saw herds of mule deer, jumped from a few rattlesnake buzzes, and witnesed unique flowers that possibly grow only in that spartan environment.

Bring water on this hike. It's dry, hot country. For that reason, early morning and early season are the best hiking times. This is not a tennis shoe hike—it's far too rugged a terrain. And although there were a few rattlesnakes, they were quite friendly. They warned you of their presence long before you stepped on them.

HIKE 20 *PAINT ROCK CREEK*

General description: A easy and gentle day or overnight hike into an exceptional canyon-country drainage of the western slopes of the Big Horn Mountains.

General location: Approximately fifty miles northeast of Worland, in the BLM lands bordering the Big Horn Mountains.

Maps: Bighorn National Forest visitors map, BLM Worland surface map, and/or USGS Hyatt Ranch and Allen Draw quads. Lake Solitude quad is optional.

Special attractions: Unique country, towering limestone cliffs above a pristine riparian creek setting. Excellent stream fishing.

For more information: Bureau of Land Management, Worland District Office, P.O. Box 119, Worland, WY, 82401, (307) 347-9871.

Finding the trailhead: Between Worland and Greybull, scenic state highway 31 travels eastward toward the Big Horn Mountains and to the tiny farming burg of Hyattville. One-half mile north of this town a paved road—the Alkali-Cold Springs Road—continues the journey. Stay on the Cold Springs paved road when the Alkali part of this road turns to gravel and jogs off to the north. Five miles later the pavement will end. Here the Cold Springs Road goes left or north up a hill, and Hyatt Lane shoots right or south. Less than a mile along Hyatt Lane sits the sign noting the Paint Rock Creek parking area.

The hike: Paint Rock Creek possibly derived its name from the Indian tribes that used the clay of variegated colors found on the creek's banks for ceremonial and war paint. Another story states that the creek was called Paintrock for the Indian pictographs found on a nearby cliff.

The first 1.7 miles of this trail is on private land that has been graciously opened to public access by the Hyatt Ranch. Stay on the road that skirts the north side of several grassy hay fields. And be sure to close all gates you pass through. Near the towering cliffs of the mouth of the canyon, BLM land is noted by a sign and fence. Hiking now becomes ideal for the next six miles. The roadbed turns into a wide trail that is being reclaimed by returning vegetation. The walking is smooth and level. The creek flows quite large and carries a powerful voice. But the prominent feature of this journey is the castle-like, massive limestone cliffs.

One can camp almost anywhere in this canyon. One can also fish the stream

Canyonlands-type cliffs tower above Paint Rock Creek.

or steeply climb and explore the various breaks in the canyon's walls. The forested bottom contains some of the largest junipers I've seen. Near the forest service boundary, North and Middle Paint Rock creeks merge, and one can hike either stream a few miles and into a confusion of four wheel drive roads that surround the area. If you are in this canyon near sunset, be sure and look up. There is an amazing amount of eagle, hawk, falcon and swallow activity between the lofty cliffs.

It's advisable to hike this area earlier in the year. For one, the Hyatts allow access only from April through September. Also, the summer is hot and the

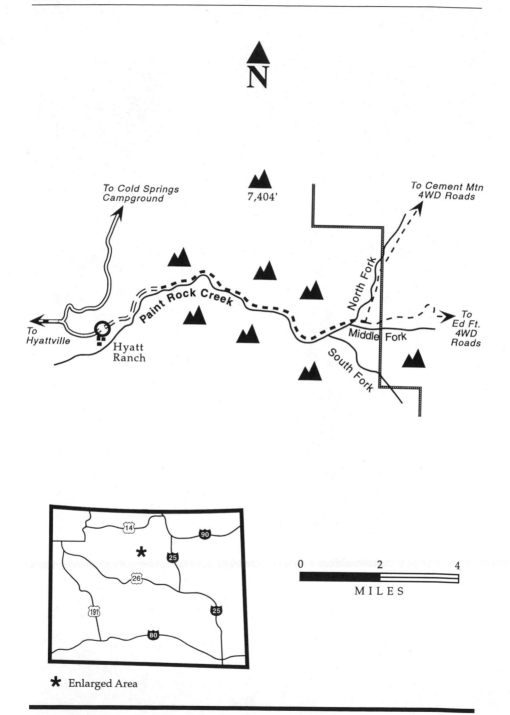

deerflies are profuse during late June and July. Another inarguable reason is that the main plant reclaiming the old road bed is cheat grass. Most folks from the west know the havoc cheat grass plays with the socks when it is dry.

Paint Rock Creek affords a Canyonlands-like experience in the middle of Wyoming. A corollary experience occurs in nearby Medicine Lodge State Archeological Site, where pictographs and petroglyphs abound.

You might consider writing the Hyatts a thank you note (Hyattville, WY, 82428) for allowing us access to such a unique area.

HIKE 21 *MIRROR LAKE AND LOST TWIN LAKES*

General description: A long day hike or perfect two- to three-day hike into high alpine lake settings in the southern end of the Cloud Peak Wilderness.
General location: Approximately fifty miles east of Worland, in the southwestern sector of the Bighorn National Forest.
Maps: Bighorn National Forest visitor map or USGS Lake Angeline and Lake Helen quads.
Special attractions: Hiking through lodgepole pine, grassy meadows and flowery, above timberline bio-successions. Several thousand foot high cliffs tower above the south shore of the Lost Twin Lakes.
For more information: Tensleep Ranger District, 2009 Bighorn Ave., Worland, WY, 82401, (307) 347-8291.
Finding the trailhead: From the tiny town of Tensleep (twenty six miles east of Worland on U.S. Highway 16) drive east on U.S. 16 through spectacular Tensleep Canyon for eighteen miles. At mile marker forty-four turn left onto Forest Service road 27. A huge "Deerhaven Lodge" sign and a "West Tensleep Lake" sign mark the road. Seven miles of northward driving along this wide gravel road brings you to another sign pointing left to the campground and right to the trailhead. There is a huge parking lot, and at its north end an information board and a sign which notes the Middle Tensleep trailhead.

The hike: West Tensleep Lake and Campground serve as beginnings for the most popular hikes into the Cloud Peak Wilderness area. A few days of hiking in this beautiful section of the Big Horns will explain its notoriety. Tensleep Canyon and Creek inherited their names from an old Indian campsite that was "ten sleeps" or ten days of travel from important points like Yellowstone and Fort Laramie.

Up a closed road .1 mile, a small "Mirror Lake" sign points north or left, toward the trail whose first miles trace along a gentle, lodgepole forest ridge. Miss this guidepost and you'll hike the road to who-knows-where. The trail then switchbacks down to an easy creek crossing. Tank up here, because the next mile is a steep and steady incline to a ridgetop view of rock-covered peaks. At 2.7 miles the trail crosses Tensleep Creek. In late June this meant a wade, but it becomes a rock hop later in the year. Mirror Lake actually seems like the lost lake, because after crossing the creek you have to leave the trail and hike a grassy ridge east for .2 mile to reach its shores. Good camping exists on the West shore of this pretty lake.

The trail now becomes a mellow walk through alpine meadows and forests. Tensleep Creek sometimes races wild and rushing, and sometimes lazes

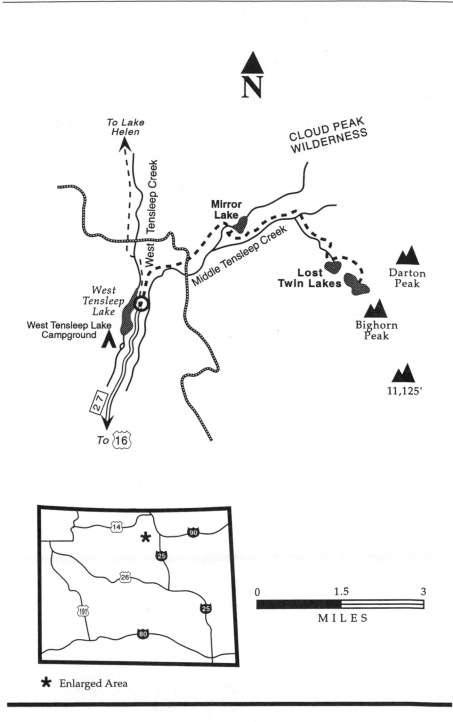

Towering cliffs surround lower Lost Twin Lake

through the gorgeous scenery. At 4.7 miles another creek crossing (or wade, depending on how far you can jump) marks the last leg to Lost Twin Lakes. After the crossing, the trail is hard to see, but simply leave the creek by journeying straight south and into the woods. For another 1.5 miles the trail climbs steeply to the first Lost Twin Lake. The thousand-foot cliff faces dropping into the peaceful and enclosed lake setting form astounding scenery to camp in.

This is simply a very nice high country hike. The area shows no signs of overuse. Using the lake as a base camp, one can hike— rock hop, actually—to the tops of the surrounding peaks.

HIKE 22 *MISTYMOON LAKE*

General description: A moderate to rugged two- to three-day hike into the alpine lake country of the Cloud Peak Wilderness. This trail serves as an enjoyable hike in itself and as a base camp hike for climbing Cloud Peak (hike 23).
General location: Approximately fifty miles east of Worland, in the southwestern sector of the Bighorn National Forest.
Maps: Bighorn National Forest map and/or USGS Lake Helen quad.
Special attractions: Perhaps the most popular trail in the Big Horns, replete with alpine and high peak scenery. Beautiful lakes and good stream and lake fishing.
For more information: Tensleep Ranger District, 2009 Bighorn Ave., Worland, WY, 82401, (307) 347-8291.

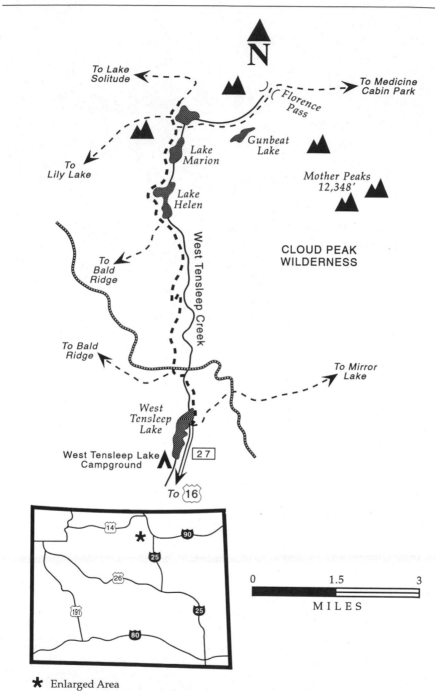

N

To Lake Solitude

To Medicine Cabin Park

Florence Pass

Gunbeat Lake

Lake Marion

To Lily Lake

Mother Peaks 12,348'

Lake Helen

West Tensleep Creek

To Bald Ridge

CLOUD PEAK WILDERNESS

To Bald Ridge

To Mirror Lake

West Tensleep Lake

West Tensleep Lake Campground

27

To 16

14

90

25

26

191

25

80

0   1.5   3
MILES

★ Enlarged Area

Finding the trailhead: Directions are the same as those to Mirror Lake/Lost Twin Lakes (hike 21).

The hike: Mistymoon is a magical, alluring name. In fact, I visited the lake under a full moon on a windless night, and magical but begins to describe the experience. At the north end of the hiker's parking lot, the West Tensleep Trail begins right beside and parallel to the Middle Tensleep Trail. A sign notes that Mistymoon lake is six miles distance. It seems like a much longer hike. Another sign notes that no fires are allowed at the lake. Camp stoves are the order.

The first two miles of the West Tensleep Trail are gentle. The next couple miles grow amazingly long and rugged, and by the time you reach Lake Helen at four miles, you may decide to camp there and day hike it to Mistymoon. Here at long Lake Helen the splendid scenery begins, with vast and rocky sub-alpine bowls merging into high peak vistas. The trail rounds the western side of Lake Helen and a mile later does the same at Marion Lake. Campsites are not lacking and water is ubiquitous. The final mile to Mistymoon Lake climbs somewhat steeply, breaking above timberline into short tundra and granite rock. It's a fragile, harsh and most beautiful environment here, and Mistymoon Lake is the gem. Its popularity is well deserved.

The best camping at this lake occurs off the trail before and below the shelf on which the lake sits. The land around Mistymoon Lake is quite exposed and carries a good slope. Dawn and sunrise by these waters, when the air is calm and the surrounding jagged peaks mirror themselves on the lake's surface, is a great time to be awake and alive. From here one can travel east to Florence Pass and into the eastern drainages of the Big Horns, or day hike the Lake Solitude/Lily Lake loop to the west.

Please walk with respect on this fragile tundra environment.

HIKE 23 *CLOUD PEAK*

General description: A taxing, exciting and especially beautiful ascent to the highest peak in the Big Horn Range. The climb is not technical but does require one to be in good physical condition.

General location: Approximately fifty miles east of Worland, in the southwestern sector of the Bighorn National Forest.

Maps: Bighorn National Forest map and/or USGS Lake Helen and Cloud Peak quads.

Special attractions: The ascent of the highest peak in the region, and spectacular scenery.

For more information: Tensleep Ranger District, 2009 Bighorn Ave., Worland, WY, 82401, (307) 347-8291.

The hike: Since a round trip from Mistymoon Lake to the top of Cloud Peak and back is an eight- to ten-hour proposition, this description assumes you have followed the directions in hike 22 to Mistymoon Lake and are beginning the journey from there. Before undertaking this climb, scan this brief checklist of commonsense needs to assure a safe trip:

- You need at least some acclimation to higher elevations.
- You need to be in fairly decent physical shape.

A view from Cloud Peak.

• Try and start early in the morning. This both gives you time to be leisurely and may allow you to beat an afternoon thunder storm.

• Carry good wind and weather gear along. Also take adequate sun protection, lunch and water.

• Heavier, waterproof boots are a necessity.

• An ice ax or a heck of a stout walking stick may be needed for the snow fields that exist into August.

• BE SKILLED AT ROCKS. The mountainside is boulder hopping at its most taxing. It's a one-step/every-step safety oriented hike. Make sure every rock you use is solid.

Park at West Tensleep Lake trailhead. Hike to Mistymoon Lake. From the lake it is 5.5 miles and five hours to the summit of Cloud Peak. From Mistymoon Lake, go north on the Solitude Loop trail to the top of the ridge. Descend, then leave the trail and cross Paintrock Creek heading for waterfall. The easiest descent is to follow the main trail west from this ridgetop for almost .5 mile. Here (by a section of trail that has been lined with large rocks and filled with gravel) you can look due north and see both the waterfall and an ascending trail to the left of it. Head north for that waterfall, cross Paint Rock Creek, which in July was an icy wade, and begin the perpetual uphill climb to the top.

The main rule now becomes "head northeast and head up." There are some cairns marking the way, but you'll probably be too busy watching your own rock-hopping footsteps to catch them all. The higher you get up the mountain, the easier it is to view the ridge you have to follow to the top.

The steep climb and rough country are not the only reason this hike takes so long. It is also so spectacular that you tend to stop every thrity feet and gaze in awe over the scenery. This country is the essence of the Cloud Peak Wilderness Area.

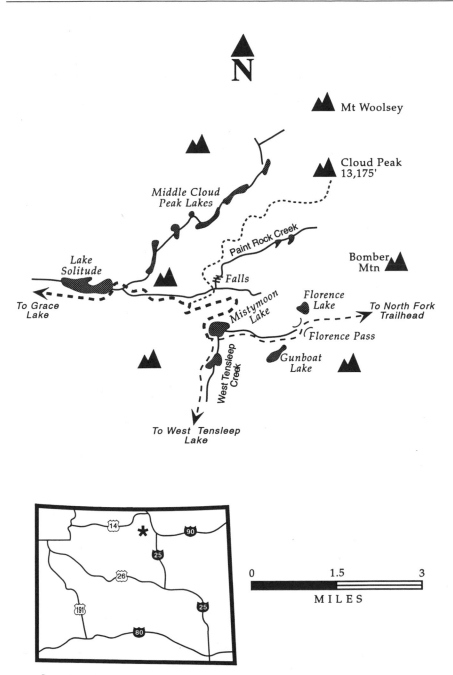

N

Mt Woolsey

Cloud Peak
13,175'

*Middle Cloud
Peak Lakes*

Paint Rock Creek

Bomber
Mtn

*Lake
Solitude*

Falls

To Grace
Lake

*Florence
Lake*

To North Fork
Trailhead

*Mistymoon
Lake*

Florence Pass

*West Tensleep
Creek*

*Gunboat
Lake*

To West Tensleep
Lake

★ Enlarged Area

0   1.5   3

M I L E S

I didn't quite make it to the summit. After pausing for a moment to add another note to the advice checklist, that being, "Don't be afraid to turn back if the weather changes," I then looked up and saw the growing tops of billowing thunderclouds building at about 800 feet per minute. It was necessary to follow my own advice. This country is too exposed and the granite is too lichen covered to want to get caught in a rainstorm. Remember that the return trip's downhill rock hopping is harder and more dangerous than the uphill scramble.

If Cloud Peak seems a bit too difficult for you, there are no lack of gentler summits around Mistymoon Lake.

HIKE 24 *BUCKING MULE FALLS NATIONAL RECREATION TRAIL*

General description: A fairly long and rugged hike along the rim of a spectacular canyon. A simple hike to the falls can be accomplished in a few hours.

General location: Approximately forty miles east of Lovell in the northwestern Big Horn Mountains.

Maps: Bighorn National Forest map and/or USGS Mexican Hill, Medicine Wheel, and Bald Mountain quads. Boyd Ridge quad is optional.

Special attractions: Stunning photographic opportunities of rock-wall encased creeks, towering waterfalls and scenic mountain panoramas.

For more information: Medicine Wheel Ranger District, P.O. Box 367, Lovell, WY, 82431.

Finding the trailhead: U.S. Highway Alt. 14 (or U.S. 14A) east of Lovell is an awe-inspiring drive across a polychromatic prairie that rises to meet the Big Horns. Approximately forty miles east from Lovell, turn north on signed Sheep Mountain Road and drive for 3.5 miles to its intersection with Devils Canyon Road. Travel west on thc gravel Devils Canyon Road seven more miles to the road end and trailhead beginning.

The hike: Bucking Mule Falls is a spectacular cascade that tumbles nearly vertically for 600 feet. Devils Canyon is a rocky obstacle of water-carved land whose rugged beauty makes the steep hiking pitches—some sloped as much as twenty percent grade—along this well-maintained trail worth the effort.

The short version of this hike, an easy walk and perfect for families, skirts the rugged southern rim of scenic Bucking Mule Canyon. From a thick lodgepole pine and Englemann Spruce beginning to incredible overhanging rock ledges and an awesome gaze across the canyon and down on to the crashing waterfalls, this hike fascinates every step of the way. It's about a mile to the falls from the trailhead, and a round trip journey takes a couple of hours.

For those who wish to journey the entire eleven-mile one-way length of the trail, the pathway is well maintained and easy to follow as it further skirts the Bucking Mule Canyon and then drops steeply down into the Porcupine Creek drainage. This crossing is your only chance to enjoy fresh water for the next 4.5 miles, as the trail just-as-steeply climbs out of inaccessible Devils

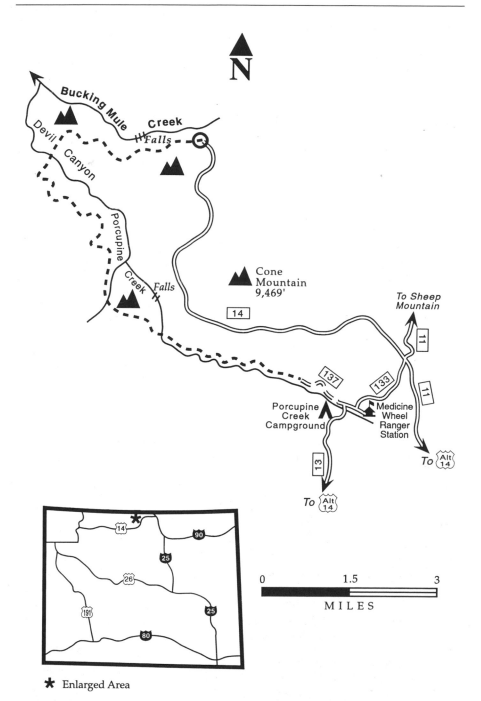

N

Bucking Mule Creek Falls

Devil Canyon

Porcupine Creek Falls

Cone
Mountain
9,469'

14

To Sheep
Mountain

11

137

133

11

Porcupine
Creek
Campground

Medicine
Wheel
Ranger
Station

13

To Alt
14

To Alt
14

14

90

25

26

191

25

80

* Enlarged Area

0   1.5   3

MILES

Canyon and again traces the southern rim of a new canyon. The views that accompany this walk are spectacular. Finally the trail again drops into the upper reaches of Porcupine Creek and follows its northern banks to the Jaws Road, ending a bit more than a mile below Porcupine Campground. Here you can try and catch a ride back to the original parking lot, or gain an entirely new perspective of this wild country by retracing your steps.

A large number of horse packers use this trail. Also, due to cliffy terrain and thick timber, camping is limited. The upper stretches of Porcupine Creek boast fair fishing.—*Susan Gilmore*

HIKE 25 *MEDICINE MOUNTAIN*

General description: A long but enjoyable day hike to a mountain summit with a considerable gain in elevation.

General location: Approximately twenty-five miles east of Lovell, on the western fringes of the northern Big Horn Mountains.

Maps: Bighorn National Forest visitors map and/or USGS Medicine Mountain quad.

Special attractions: Fabulous view of the Bighorn Basin prairies to the west. Close to the fascinating and enigmatic Medicine Wheel archaeological site.

For more information: Medicine Wheel Ranger District, P.O. Box 367, Lovell, WY, 82431; Worland District BLM Office, 101 South 23rd, P.O. Box 119, Worland, WY, 82401, (307) 347-9871.

Finding the trailhead: Located twenty-five miles east of Lovell on U.S. Highway Alternative 14, the BLM Five Springs Road leads to a nature trail at Five Springs Falls, where there is water, three camps, two picnic sites and no fee. The trail begins past the campground at the end of the road.

The hike: Medicine Mountain sits above a prehistoric wonder of a Sheepeater Tribe's stone medicine wheel. The origin and significance of this stone relic is still unknown, but it is believed to be part of ancient religious ceremonies. A Crow Indian legend states that the wheel was built by "people who had no iron." The wheel is an almost perfect circle of stones seventy feet in diameter and having twenty-eight stone spokes that radiate out from a central stone cairn. Discovered in the 1880's, the site has been so vandalized and molested by souvenir hunters that a protective fence now surrounds the monument. Not visible from the top of the namesake mountain that it sits on, the site is certainly worth a visit.

A road does ascend Medicine Mountain from its eastern flanks, and a space-age FAA radar geodesic dome stands atop the mountain, monitoring air traffic in a three-state area. But the wonderful six-mile climb to the top of the mountain via this little-used trail offers spectacular vistas of the Big Horns from the nearby cliffs to west of the Medicine Wheel. The trail is easy to follow, and the hike significantly and continuously climbs through open meadows and sporadic timberland to the summit of 9,962-foot Medicine Mountain. Do carry some water on this hike.—*Susan Gilmore*

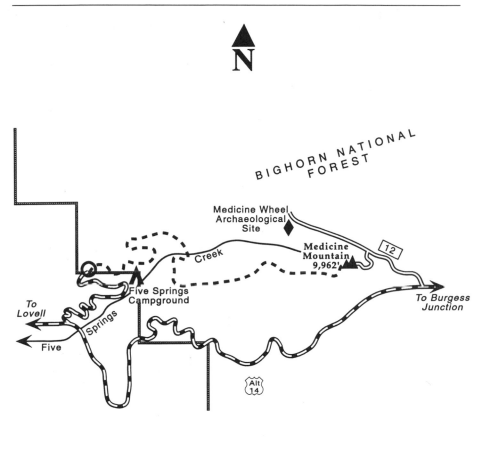

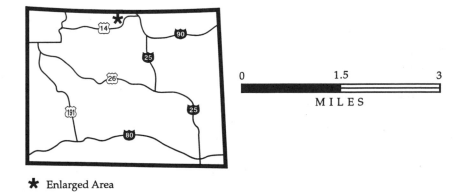

* Enlarged Area

WEST-CENTRAL WYOMING
The Wind River Range

Welcome to the roof of Wyoming. For over 100 miles, from Togwotee Pass on U.S. Highway 287 to South Pass now straddled by Wyoming Highway 28, the Wind Rivers form an unbroken and supreme expression of mountain beauty, geology, glaciers, wildlife, and wilderness. Forty-seven peaks touch or exceed the 13,000-foot elevation barrier. Sixty-three glaciers in this range cover a total of seventeen square miles of mountain.

Geology buffs can study thrust faults that were so severe the rock folds literally faulted over on themselves. Tremendous ice age glaciation bulldozed large canyons into the range while sculpting the granite peaks into an awesome display of cliff-art. And speaking of granite cliffs, rock climbers have found their Shangri-La in the towering and varied headwalls, spires, chimneys and shear summits of the Wind River Mountains.

The human history of these mountains, from Indian to fur trapper to late nineteenth century immigrants and gold miners, is far richer than the accumulated bounty of fur pelts and precious minerals extracted from the land. More than 300,000 people and their wagons poured through South Pass between 1843 and 1863, following hopeful promises and improbable dreams.

But by far the greatest treasure of the Wind Rivers lies in its vast acreage of officially classified wilderness. Three major wilderness areas plus the de facto wilderness of the Wind River Indian Reservation create over a million acres of contiguous wilderness.

Recent Environmental Protection Agency studies have concluded that the high wilderness lakes in the Wind Rivers are susceptible to damage and contamination from acid rain. The pure waters have a low alkalinity and sport little ability to buffer the nitrates and sulfides of the nearby coal-fired Jim Bridger electric plant. A second, more immediate threat challenges portions of these mountains in the form of human hikers coalescing in greater numbers than an area can accomodate. Even the roof of Wyoming, classified and protected as it is, needs help if it is to survive as a viable remnant of wild country.

Keep a few general considerations in mind when planning any journey into the Wind River Range. The western side of the Winds fall under the auspices of the Bridger-Teton National Forest. The forest maps of this national forest are the finest maps any individual forest offers. The eastern slopes of the Wind Rivers are administered by the Shoshone National Forest. Be sure and obtain the new version of the Shoshone Forest's north and south visitor maps. They lack great detail, but do portray the roads and trails and creek drainages and a few high mountain points.

HIKE 26 *SINKS CANYON*

General description: An easy and fairly gentle day hike that explores the refreshing environments of the foothills of the eastern Wind River Mountains.
General location: Approximately seven miles southwest of Lander, on the Middle Fork of the Popo Agie River.
Maps: Obtain a Sinks Canyon Volksmarch Trail Map from the state park visitor center. The topography is on USGS Fossil Hill quad (which will not show this trail).
Special attractions: Disappearing rivers and other extraordinary geological features. Also, lower mountain settings with pretty, diverse hiking.
For more information: Sinks Canyon State Park, 3079 Sinks Canyon Rd, Rt, 63, Lander, WY, 82520, (307) 332-6333.
Finding the trailhead: U.S. highway 287 forms the main drag of Lander. On Fifth Street, which is also Wyoming highway 131 and well marked with a brown and yellow state recreation sign, turn south. It's a simple matter of following the Wyoming 131 and Sinks Canyon Park signs for seven miles to the park boundaries.

The hike: This hike constitutes another of the Wyoming State Park Volksmarch walks, and it is one of the best. The park is founded around a natural phenomenon where the entire Middle Popo Agie River plunges and disappears into a limestone cavern, the Sinks. The river reappears .5 mile later as large spring named The Rise. It's interesting to note that the volume of The Rise is greater than the water volume vanishing into The Sinks. When a harmless dye was released into The Sinks, it took over two hours before it reappeared at The Rise. Where the extra water comes from, and why the swiftly moving river requires such a time period to travel a half mile remain mysteries.

The trail officially begins at the visitor center. Here also you can hike a short distance to the river and view the earth swallowing the cascading waters.

Like several Volksmarch trails, this one incorporates a bit of roadway into it. The first .6 mile trace the main highway west to the Popo Agie Campground. Then you must follow the campground gravel roads west as far as possible (.2 mile) to the Nature Trail parking area. Here a wild suspension bridge spans the river, and the true hiking trail begins with a standard IVV brown and yellow sign. If one is not after Volksmarch accreditation, one could eliminate over a mile of this trail by driving to the parking lot and starting at the suspension bridge.

The trail forms a figure eight with a third loop attached to it. The main rule to follow at trail intersections is to always go left. Arrows on IVV signs point the way, but if there's any doubt, go left. The first mile has a slight climb as you journey into the unique habitats of the Wind River foothills. It's actually country few people see, having set their sights on the high peaks to the west. It's also a country that is splendid in its own special way. Lush (by Wyoming standards) meadows and gentle forests, riparian aspen groves and extended views of cliff-encompassed Sinks Canyon keep the hiker entranced. In late June the river wears a wild white robe and the flowers almost over decorate the hillsides and meadows. Where the trail is a bit

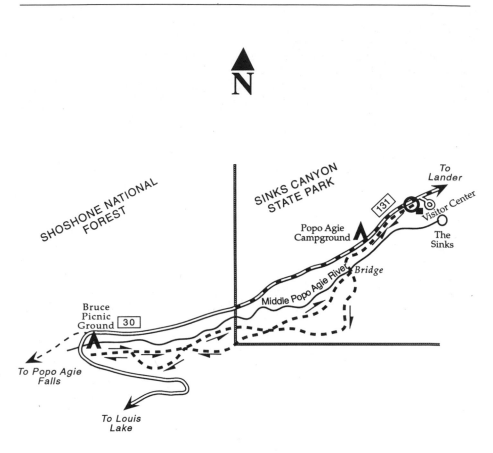

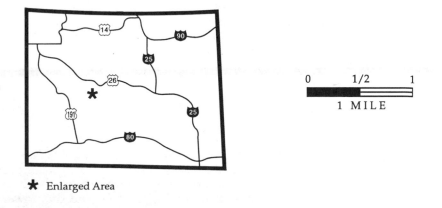

* Enlarged Area

difficult to follow, look for the IVV signs and for blue diamond ski trail markers.

The trail turns back on itself at Bruce Campground. Much of the return journey treads through special river environments. The only slightly confusing area occurs at the return end of the western loop near the University of Missouri's Geology camp. Cross the little log foot bridge that spans an offshoot rivulet, but don't cross the suspension bridge or main river. Continue on the trail parallel to the river.

This is a most enjoyable hike. It can be used to get the legs into shape for the long and rugged trails into the nearby wilderness area. It also forms a great trek for easy walking, open views and welcome solitude.

Sinks Canyon State Park sports two other short nature/interpretive trails. Descriptive pamphlets are available at the visitor center, which is open Memorial Day through Labor Day.

HIKE 27 MIDDLE FORK OF THE POPO AGIE RIVER/ TAYO PARK LOOP TRAIL

General description: A quite rugged five day or longer backpacking loop into high country lakes surrounded by majestic peaks. Wind River Peak is a 13,000 foot, non-technical but strenuous cross-country climb.

General location: The trailhead begins approximately twelve miles southwest of Lander. Deep Creek Lakes are about twenty trail miles west of the trailhead.

Maps: Shoshone National Forest South Half visitors map and USGS Fossil Hill, Cony Mountain and Sweetwater Gap quads. Also, Earthwalk Press has an excellent overview topography and trail map of the Southern Wind Rivers. It's available at most local sporting goods and outfitting stores.

Special attractions: Long and continuous hiking, open parks and meadows, astonishing vistas into panoramic peak and alpine lake settings. Deep Creek Lakes are rumored to contain Golden Trout.

For more information: Lander Ranger District, 600 North Highway 287, Lander, WY, 82520, (307) 332-5460.

Finding the trailhead: An official Wyoming Highway, 131, (the Sinks Canyon State Park road, described in hike 26) now leaves Lander at Fifth Street, and ten of the eleven miles to the trailhead are paved. The last mile, Forest Service Road 300 is wide and graveled. Just past the Bruce Picnic Ground the road turns southward and crosses the Middle Fork of the Popo Agie River. South of and across the bridge is a several-acre parking lot geared to accomodate the many hikers, packers and horse packers that now use the trail.

The hike: 1971 marked the first time I traveled this major access trail into the Popo Agie Wilderness Area. Then, a grimy little dirt road out of Lander led to an unmarked and obscure trailhead. A few horsepackers and a survival school named NOLS were practically the only users of the wilderness. For five weeks we traveled these mountains, meeting almost no people and experiencing wild beauty beyond comprehension. Twenty years later, the excitement of memory permeated my footsteps as I again set foot into the Popo Agie via the Middle Fork Trail.

This Middle Fork trail not only serves as a gracious introduction to the Wind Rivers, but it forms the major access route into the Popo Agie Wilderness. A map posted on that trailhead sign shows a system of twenty eight different

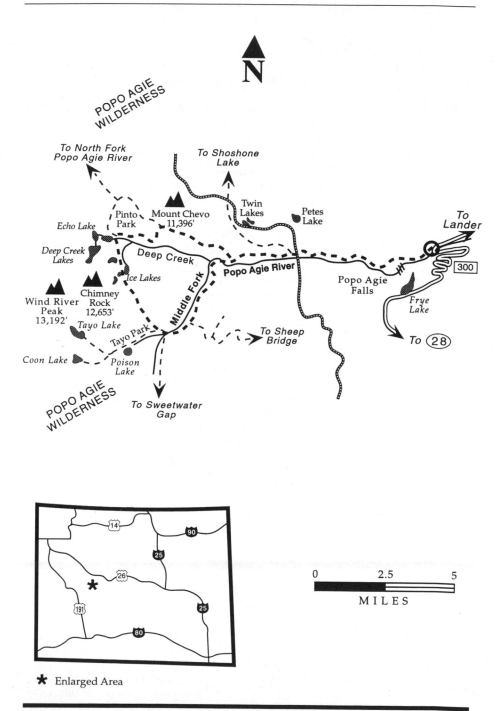

N

To North Fork
Popo Agie River

To Shoshone
Lake

POPO AGIE
WILDERNESS

Pinto
Park

Mount Chevo
11,396'

Twin
Lakes

Petes
Lake

To
Lander

Echo Lake

Deep Creek

Popo Agie River

Deep Creek
Lakes

Ice Lakes

Middle Fork

Popo Agie
Falls

300

Wind River
Peak
13,192'

Chimney
Rock
12,653'

Tayo Lake

Tayo Park

To Sheep
Bridge

Frye
Lake

To 28

Coon Lake

Poison
Lake

POPO AGIE
WILDERNESS

To Sweetwater
Gap

14

90

25

26

25

191

80

0   2.5   5

MILES

★ Enlarged Area

trails, with this one trailhead as the gateway to all. Bear in mind that the hike to Popo Agie Falls, the first mile of the trail, is the goal of over half the people using the trail.

The steep and rocky beginning, in a mile, takes you 600 feet higher to where a short side trail journeys off for a view of the impressive Popo Agie Falls.

A decision needs to be made periodically, if you haven't pre-planned your trip, on which side-trail to take. I present this hike as a journey up the Middle Fork to Three Forks park, a jog along the Pinto Park trail, a slice over to the Deep Creek and Ice Creek Lakes, a journey into Tayo Park and a loop back down the Popo Agie River, again to Three Forks Park and out the main trail. But this forms the basic introduction, and many other possibilities present themselves along the route.

The wilderness boundary begins about six miles after the trailhead. This wilderness has a "no camping within 200 feet of trail, lakes and streams" rule, and between that and the extremely rugged, rocky and timbered countryside, it's another four miles to good camping at Three Forks Park. The trail is well signed from here to Pinto Park. In four miles the Deep Creek Cutoff Trail jogs south, and the rewards for your long hiking efforts begin. The Deep Creek Lakes, the Ice Lakes and upper Tayo Park are set in almost dreamlike high alpine meadows that lie beneath the base of giant peaks and shear granite cliffs.

Wind River Peak, at 13,192 feet, affords a challenging cross-country peak climb without any technical gear required. Its gentle ridges are accessible from the southern shores of the upper Deep Creek Lake. Be aware that there are several creek crossings between the Echo Lakes and Tayo Park, and a major creek crossing occurs on the Middle Fork Trail before you reenter Three Forks Park from the west. These waters are swift and icy. In fact, Ice Lakes can still be solidly frozen in mid July. Wind River Peak may be a snow climb up to that time, and an ice ax would be useful.

It would take a book-length description to do justice to the vast beauty encompassed by this hike. It forms an excellent first taste of the southern Wind Rivers and will surely pique your adventure buds into wanting more. The trail intersections are well-signed, but it's still advisable carry a topog map. Signs do have a habit of disappearing.

HIKE 28 SOUTH PASS CITY

General description: A nice day hike in historic, high altitude, rolling prairie country.

General location: Approximately thirty-five miles south of Lander, in the southernmost foothills of the Wind River Range.

Maps: Obtain a Volksmarch map from the supervisor of the South Pass City Historic Site. The topography is located on USGS South Pass City quad.

Special attractions: An opportune chance to explore the dazzling mining and settlement history of Wyoming. Prairie canyon and ridgetop hiking at its best.

For more information: South Pass City State Historical Site, Route 62, Box 170, Lander, WY, 82520, (307) 332-3684.

Finding the trailhead: Leave Lander driving south on U.S. 287. Nine miles from the town, Wyoming Highway 28 forks westward. Twenty-five miles of this most scenic highway takes you to a South Pass City State Historical Site

High Wyoming Prairie near South Pass City.

sign, where you turn south and follow a gravel road 2.5 miles to a large parking lot beside the historic city.

The hike: Wyoming has made excellent efforts to preserve its heritage, and here is an area where history and hiking now merge. In the late 1860s, the Carissa Mine began producing gold, and a rush to the South Pass area began. Within two years South Pass City, Atlantic City and a burg named Miner's Delight were built. As businessmen arrived to meet the prospectors' needs, the South Pass area soon boasted over 2,000 inhabitants. Mining busts and booms bounced the populations of the area for nearly a hundred years. Today, few mines are active. But a fascinating restoration of South Pass City has created a unique piece of living history. Recently, what I consider the best of the state's Volksmarch trails, has been added to the site.

The six-mile Volksmarch trail begins in the townsite, and for a complete exploration of all aspects of this area, leave enough time to explore the restored buildings and historical markers. You can obtain information, maps and, if desired, official Volksmarch trail registration at the 1848 Smith-Sherlock Co. Store on "Main Street." (Open Memorial Day through Labor Day, usually until six p.m.)

Volksmarches are nice because they create trails in country where there would otherwise be no hiking. Just east of the townsite, well-signed by the brown and yellow IVV signs, the trail follows aptly named Willow Creek for nearly 2.5 miles. Here is a landscape where the last of the Wind River Mountains and the first of the high prairies seem to be competing with each other for dominance.

Then the trail leaves the creek, climbs an aspen-lined ravine to the north and enters the windswept, short-grass sage prairie that rules so much of Wyoming. Topping a ridge, the trail passes by an old mine where one fissure

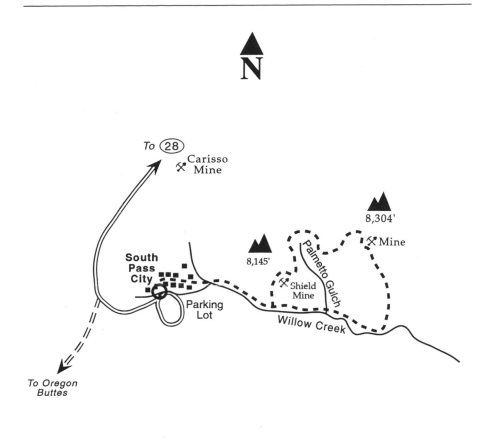

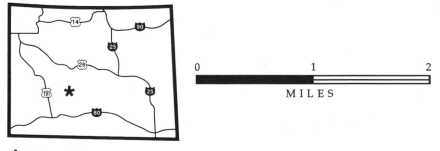

* Enlarged Area

was so deep, I couldn't hear a dropped rock hit the bottom. You should be extremely careful around mine shafts.

An old road bed now constitutes the trail and guides you into the headwaters of Palmento Gulch with it's musical aspen groves and copious evidence of beaver activity. Another rocky ridge, another mine and a staggering view of Willow Creek surrounded by the prairie it cuts through, and the trail returns to the creek bottom and back to South Pass City.

This is a day hike worth seeking and hiking. Its uniqueness and beauty won't disappoint you. Be advised that this is probably some of the windiest country in the world.

HIKE 29 *SWEETWATER CANYON*

General description: A very wild, isolated and trailless two- or three-day exploration into a little known prairie canyon.

General location: Approximately forty miles southeast of Lander, along the banks of the Sweetwater River.

Maps: Bureau of Land Managemant South Passs and Lander 1:100,000 surface management maps and USGS Lewiston Lakes and Radium Springs quads.

Special attractions: A prairie wilderness river that few persons know about. Fishing is excellent, geology remarkable and isolation complete.

For more information: Outdoor Recreation Planner, Lander Resource Area, Bureau of Land Management, P.O. Box 589, Lander, WY, 82520, (307) 332-7822.

Finding the trailhead: I highly recommend contacting the Lander BLM office for directions before journeying there. Be aware that a drive to Sweetwater Canyon by whatever route requires a high clearance vehicle, good rut driving skills, and an awareness that if it rains, there you will be stuck until the sun again shines.

Following the directions from Lander to South Pass City (Hike 28), drive to the abandoned Carissa gold mine. Here, instead of continuing toward South Pass City, a graveled and graded BLM road journeys eastward toward Atlantic City. About two miles later, by another abandoned mine and totally dilapidated shack, the Pickaxe Road is signed and journeys south. Follow this graded road 4.9 miles to an intersection labeled the Lewiston Road. Even though the sign here notes the Sweetwater River is six miles further south on Pickaxe Road, turn east onto the dirt Lewiston Road. This road slowly deteriorates in width and quality.

After 7.6 miles, by an Oregon Trail/Pony Express concrete marker, it branches into three equally unalluring directions. The landmark at this intersection is two log cabins directly to the north that cannot be seen from the intersection but are visible .5 mile before the junction. Turn right or south onto a two-track road and head up a hill. At the top of the hill, take the two-track to the left, and .25 mile later, take the fading two-track that goes right. .75 mile later at a dilapidated mining cabin, you venture left away and downhill from the cabin. My two-wheel drive 1976 Toyota did negotiate the ruts of the next two miles, but it was pushed to the limit.

Two miles later, after turning left or east at every intersection on the way, you can park and camp at a nice grassy flat beside the clear waters of the Sweetwater River and the tailings of Wilson Bar Mine.

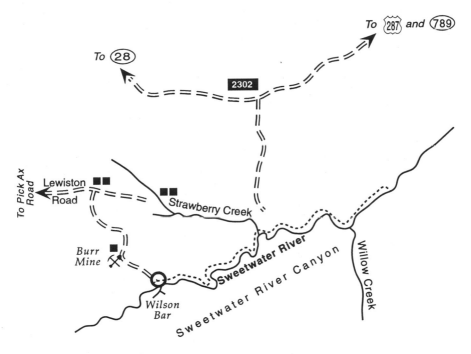

To ⑳ and ⑲

To ㉘

2302

To Pick Ax Road

Lewiston Road

Strawberry Creek

Burr Mine

Sweetwater River

Sweetwater River Canyon

Willow Creek

Wilson Bar

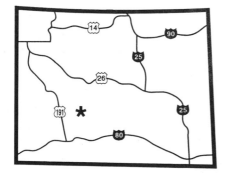

0   1.5   3

MILES

★ Enlarged Area

The hike: Sweetwater is the name that dominates central and southwestern Wyoming. Most stories attribute its naming to the fresh water which tasted sweet to trappers and settlers after weeks of drinking alkali water. But there is a story circulating that claims a mule toting a load of sugar fell into the river and hence the name.

This hike is one of those rare gems, unknown, untrammeled, untrailed and hard to find and access. Sweetwater Canyon forms an unusual scenic prairie canyon of about eleven miles length. The area is a BLM wilderness study area.

Even if one survives the drive, this is not a hike for everyone. Other than an occasional cattle path, there is no trail to follow. Hiking is extremely rugged cross-country, sometimes through thick brush, across and over dangerously loose rock slopes along the shores of the river. You are also as isolated and as far away from everything as you can get.

The rather bald sage slopes and rocky cliffs that lead to the river are dotted with old mines. The bird life is abundant and varied. And the country is wilderness wandering at its best. Four miles into the canyon, a trickle of exceptionally clear water from the north marks the half-way point. East of Strawberry Creek the canyon broadens and the hiking becomes somewhat easier. My favorite area was the distance west of this creek, with its narrower widths and rushing waters. Driving to the canyon via the Strawberry Creek road would allow you to dayhike both up and down the canyon.

There are lots of ticks, deer and horse flies in the summer. When the river's waters are high and you can't wade them, you must fourth-class climb a few of those fractured and very crumbly rock cliffs to skirt the river's shore. If you are not versed in rock climbing, you should probably try the hike when the water is lower.

The Eastern Wind Rivers, North

The absolute best trail and topog map of the Wind River Range is published by Earthwalk Press, 2239 Union Street, Eureka, CA, 95501. They carry a northern and a southern Wind River Range Hiking Map and Guide Series, each one condensing 15 or more 7.5 minute USGS quadrangles into a single 1:48,000 overview map. Topography is not lost while large overviews are gained. The maps are available at most sporting goods stores in towns around the range.

HIKE 30 *LAKE LOUISE*

General description: A shorter day hike to a most pretty and serene lake. Overnight camping is an enjoyable option.
General location: Approximately fourteen miles south and east of Dubois, in the northeast section of the Wind River Range.
Maps: Shoshone National Forest south half visitors map and USGS Torrey Lake and Simpson Lake quads.
Special attractions: Excellent fishing in a deep lake. A hot fire charred the valley above this lake in 1976, and the natural forest regeneration is interesting to witness.

For more information: Wind River Ranger District, 209 E. Ramshorn, P.O. Box 186, Dubois, WY, 82513, (307) 455-2466.

Finding the trailhead: The sign isn't very big, 3.8 miles east of downtown Dubois along U.S. highway 287 and 26, so watch carefully for it on the southern side of the road. It notes a Wyoming Game and Fish Department fish hatchery location. As you turn off the highway to the south, the road immediately forks—the right or west fork journeying to the fish hatchery and the left or southeast branch following another smallish sign that points to a conservation camp. Follow this second route toward the camp, and enjoy the ensuing 2.5 miles of washboard gravel road. At the Wyoming Game and Fish Department sheep range sign, the road again forks. The conservation camp sign you want to follow points eastward, and the next 3.5 miles of driving becomes the worst road in America that a two-wheel drive rig can still negotiate. The private property owners haven't graded this rock garden of a road since its birth, and it will truly test your driving and patience.

At the conservation camp, almost six miles after leaving the highway, the road forks again. Go right or northwest, following the Glacier Trail sign. Another couple of miles places you in a huge Fitzpatrick Wilderness Trailhead parking area. The Glacier Trail, the Whiskey Mountain Trail and the Lake Louise Trail begin as one path at the western end of this lot.

The hike: This little hike often serves as a primer to the long Glacier Trail/Gannett Peak hike (hike 31). It allows folks to test their boots or firm their muscles a bit before undertaking a rather colossal mountain trail. But Louise Lake is a great introduction to and escape into the rocky northernmost corner of the Wind Rivers.

Cliff-immured Lake Louise.

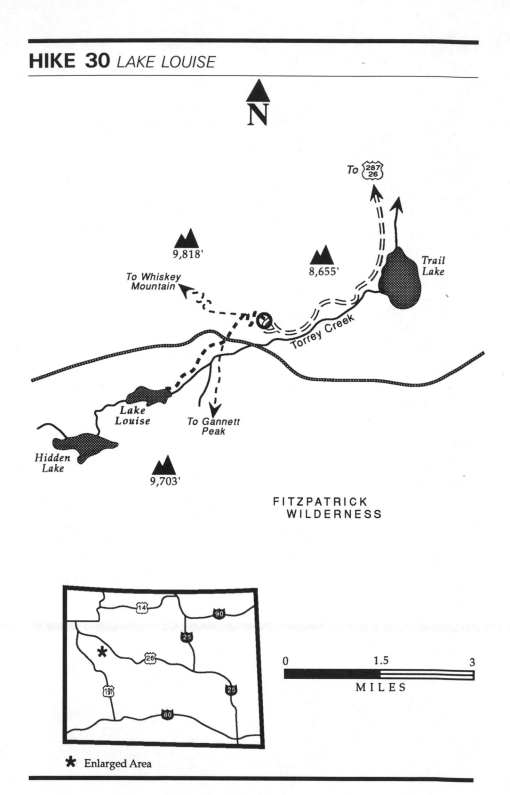

Short doesn't necessarily mean easy. The first .4 mile of trail switchbacks steeply uphill. Here The Whiskey Mountain Trail branches to the northwest. Continue along the Glacier Trail for another .2 mile and a sign will soon direct you westward toward Lake Louise.

The next two miles of trail are easy to follow but somewhat breathy to walk as the trail wanders into, over and around these impressive waves of rosy-colored granite rock. It weaves into meadowed and forested microenvironments located between the rock-wave troughs. And it passes beside some incredible Torrey Creek cascades. The last several hundred yards of the trail leading to the lake is granite shelf walking.

The deep waters of Lake Louise are completely imprisoned by restricting granite cliffs. One can traverse the lake's distance by either crossing the log jam at the foot of the lake and circumventing the southern shores, or by picking a way around the northern cliffs of the lake. Both routes require some scrambling and a little climbing. The southern shore option contains some excellent campsites and is a bit easier.

In 1976 a fire burned the forested area between Lake Louise and Hidden Lake. Rejuvenation has been slow, due to the sterile and rugged environment. But a cross-country journey between the lakes and along Torrey Creek is possible albeit exacting. For the fisherman, it may be worth the effort. I've seen Hidden Lake boil like a pot of tea during a fish frenzy-feeding on some recent hatch.

HIKE 31 *GLACIER TRAIL*

General description: A five- to eight-day or longer, quite rugged, ineffably beautiful hike to the largest glacier area and highest peak in Wyoming.

General location: Approximately fifteen miles south and east of Dubois, in the northeast section of the Wind River Range.

Maps: Shoshone National Forest Southern Half map and USGS Torrey Lake, Inkwells, Fremont Peak North and Gannett Peak quads. USGS Downs Mountain quad is optional. Earthwalk Press's northern Wind River Range hiking map and guide covers all these quads and more.

Special attractions: The biggest glaciers, the highest peaks, the deepest, cliff-encased valleys and the most beautiful blue-green glacier-milk creek weaving a channel through it all.

For more information: Wind River Ranger District, 209 E. Ramshorn, P.O. Box 186, Dubois, WY, 82513, (307) 455-2466.

Finding the trailhead: Access via car is exactly the same—including the super rough road—as the Louise Lake route (Hike 30). The trailhead begins at the west end of the parking lot.

The hike: The Fitzpatrick Wilderness, 198,838 acres of high-elevation, mountainous rock wonder, was designated in 1976 from what was originally named the Glacier Primitive Area. The area encompasses the northern portion of the Wind Rivers east of the divide. Tom Fitzpatrick was a contemporary of Jim Bridger, and naming agencies decided to place the wilderness appellations of the two trail blazers side-by-side.

The Glacier Trail forms a twenty-eight mile (one way) adventure. Numerous

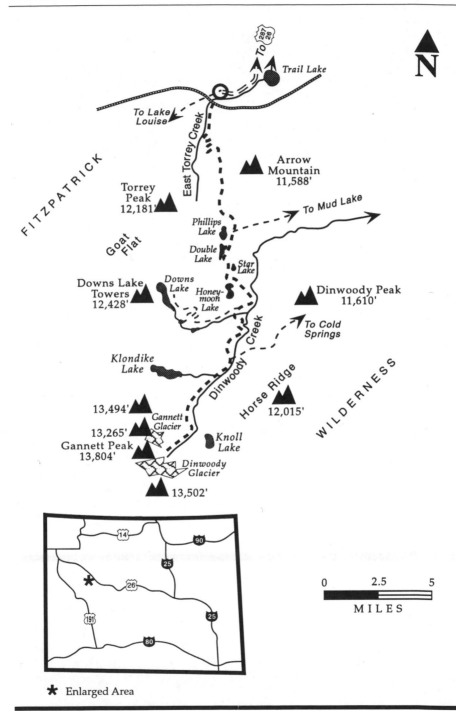

Mountainous country west of Gannett Peak. PAUL DONHARL PHOTO.

side trails and cross-country explorations are possible in this region, and anyone hiking in for less than a week's time can expect to miss a great deal of adventure and scenery. This is a most popular and sometimes crowded trail. Count on viewing many overused campsites and on encountering many other hikers as you travel. The land, though, is large enough to swallow all who enter it.

Many older and current maps show the trail beginning with a sinuous switchback up the southern sides of Arrow Mountain. In 1976 a massive rockslide wiped out a large section of that mountainside. You can see its scar if you look south-southwest from the parking area. The next year the Forest Service built the current parking facilities and rerouted the trail up the eastern side of East Torrey Creek. This proves to be a less steep, less waterless and less taxing beginning than the old trail. The original route tended to desicate and annihilate first-time and/or out-of-shape hikers.

A lot of elevation gain accompanies the first seven or eight miles of the hike. From a 7,500-foot creek-bottom beginning to a 10,895-foot pass above Burro Flat, new trail or not, it's a huff-and-puffer. Above what's called Williamson Corrals, water and tree shelter vanish. The open alpine is amazingly beautiful and quite exposed. Hikers need to be aware that it's ten or eleven miles to the first water and tree camping around the Phillips and Dinwoody Lakes area. Because this area—from Upper Phillips to and including Star Lake—forms the first respite after miles of hard hiking, overuse has heavily scarred it. Livestock camping and campfires are now prohibited in this area.

From Double Lake southward the trail begins a rugged descent into the Dinwoody Creek drainage. Downs Fork Meadows serves as the introduction to the exceptionally colored, milky-green creek that will be a companion much of the rest of the journey. Camping is a wherever, whenever choice from now on (as long as you're 100 feet from trails and streams). At Big Meadows, a few miles beyond the Downs Fork Trail intersection, the huge granite monoliths and castles begin to encase the milky-creeked valley. After you pass the Ink Wells Trail intersection, close to twenty miles into this hike, the forests part and the high peaks of Gannett (13,804 feet) and Woodrow Wilson (13,502 feet) begin to rule the western skyline. It all gets bigger and better and more open the farther you hike. Even though you're continually loomed over and towered above and tucked in a deeper valley, you still tend to feel you're on top of the world.

The Glacier Trail is well-signed and maintained its entire distance. Some of the side hikes—Inkwells, Downs Fork and Klondike Lake—may not be. Good topographic maps are a must on this trip.

Beyond Floyd Wilson Meadows, which contains the last stands of diminishing trees, the trail continues a few miles along the northern banks of a southern branch of Dinwoody Creek. Then it ends as Dinwoody Glacier moraine becomes too unpredictable to build on. One can continue over Dinwoody Glacier to what's labeled Glacier Pass and drop into the Titcomb Lakes Basin in the Bridger Wilderness. This is close to a fourth class scramble over the most rugged of rocky country and may require an ice axe to safely surmount the huge glacier.

The Western Wind Rivers, South and North

In 1931, 428,169 acres of scenic wildland in the western Wind River Range was set aside as a primitive area. In 1964, that wonderful year of passage of the National Wilderness Act, this acreage became the Bridger Wilderness. The area's roadless, unspoiled ninety-mile length nestles against a portion of the Continental Divide whose shear ruggedness truly exemplifies the term "backbone of the nation." Approximately 500 miles of intersecting trails leave little of this wilderness inaccessable to hikers, yet cross-country treks to isolated peaks, neighboring creek drainages and untrailed lakes are easily possible. Please tred lightly across the high-altitude environments if you leave the trail. More than 1,300 lakes dot the wilderness landscape. Until the 1920s, these lakes supported no fish. Several successful stocking programs have resulted in six trout species, grayling and/or mountain whitefish inhabiting many of the waterways. Fishing is often superb.

It is advised that you to check in with the Pinedale Ranger District before venturing into the Bridger Wilderness. They sport rules that are a bit more stringent than most forests, and they have identified seven special management areas inside the wilderness where: "groups cannot exceed ten people in number; building or using an open fire is prohibited; permits are required for organized groups; and camping is prohibited in a location visible from any lake or trail, unless that location is more than 200 feet from that lake or trail."

HIKE 32 *LITTLE SANDY LAKE*

General description: A moderate but not too long day hike or an easy over-nighter to a spectacular lake setting.

General location: Approximately fifty miles northeast of Farson or sixty miles southeast of Pinedale, in the extreme southeastern corner of the Bridger Wilderness.

Maps: Bridger-Teton National Forest Pinedale Ranger District map and/or USGS Sweetwater Needles, Sweetwater Gap and Temple Peak quads.

Special attractions: One of the shortest hikes granting access to the spectacular peak and lake country of the southern Wind Rivers. Can be used as a jump-off point for longer ventures into the deep wilderness.

For more information: Pinedale Ranger District, 210 W, Pine Street, P.O. Box 220, Pinedale, WY, 82941, (307) 367-4326.

Finding the trailhead: One half mile east of South Pass on Wyoming highway 28, three signs—a Sweetwater Gap Ranch sign, a Bridger Wilderness Big Sandy Entrance sign and a county road sign noting the Lander Cutoff Road—direct you onto the Lander Cutoff Road. Drive 15.4 miles northwest along the rolling hills of this graded road. Here, at the first graded road heading northward, an ancient BLM sign points to the Juel Ranch and Sweetwater Gap. Follow this road north, but don't take the BLM road jutting to the west at 3.5 miles. Continue northward for another 2.5 miles until another BLM sign directs you left or north to the Bridger National Forest. At 8.5 miles a Forest Service sign will note that it's still six miles to the "Sweetwater Wilderness Area," which makes no sense because there is no such beast. But do turn left or west on this road, which immediately becomes a jeep road. My little two-wheel drive trucklet made it up some serious grades in the roads's two mile distance, but a lesser clearance vehicle will require you to park and hike these couple miles. At the road's end, a sign points north to the trail and east to a tiny parking lot.

The hike: In 1988, a massive forest fire swept through several thousand acres of the southeastern corner of the Wind Rivers. The burn generated a heat so intense it actually sterilized the soil, creating a condition of extreme erodability. The beginnings of this route to Little Sandy Lake and to the Sweetwater Gap (hike 33) provide excellent on-site fire ecology lessons. The earth is just now beginning plant successions that will ultimately reforest the area.

Little Sandy Lake constitutes one of those seven special management areas in the Bridger Wilderness mentioned in the above introduction. This particular trail is a more lightly-used pathway than the popular trail from the Big Sandy access. It's also one of the shortest hiking accesses into the heart of the high peak country.

In but a .1 mile distance, beside a wilderness register sign, the trail forks. There is no direction sign at this fork, but the Little Sandy Lake Trail heads left while the Sweetwater Gap Trail goes right. After a short downhill wander and into a meadow, the Little Sandy Trail almost vanishes. The trick here is to cut straight northwest across the meadow (it's a swamp, actually). A cairn marks the trail's meadow exit, and the track of the trail visibly cuts into the burned forest above the grassy and open area.

The next mile forms an intense experience in fire-transformed landscapes.

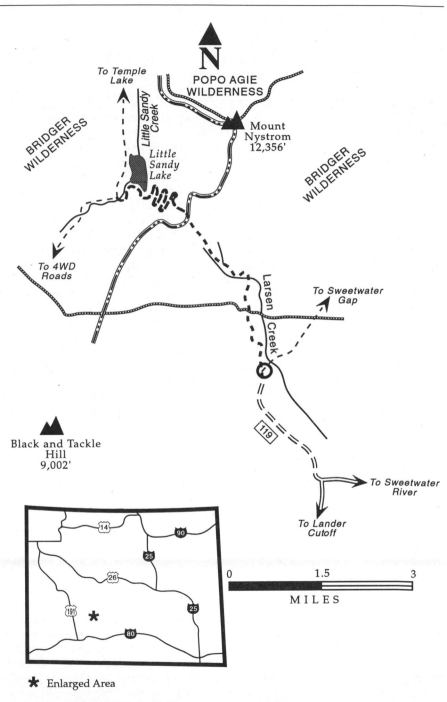

Near the Bridger Wilderness boundary, the burn stops. One step has you hiking a used-match forest and the next places you beneath a green bower, as if no burn ever occured. The trail is gentle for the first 1.5 miles. Then it seems to remember it has a pass to climb, and the next two miles ascend a steep grade. Take time to view the surrounding lodgepole forests. Some amazing burls have formed on these trees. The Continental Divide crossing into the Little Sandy drainage is thickly forested and unspectacular, but the descending trail's occasional views of the striking walls and cliffs and high pinnacles of the peaks towering over the lake make up for that. A little over a mile of steep downhill switchbacking places you in a Wind River scenic wonderland.

Camping spots are a bit sparse beside Little Sandy Lake. The trail leading into the high peak heart of this area skirts the southern shores of the lake and crosses Little Sandy Creek before venturing north. If you hike this trip as a day hike, remember the climb and return distance you have yet to cover before day's end.

HIKE 33 *SWEETWATER GAP*

General description: A long but quite enjoyable day hike or a leisurely over-nighter to a high pass that accesses the Popo Agie Wilderness from the south.
General location: Approximately fifty miles northeast of Farson or sixty miles southeast of Pinedale, in the extreme southeastern corner of the Bridger Wilderness.
Maps: Bridger-Teton National Forest Pinedale Ranger District-Bridger Wilderness map and/or USGS Sweetwater Needles and Sweetwater Gap quads.
Special attractions: A lightly-used trail, wonderful stream fishing, pretty meadow camping and incomparable views .
For more information: Pinedale Ranger District, 210 W, Pine Street, P.O. Box 220, Pinedale, WY, 82941, (307) 367-4326.
Finding the trailhead: Driving-to-trailhead directions are identical to those in the Little Sandy Lake Trail (hike 32).

The hike: Sweetwater Gap is a fun adventure into the headwater beginnings of that untamed river. After hiking the beginning .1 mile, by the registration sign, be certain to take the right or east fork. Like its counterpart to the west, this trail also journeys through the blackened landscape of a recent forest fire. The first 1.3 miles to the Bridger Wilderness boundary is quite a charred-wood experience. Beyond that, green and healthy forest dominates the scenery. So do the gentle pools and still pockets of the Sweetwater River. Several peaceful meadows dress the forest and offer ideal camping and stream fishing spots.

The trail wanders gently uphill for over five miles. Then the lodgepole pine turns to limber pine, and the sub-alpine spruce claims hillside dominance. The final two miles to Sweetwater Gap become a moderate climb. The pass itself is a large and broad meadow with excellent views toward Wind River Peak.

This trail is a most typical Wind River trail. You hike and hike, mostly over rocky path and through obscure lodgepole forests. Occasional glimpses of large

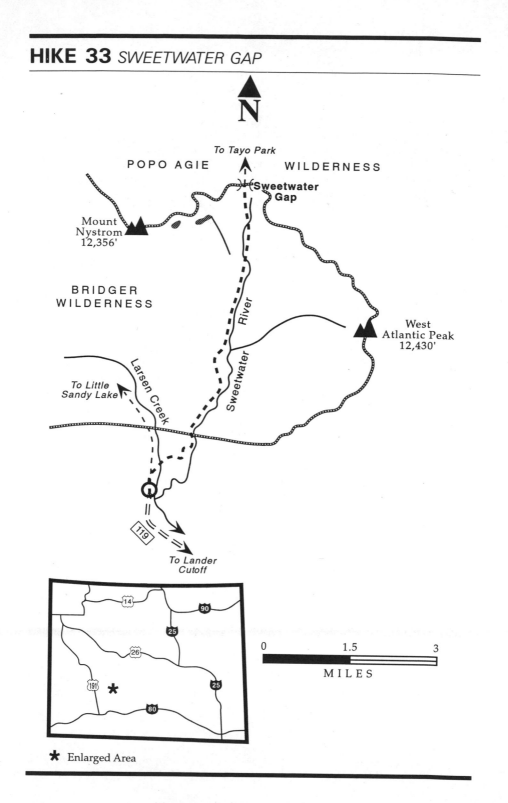

N

POPO AGIE   *To Tayo Park*   WILDERNESS

Sweetwater
Gap

Mount
Nystrom
12,356'

BRIDGER
WILDERNESS

West
Atlantic Peak
12,430'

Sweetwater River

Larsen Creek

*To Little
Sandy Lake*

119

*To Lander
Cutoff*

14   90

25

26

191   25

80

0   1.5   3

MILES

★ Enlarged Area

peaks present themselves, but the views rarely last more than a moment, until near the summit. Sweetwater Gap from this approach offers a shorter and less-used access into the Tayo Park/Ice Lakes high country of the southern Popo Agie Wilderness. Fine camping spots are available the entire length of the trail, including around the open meadows near the pass.

HIKE 34 *ALPINE LAKES*

General description: A six- to ten-day very rugged trek for experienced hikers. Map reading abilities are a must on this complex journey.
General location: About twenty-five miles northeast of Pinedale, in the central part of the Wind River Range.
Maps: Bridger-Teton National Forest Pinedale Ranger District and Shoshone National Forest south half visitors maps and USGS Fremont Peak South, Bridger Lakes and Horseshoe Lakes quads.
Special attractions: Highest alpine peaks, cross-country glacier walks and several days in seldom visited and sometimes untrailed terrain.
For more information: Pinedale Ranger District, 210 W. Pine Street, P.O. Box 220, Pinedale, WY, 82941, (307) 367-4326, and Lander Ranger District (for southern Fitzpatrick Wilderness), 600 North Highway 287, Lander, WY, 82520, (307) 332-5460.
Finding the trailhead: The trailhead starts at Elkhart Park, fourteen miles northeast of Pinedale. Take County Road 134 east and out of Pinedale, passing Fremont and Halfmoon Lakes. The road deadends at the Trails End Campground. The trailhead is located at the northeast corner of the parking lot, between the campground and the Ranger's station.

The hike: This is a rugged forty-five-mile loop into the central section of the Wind River Range. It crosses the Continental Divide twice and follows a seldom-visited, high glacial valley. It is best to give yourself a minimum of six days of travel due to the nature of the terrain and the unpredictability of the weather.

Begin on the Pole Creek Trail, which heads east through the woods following Faler Creek for a mile. It then turns northeast and reaches Miller Park after four miles. Here a trail to Miller Lake cuts off to the right. Pole Creek Trail reenters the woods for about a mile and comes out on Photographers Point, which affords spectacular views of Gorge Lake and the Continental Divide to the east.

Another meadow appears in .5 mile where the Sweeney Lake Trail cuts to the right. The main trail then rounds a knob and drops down to Eklund Lake. At the north end of the lake, Pole Creek Trail turns right and heads east. The Seneca Lake Trail—your new route—turns left and drops down around the west side of Barbara Lake. This trail then descends several switchbacks and climbs back up to Hobbs Lake.

One half mile beyond Hobbs Lake the trail crosses Seneca Creek, which must be forded farther upstream during high water in the early part of the season. The trail passes several small lakes in the next mile and drops into a small basin before climbing up to Seneca Lake. You're now about eight miles from Elkhart Park. Several excellent campsites exist on the southwest end of

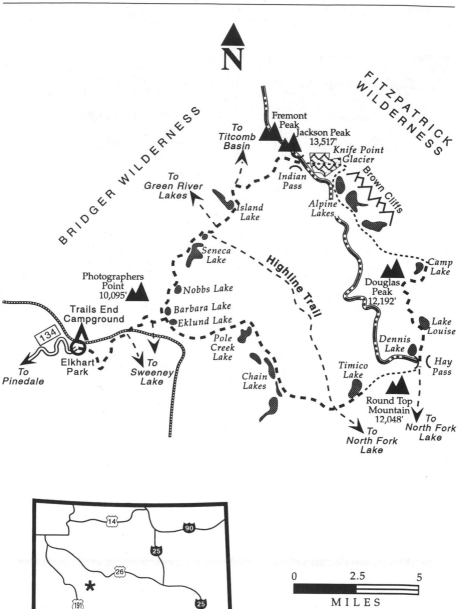

N

FITZPATRICK WILDERNESS

BRIDGER WILDERNESS

Fremont Peak

Jackson Peak 13,517'

To Titcomb Basin

Knife Point Glacier

Indian Pass

To Green River Lakes

Island Lake

Alpine Lakes

Brown Cliffs

Seneca Lake

Highline Trail

Camp Lake

Photographers Point 10,095'

Nobbs Lake

Douglas Peak 12,192'

Trails End Campground

Barbara Lake

Eklund Lake

Lake Louise

134

Pole Creek Lake

Dennis Lake

Hay Pass

To Pinedale

Elkhart Park

To Sweeney Lake

Chain Lakes

Timico Lake

Round Top Mountain 12,048'

To North Fork Lake

To North Fork Lake

To North Fork Lake

14

90

25

26

191

25

80

0   2.5   5

M I L E S

★ Enlarged Area

Alpine splendor at Alpine Lakes. PAUL DONHARL PHOTO.

the lake. Fremont and Jackson peaks dominate the eastern skyline.

From here the Seneca Lake Trail continues along the shoreline of the western side of the lake. High water early in the season may force a higher route by scrambling over the rocks above the shore. At the north end of the lake the Lost Lake Trail heads left and the Seneca Lake Trail continues to Little Seneca Lake, beyond which it ascends to meet the Highline Trail.

The Highline Trail runs north and south at about timberline for the entire length of the Wind River Range. Follow this trail north up a series of switchbacks to a saddle where the Highline Trail continues north and the Indian Pass Trail—your new route—turns east toward Island Lake.

You'll reach Island Lake in about a 1.5 miles. This is a popular area, with many campsites on the southeastern shore. The Indian Pass Trail skirts the southern shore and then starts a gradual climb for .75 mile to the cutoff for Titcomb Basin. The Titcomb Basin Trail is quite heavily used and continues north. The Indian Pass Trail turns to the right. The trail sign will note that Indian Pass is six miles distance when actually it's just over three miles.

Indian Pass Trail climbs about 200 feet in the first mile to Indian Basin. Here there are suitable campsites around the several Lakes in the basin. However, the weather is very unpredictable at this elevation, with frequent afternoon showers, lightning, hail and possibly snow. The trail climbs over 1,000 feet in the next two miles, passing under the bases of Fremont (13,745 feet) and Jackson (13,517 feet) peaks. At Indian Pass, 12,100 feet, the trail ends.

At Indian Pass, cross-country and wilderness adventure begin. A knowledge of cross-country and glacier travel with appropriate equipment is a prerequisite for this part of the journey. Descend east onto Knife Point Glacier. An ice axe is necessary, and crampons are highly recommended. Journey east past the large rock knobs and then turn southeast toward a looming 12,860-foot unnamed peak. After a mile of glacier crossing, begin a steep ascent to a saddle which lies at 12,120 feet. Maps label this Alpine Pass.

From the top of this saddle it is a fairly steep descent to the highest of the three Alpine Lakes. There is a good area for a campsite at the north end of this lake. The Brown Cliffs rise almost 1,500 vertical feet on the east, as does the Continental Divide on the west.

From the north end of the lake, climb up the western wall to just below the snout of an ice field and stay high above the lake for the next two miles. Be prepared to scramble over some "Volkswagen" sized boulders on the way.

At the north end of the lowest Alpine Lake, some maps show a suggested route which follows the eastern shore. This will result in a 100-foot walk through the lake and in chest-deep water. An alternative is to follow the western shore for about .75 mile to the drainage from a lake at the base of Douglas Peak. Go to the lake and turn east, climb about 100 feet to a small saddle and descend, following the drainage to the three small and unnamed lakes just above Camp Lake.

A real trail appears on the eastern shore of Camp Lake. Follow this trail south and begin a 600-foot climb to two small but deep lakes at the southern base of Douglas Peak. Cross the saddle and descend into the Middle Fork of the Bull Lake Creek drainage which contains Upper Golden, Louise and Golden lakes respectively. The trail follows the northern shores of these lakes and begins a 700-foot climb to Hay Pass.

At Hay Pass, 10,960 feet, the trail drops into the North Fork of Boulder Creek and eventually meets the cutoff to the Timico Lake Trail. A many-mile-saving alternative to this route is to bushwhack around the northern slopes of Round Top Mountain from Hay Pass. Head southwest from the lake west of Hay Pass to the meadows at 11,000 feet and follow this elevation around to the saddle where you rejoin the trail to Timico Lake. Keep an eye out for bighorn sheep. At Timico Lake there are several good campsites at the northern end and on the eastern shores.

The trail crosses the Fremont Trail about a mile west of Timico Lake. At the signpost, head almost due west on the Bell Lakes Trail which drops down to Chain Lakes in three miles. At Chain Lakes the trail junctions with the Highline Trail. Follow the Highline Trail north about two miles to the lower ford of Pole Creek. About .25 mile past this ford, the Pole Creek Trail is reached. Eklund Lake lies about 3.5 miles west on the trail which passes several small lakes, including Mary's Lake and its excellent campsites. Once at Eklund Lake, Elkhart Park is but six more miles west.—*Paul Donharl*

HIKE 35 *CLEAR CREEK NATURAL BRIDGE*

General description: An especially beautiful and peaceful day hike to an awesome geological sculpture surrounded by wild and rugged scenery.

General location: Approximately fifty miles north of Pinedale, in the northern section of the Bridger Wilderness.

Maps: Bridger-Teton National Forest Pinedale Ranger District Map and/or USGS Green River Lakes quad.

Special attractions: Waterfalls, springs, crystal creeks, a monumental natural bridge and towering mountain cliffs immuring it all. A wonderful family hike.

For more information: Pinedale Ranger District, 210 W, Pine Street, P.O. Box 220, Pinedale, WY, 82941, (307) 367-4326.

Finding the trailhead: From Pinedale drive six miles west on U.S. Highway 191 to a Bridger Wilderness Green River Access sign. This is also Wyoming highway 352, and it wanders northward for 26.4 miles before the pavement ends and the road transforms into graveled Forest Service Road 091. Another long twenty miles of this road brings you to the Green River Lakes Campground. Just before driving into the fee campground area, a large sign directs hikers to a wilderness parking area.

The hike: Anyone who has floated through Dinosaur National Monument or witnessed the amazing confluence of the Green and Colorado rivers in Canyonlands National Park knows what a mighty body of moving water the Green River becomes. What fun it is to trace that full-grown river to its bubbling spring beginnings amid the flanks of precipitous Wyoming mountains. The following three hikes guide you into the different settings and personalities of the various sources of the Green River. Clear Creek Natural Bridge is the wonderful kind of day hike that allows for easy wandering while permiting you to see a fair amount of incredible scenery. It's also a great first-day, get-the-legs-strengthened hike for the long and rugged journeys one can choose to travel from this location.

In the middle of the large parking lot, a wilderness information sign stands, and directly southeast or behind this sign, a trail cuts into the woods and parallels the buck-and-pole fence surrounding the campground. But .1 mile of following this path brings you to a signed intersection. The Lakeside Trail continues southeast, and the access to the Granite Highline Trail jogs left or eastward. Follow this second trail east .3 mile to a major steel bridge that spans the already-huge Green River. Just across the bridge, the trail to Clear Creek Natural Bridge is signed and journeys to the right or southeast.

This trail skirts the south-facing shores of Lower Green River Lake for nearly two miles. Southeast of the trailhead .10 mile be sure and take the main trail to the right, not the hunting trail to the left. Otherwise, simply enjoy an easy-going stroll in open grassy and sage meadows where the only concern is that there are too many scenic wonders to see.

Two miles from the bridge a sign directs the trail eastward and into the Clear Creek drainage. The trail gently switchbacks along a canyon wall that offers great views of cascading Clear Creek Falls. Then it enters into a vast mountain-encompassed meadowland where gentle Clear Creek snakes through the middle of the scenery. 1.3 miles of this hiking places you at the Slide Creek

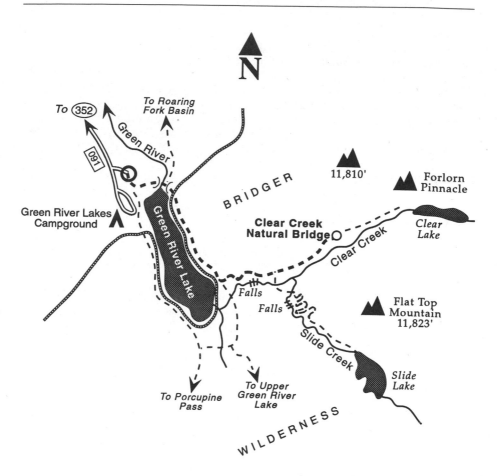

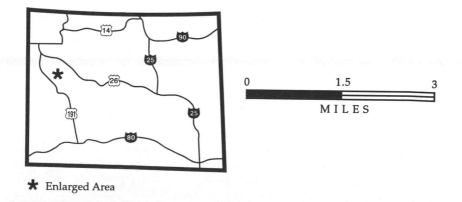

* Enlarged Area

Water flows from beneath Clear Creek Natural Bridge.

Lake Trail intersection. A log bridge does span the river. A couple of long miles of wooded and steep uphill hiking brings you to the large bowl holding aptly-named Slide Lake.

Continuing up Clear Creek for another 1.2 miles, you face the natural bridge, a massive, building-sized rectangle of rock that the creek decided to burrow under rather than weave a way around or carve a channel through. Ponderous Flat Top Mountain rules the eastern horizon, and a lofty crag of granite spires named Forlorn Pinnacle grabs all upstream attention. The last mile of hiking to the bridge is through a forest fire burn, but ample camping exists anywhere below that area. Be sure and follow the trail around to the other side of the bridge where the water funnels under the rock.

The trail does continue in an unmaintained manner up the creek to Clear Lake, and many adventurers use this area as a step-off into the alpine Bear Basin area. The entire Clear Creek drainage falls under a special management classification that prohibits campfires.

HIKE 36 *GREEN RIVER LAKES TO SUMMIT LAKE*

General description: A multi-day, fairly long and adventurous backpack into the rocky and high headwaters of the Green River.

General location: Approximately fifty miles north of Pinedale, in the northern section of the Bridger Wilderness.

Maps: Bridger-Teton National Forest Pinedale Ranger District Map and/or USGS Green River Lakes, Squaretop Mountain and Gannett Peak quads. Earthwalk Press's Northern Wind River Range Hiking and Guide affords an excellent topographic overview of the area.

Special attractions: This is the breath-taking country that promotional bureaus photograph for their "Visit Wild Wyoming" brochures. The vistas and west-side views of the Gannett area peaks are dazzling.

For more information: Pinedale Ranger District, 210 W, Pine Street, P.O. Box 220, Pinedale, WY, 82941, (307) 367-4326.

Finding the trailhead: Road access directions are identical to those in the Clear Creek Natural Bridge hike description, (Hike 35).

The hike: So many hiking options exist here, so much outstanding and spectacular beauty abounds that a week will barely allow you to see and feel the country. Take at least five days. Take ten days. This is not country you want to rush into and through. The Green River Valley offers awesome views and settings. Summit Lake shouldn't be a final goal but a basecamp from which to expand into the surrounding peaks, glaciers and alpine lakes.

For this trail, you'll need to journey around the southwest shores of Lower Green River Lake, along the Lakeside Trail. The bridge over large and swift Clear Creek on the northern shore Highline Trail was washed out. It was scheduled for replacement fall 1991. Check with the Pinedale Ranger District or look for information signs posted on the trailhead boards to determine if this has occured. To reach the Lakeside Trail, simply continue southeast along the trail that skirts the campground, or walk through the campground to its eastern edges. Beyond campsite 10 you'll see a fence ladder over the pole fence and a trail sign noting the Lakeside Trail.

The first 2.5 miles of this level trail skirt the lake's shores, but the forest hides the surrounding views. After you walk across the meadow at the head of the lake, cross the quite large bridge spanning huge and aquamarine-tinted Green River, and hike a total of three miles to Upper Green River Lake, the limitless panoramas begin, and from here on they never end. This area is actually one of the most-photographed scenes in Wyoming. Towering Squaretop Mountain creates a magnificent backdrop to this scenic lake. For 2.5 miles beyond the upper lake, large and open meadows rule the valley bottom. Camping is an anywhere-you-want proposition, and as you hike, Squaretop Mountain grows from a distant centerpiece to a looming overhead projection.

After six miles of level hiking, the meadows end and the trail becomes typical Wind River valley hiking. Thick forests and rocky trails sneak beneath the shear and towering rocky faces of surrounding cliffs. You cross the river back to the west side at 9.8 miles. This is quite a crossing. Two not-too-large logs are wired together and end atop a large rock in the middle of the swift-moving river. Two more wired logs then span the remaining half of the river. It takes

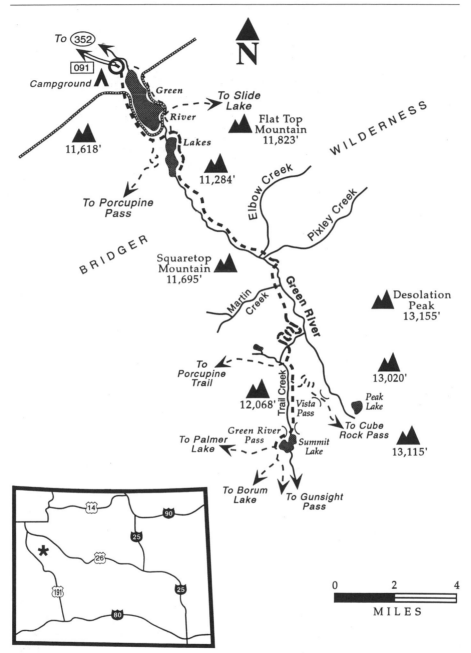

a sturdy frame of mind to bob across these logs in ideal weather. If they are wet, say from a rain, waiting until they dry out is advisable.

You reach Three Forks Park 1.5 miles after the crossing—a glorious breath of meadowed country that affords numerous camping opportunities. So far the eleven miles of trail has been mostly level. Beyond Three Forks Park it begins a steep switchback for two miles. Here you encounter Trail Creek, a too-wide-to-jump gush of crystaline water. In 1991, thirty-five yards upstream, three small and half-rotten poles bound together with nylon cord spanned the waterway. No guarantees are offered that they will still be there when you reach this creek crossing.

About a mile beyond the Trail Creek crossing, a signed intersection offers a route westward to the Porcupine Trail (HIKE 37). You've hiked over thirteen miles to this point, and the high, jagged and spectacular country is just beginning. There are now numerous options and decisions to consider. Great camping exists in this Trail Creek Park area, allowing a base camp from which to explore. Two of the three miles south to Green River Pass and Summit Lake are above timberline. At the lake the land is wide, flat, open and above it all. Along the way a wonderful trail jogs westward to Vista, Cube Rock and Shannon passes, and every step of this trail places you in the western shadows of the highest Wind River Peaks.

Be sure and carry a good map for an overview of all the hiking options in this grandest of mountain high country. Be aware that all of this area is special management, and campfires are prohibited.

HIKE 37 *PORCUPINE CREEK TO PORCUPINE PASS*

General description: A three (or more) day, less known and less traveled sister hike to the Green River Trail (HIKE 36).
General location: Approximately fifty miles north of Pinedale, in the northern section of the Bridger Wilderness.
Maps: Bridger-Teton National Forest Pinedale Ranger District Map and/or USGS Green River Lakes and Squaretop Mountain quads.
Special attractions: Offers a quicker, wilder and less-used pathway to access the unique Wind River high country. Many additional routes branch off from this trail.
For more information: Pinedale Ranger District, 210 W, Pine Street, P.O. Box 220, Pinedale, WY, 82941, (307) 367-4326.
Finding the trailhead: To gain access to remote and rugged Porcupine Creek, follow the road directions in hike 35, the Clear Creek Natural Bridge hike.

The hike: The Continental Divide backbone of the Wind Rivers forms the most spectacular, jagged and awesome line of mountainous crags imaginable. No less captivating are the unique peaks and cirques, flats and drainages within the range that lie outside the immediate sphere of these highest granite steeples. In fact, much of the range's wildlife lives within these encircling boundaries. The mountains surrounding Porcupine Creek project a more rounded and flat-topped look than the high neighbors to the east. The cliffs overlooking the drainage emminate an untamed, almost ferocious beauty.

Trace the first 2.3 miles of the Lakeside Trail along the beginning of the Green

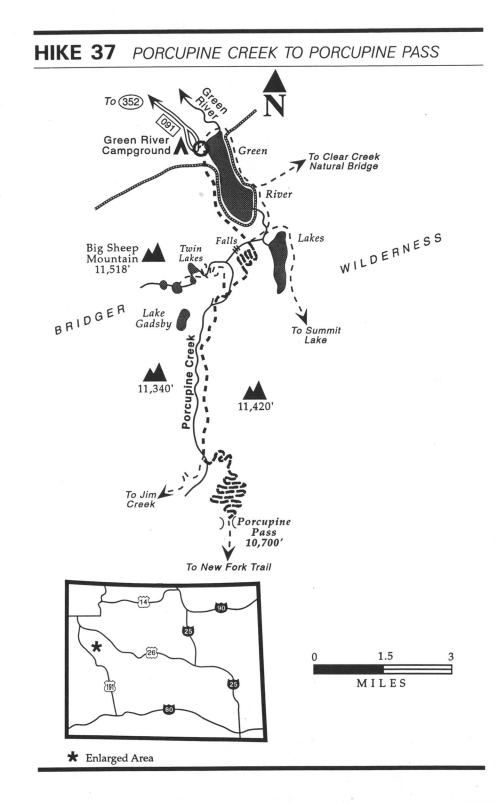

River Lakes hike (HIKE 36). At this point, near the head of Lower Green River Lake, a sign will direct you southward and onto the Porcupine Trail.

After .2 mile of level meadow skirting, you meet the first crossing Porcupine Creek. Look upstream, as there may be some hefty spruce trees spanning the waters and facilitating an easier crossing. The next 1.5 miles switchback quite steeply through a basic no-view lodgepole forest. Finishing this ascent, it's time to again cross the creek. Whether or not the half-rotten splay of logs that afforded a tenuous dry crossing will survive next winter's runoff is a wilderness variable. Immediately beyond this ford, the Twin Lakes Trail breaks away to the west and will, in a bit more than a mile's steep uphill distance, take you into a small mountain bowl hiding four reclusive lakes.

The main trail continues southward and now begins breaking into various meadows and their associated views of the surrounding cliffs. Beyond the Twin Lakes intersection .3 mile count on wading the creek, but also know that your hiking efforts are about to be rewarded. The meadows become vast and open, and the towering mountains stand tall and beautiful around them. The next couple miles distance has the hiker walking a gentle to moderate slope through deepening forests and into many slide areas where the trees have been obliterated by winter avalanches.

Another east-to-west creek crossing occurs almost four miles after the the beginning of Porcupine Trail. Here you start to penetrate the subalpine country. The trail recrosses the creek .2 mile later for a last time. There is an intersecting trail at this crossing, the Jim Creek Trail, but it's unsigned and a hard one to locate. The main trail jogs east and begins a steep switchbacking ascent toward Porcupine Pass. The last section of this journey forms a phenomenal zigzag that climbs about .2 mile of mountain in 1.5 miles of switchbacks. Porcupine Pass, at 10,700 feet, is small in area and offers no available liquid, so water needs to be carried if you feel the urge to camp on the summit.

The trail continues south of the pass, providing access to the New Fork Lakes area, and loop access to numerous lakes, canyons and peaks in the Bridger Wilderness. Following the New Fork Trail east past the Lozier Lakes, over Greely Point and into Trail Creek Park not only offers a nice loop hike back to the Green River Lakes, but it also provides excellent views of the western faces of the high mountains. Good maps are essential to show you all the possibilities.

Salt River Range

Not all of Wyoming's many mountain ranges are granite cored. A different, softer and subtler beauty distinguishes high mountains composed of sedimentary sea remnants. In the southwestern sector of Wyoming, two exceptional parallel mountain chains offer remote and unpublished hiking opportunities amid the crumpled and steeply tilted rock layers of the Salt River and Wyoming Ranges. Divided by the Greys River, these two north-south ranges of the geologically wild Overthrust Belt are actually part of an identical structural mountain-chain formation.

Geologists are not certain where these mountain ranges originated. Thick sections of thrust-deformed sedimentary rocks, later to be named the Salt River and Wyoming Ranges, slid into Wyoming and piled against the Gros Ventre and Teton ranges. But from whence they slid still remains a mystery.

The Overthrust Belt tells a sad story for many Wyoming conservationists. Nearly 700,000 acres of wilderness were identified in this area during the RARE studies. This wasn't only quality wilderness, but quiet wilderness—isolated and untrodden wilderness. But a USGS 1984 study claimed the Overthrust area "to be highly favorable for the occurrence of gas and oil. The Wyoming congressional delegation proposed but one fifth of the acreage for wilderness study. These ranges are now blanketed with oil, gas and mineral leases.

The Bridger-Teton National Forest map for this area is the Big Piney, Greys River and Kemmerer Ranger Districts map. The Big Piney District is located in Big Piney, the Greys River District in Afton, and the Kemmerer District in Kemmerer. The map is excellent in contour detail, but wisdom dictates checking with these districts when planning a new and undocumented hike into these ranges. Trails very often have been converted into roads that lead to new drillholes. Also, ATVs have claimed many of the former hiking trails as motorized domain, and the map doesn't note the occurance.

On the other hand, this section of Wyoming still offers a kind of exploration rare to experience these days. The country is very big, people are quite rare, and hikers can create trips that are not defined by the thousands who tread before them.

HIKE 38 POKER CREEK TRAIL TO ALICE LAKE

General description: A two- to three-day, long and steeply rugged journey into one of the few lakes in the Commissary Ridge/Salt River Range area.
General location: Approximately forty miles west of Big Piney, near the northern beginnings of Commissary Ridge in the Bridger-Teton National Forest.
Maps: Bridger-Teton National Forest Big Piney, Greys River and Kemmerer Districts map and/or USGS Graham Peak quads.
Special attractions: Scenic hiking on a little-used trail. Incredibly wild and varied mountain country. A beautiful and large lake to play on/in/at.
For more information: Kemmerer Ranger District, Highway 189, P.O. Box 31, Kemmerer, WY, 83101, (307) 877-4415.
Finding the trailhead: I highly recommend when driving roads to trailheads

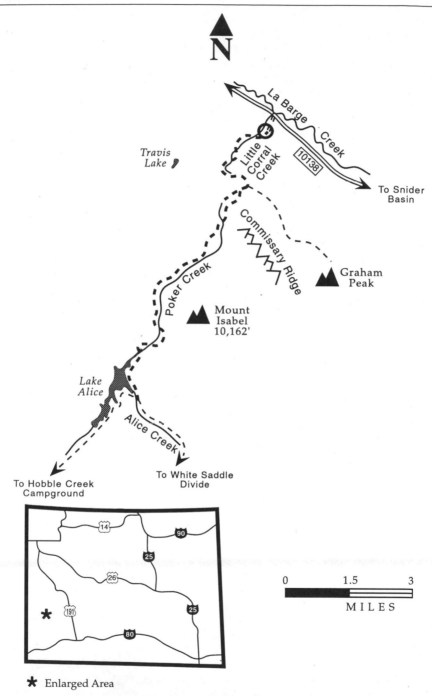

La Barge Creek

Travis
Lake

Little Corral Creek

10138

To Snider
Basin

Commissary Ridge

Graham
Peak

Poker Creek

Mount
Isabel
10,162'

Lake
Alice

Alice Creek

To Hobble Creek
Campground

To White Saddle
Divide

14

90

25

26

191

25

80

0   1.5   3

M I L E S

★ Enlarged Area

The glorious and unknown Salt River Range

in this sector of the forest that you have the forest visitors map in your lap and trace every mile of the journey, especially marking off all intersections. Someone is creating havoc for newcomers by stealing or vandalizing some of the road junction signs.

From Big Piney, turn west on Wyoming highway 310. It's paved for nearly eleven miles. Then Sublette County Road 142 begins as you follow the signs left or south toward Snyder Basin. La Barge Meadows is your final goal, so any sign with this name is a direction sign. The county road ends after 4.4 miles, and a one-mile section of private road with some gruesome speedbumps follows. After this section you cross a cattleguard and come upon an unsigned intersection. Turn left or south, continuing beside South Piney Creek. Forest Service land begins 5.5 miles later, and FS Road 10128 is a welcome relief after the bumps of the preceeding BLM road. Follow this road past the Snyder Guard Station. 6.1 miles after the forest boundary, at a sign-removed intersection, turn right, and 1.4 miles later turn right again, into the Kemmerer Ranger District and over what is labeled Witherspoon Pass. Three miles later the road

T's into FS Road 10138. Another right or west turn and 6.5 miles of driving places you at a huge commemorative "La Barge Meadows" sign, and .5 mile farther west another sign notes the "Poker Creek Trail". Just west of this marker is a road that parallels the east side of Little Corral Creek. Any two-wheel-drive can handle this rough road the few tenths of a mile to the trailhead if you are good at straddling ruts.

Another and easier access route, if you happen to be journeying from Jackson, is to drive approximately sixteen miles south of Afton on U.S. highway 89. Just beyond the forest boundary turn east onto FS Road 10072, the Smiths Fork Road. This graded and graveled road weaves through the mountains for twenty-four miles to the Tri Basin Divide intersection. Turn southward and drive toward La Barge Meadows (on FS Road 10138) for a bit over a mile. Little Corral Creek is signed, and the road leading to the trail is just east the creek.

The hike: Hiking the more southern portions of the massive Bridger-Teton Forest requires arduous drives over military roads. Consequently, fewer of the casual explorers venture here. Commissary Ridge, named after the commissary or supply wagons hauled into this country by the stockmen who grazed sheep here in the 1880s, is a many-mile crest of 9-10,000-foot ridge elevations and open forests that extends from LaBarge Meadows south to Fossil Butte (HIKE 18). Not an official wilderness area, this unique roadless area finds its edges being ever encroached upon by piecemeal development. Lake Alice, one of the few lakes to grace this volcanic mountain area, is named for the wife of a copper miner who discovered a lode and worked a nearby mine for a few years.

The trail begins along the eastern shores of Little Corral Creek, and passes beneath a towering, monsterous spruce forest—trees so huge three people as one unit couldn't hug them. There are several creek crossings in the two miles to the top of Commissary Ridge, but they are simple hops. No ridge walking occurs after this first climb, as the trail immediately and steeply descends into an incredible ravine-like Poker Canyon. This gorge is awesome in depth while shy in width, and offers animated scenery to match its ruggedness. It's over five miles of bold downhill to Lake Alice. A mile before the lake, the trail crosses the stream in a wade, and then a half mile later, by a permanent hunting camp, it recrosses. This second crossing, in July, is a watery and willowed jungle that is almost impossible to negotiate. I had to backtrack and recross Poker Creek upstream. On the return hike I easily avoided both creek crossings by staying on the western shore of the creek.

The best camping occurs in the meadows near the Poker Creek's inlet into the lake. Being a reservoir, the sides of the lake extend up the steep and forested hillsides and camping is non-existant. Also note that around the first of July, due to high runoff, the trails around both sides of the lake were under water in places. This situation corrects itself as summer wears on. A second trail to the outlet of Lake Alice is a few-mile hike from the Hobble Creek Campground west of the lake. It's a much more spectacular and isolated journey to touch the clear, deep and blue waters of Lake Alice via the back entrance.

The soil in this country is a bizzare kind of clay that turns to pure goosh when it's wet and concrete when it dries. It can be really rough walking if horse and game hooves have cratered the ground and the ground later dries in that shape. Also, stinging nettles occasionally line the trail. Be wary if you have a particular reaction to their touch.

114

HIKE 39 *LANDER CUTOFF or THE WAY TRAIL*

General description: An easy and enjoyable day hike along a historic Oregon Trail route.

General location: Approximately forty-five miles west of Big Piney, near the southern end of the Salt River Range and northern beginning of Commissary Ridge, in the Bridger-Teton National Forest.

Maps: Bridger-Teton National Forest Big Piney, Greys River and Kemmerer Districts map and/or USGS Poison Meadows quad.

Special attractions: A little-known hike along the famous coverd-wagon route of the mid 1800s.

For more information: Kemmerer Ranger District, Highway 189, P.O. Box 31, Kemmerer, WY, 83101, (307) 877-4415.

Finding the trailhead: If you come from the east and Big Piney, follow the directions to Little Corral Creek/Poker Creek as given in hike 38. Continue west one more mile to a major road intersection, Tri Basin Divide. Turn west onto the Smiths Fork Road and travel .6 mile to the well-signed and visible La Barge Meadows Guard Station. Turning south on this road places you by the signed "Old Lander Trail."

If you drive from Afton, again follow the second set of directions in hike 38, turning onto the Smiths Fork Road and driving approximately 23.5 miles to the same La Barge Guard Station Sign.

The hike: The Oregon Trail certainly forms the most famous of the many wagon routes to and through the west. From 1834 to 1868 more than 30,000 travelers a year strained a passage through the inhospitable country that later became the state of Wyoming. In 1858 General F. W. Lander directed construction of an Oregon Trail shortcut route that both shortened the journey's distance by 200 miles and stayed closer to the welcome wood and water of the southern Wind River and Wyoming ranges. But a tiny portion of the Lander Cutoff isn't part of or quite close to a modern-day roadway. The Old Lander Trail affords an unequalled opportunity to retrace a portion of that history.

This trail is as much a journey into your mind as it is a pleasant physical walk. The more you've read and know about the Oregon Trail and its trials and hardships, the more you'll sense the creaking wagons and hope behind the incredibly arduous journey you're reliving. After an uphill mile to Commissary Ridge at Wagner Pass, and another mile down into the Hobble Creek drainage, you too will be in awe of what the forefathers managed to do and where they managed to go. All the while there is also the bonus of exceptionally beautiful and peaceful mountains with great valley views and huge trees.

I hiked but a couple of miles of this seven-mile trail. It's a good thing I wasn't hired as General Lander's expedition scout. I couldn't find where the emigrant's trail left the Hobble Creek drainage. One mile beyond my frustrated ending there supposedly sits a square stone noting "Estella Brown, layed(sic) two(sic) rest, July 29, 1891." A first impulse was to chuck this hike description until the Kemmerer District caught up with its trail maintainence and I could present the entire trek. But even those first two miles turned out to be such a splendid and enjoyable hike, both physically and mentally, that I

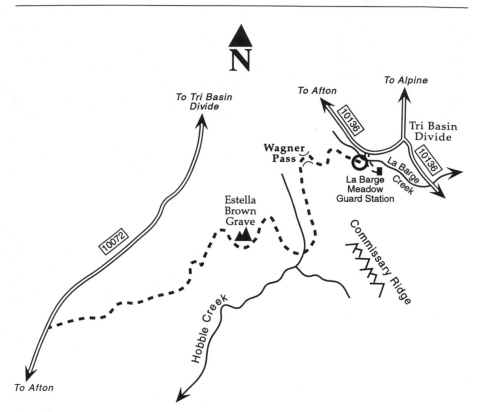

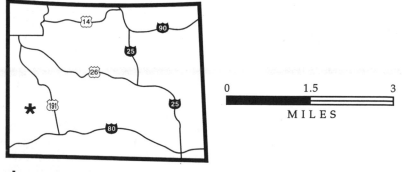

* Enlarged Area

include it here and make it known to other hikers. A lot of history lives on that trail. And perhaps your pioneering instincts are a bit sharper than mine, and you will enjoy the challenge of finding the way.

HIKE 40 *CROW CREEK*

General description: An enjoyable and not too steep day hike into a lovely high mountain setting. This picturesque area offers great camping for an enjoyable overnight trip.

General location: Approximately forty-five miles east and south of Alpine Junction along the Greys River Road, in the central section of the Salt River Range.

Maps: Bridger-Teton National Forest Big Piney, Greys River and Kemmerer Ranger Districts map and/or USGS Box Canyon Creek and Red Top Mountain quads.

Special attractions: Enjoyable, easy hiking into lushly forested hills. Great meadows and impressive views reside at the foot of spectacular Mount Fitzpatrick.

For more information: Greys River Ranger District, 125 Washington, P.O. Box 339, Afton, WY, 83110, (307) 886-3166.

Finding the trailhead: Driving west from Alpine on the Grey's River Road, travel forty-one miles southward and upstream. All the perpendicular creek crossings along this road are well-signed, and the "Crow Creek" sign sits across from mile marker 41. The map shows the trail beginning a mile to the north of the creek. That is actually an old road that is accessed by an older bridge that doesn't appear too drivable. One mile north of this unmarked road and bridge, by the "Crow Creek" sign, there is a small parking area on the west side of the road. Another and newer footbridge that spans the Greys River is visible to the southwest. This is the hiking trailhead.

The hike: The problem with coming upon a topographical name like "Crow Creek" is that in this country you don't really know if it commemorates a sub-tribe of Indians or a flock of birds. A more leisurely hike through easygoing mountain country landscape does not exist.

Once across the river, you need to wander cross-country and southwest for a few tenths of a mile, toward the mouth of Crow Creek Canyon. Here the trail becomes visible as it follows the north side of the creek. At about .7 mile from the bridge, the trail crosses the creek, and a few tenths of a mile later it recrosses, back to the north side. It is possible to avoid these two wades by skirting the north bank of the creek, but one wall of conglomerate dirt and rock slopes toward the creek at seventy degrees and is quite tricky to cross with a backpack. The remaining four miles of this not-too-used trail form a wonderful, unhurried, gentle climbing walk through quiescent forests. High country meadows create great camping spots below the foot of the impressive cliffs of Mount Fitzpatrick. Since this trail is but 5.5 miles north of the Wyoming Range's Box Creek Trailhead (HIKE 42), these two day hikes—one the epitome of rushing waters and towering cliffs, the other filled with almost inert beauty—make interesting mountain range comparison hikes.

The abundance of wildlife in this drainage is visible everywhere. The

N

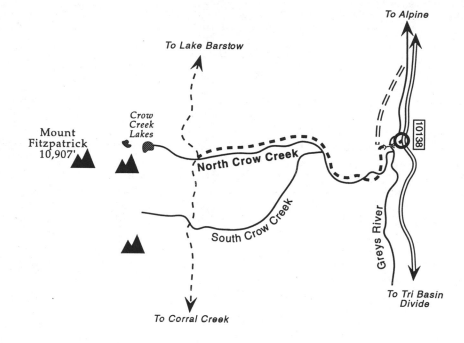

To Alpine

To Lake Barstow

Mount
Fitzpatrick
10,907'

Crow
Creek
Lakes

North Crow Creek

South Crow Creek

Greys River

10138

To Tri Basin
Divide

To Corral Creek

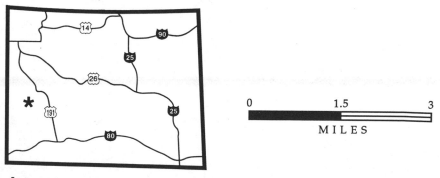

14

90

25

26

191

25

80

0   1.5   3

M I L E S

★ Enlarged Area

Mellow meadow walking above Crow Creek.

meadows below Mount Fitzpatrick make an excellent base from which to experience a fairly rugged yet not-too-difficult cross-country peak climb (see HIKE 41).

HIKE 41 *MOUNT FITZPATRICK*

General description: A wonderful example of a cross-country peak climbing/hiking. It's easy to complete in a day from the meadows along North Crow Creek.

General location: Five miles west of the Crow Creek Trailhead in the Salt River Range.

Maps: Bridger-Teton National Forest Big Piney, Greys River and Kemmerer Ranger Districts map and/or USGS Box Canyon Creek and Red Top Mountain quads.

Special attractions: A hard-earned and breathtaking view of the Wyoming world from over 10,000 feet.

For more information: Greys River Ranger District, 125 Washington, P.O. Box 339, Afton, WY, 83110, (307) 886-3166. (Since this hike is cross-country and quite an offshoot route, the Forest Service probably knows little about it.)

Finding the trailhead: Same as HIKE 40.

The hike: When I first began hiking, twenty-five years ago, I joined a mountaineer club whose members were gung ho about hiking to the tops of peaks. Every week we climbed a different mountain summit. The untrailed, difficult and unforgiving alpine terrain imparted in us beginners a kind of special confidence and verve.

Realizing that a very large portion of the Wyoming landscape is composed of peak tops, I've endeavored to include a few examples of this form of hiking in this guidebook. This hike is geared for the kind of people who love challenging cross-country adventures. While this particular hike is quite suitable for beginners, it's advised that rookies do travel with someone more experienced.

Follow the directions for the Crow Creek Trail (HIKE 40) and begin at the meadows at the foot of Mount Fitzpatrick. The maps show the trail T-ing here. But there is no sign and there are so many game trails crossing the faded main trail that its hard to distinguish the intersection. Continue along the main-ish trail a few tenths of a mile farther until you notice it climbing up hill and venturing to the north. Here look south and downhill to Crow Creek, and you'll see a quite visible trail crossing the creek. Head south to that trail, cross the creek, and notice that the trail immediately disappears again. Now angle southwest toward the mountain for twenty yards and watch the trail reappear where it journeys southward into the forest. The next mile's distance is very steep, and trail maintenance happened years ago, so a lot of fallen trees impede the hike.

At the ridgetop, one mile south and beyond Crow Creek, the landscape levels out. Here the trail continues to the south, but you want to turn west and follow this ridge through the forest. A short distance later the landscape tilts steeply upward, and a short but tricky, almost-fourth-class scramble places you onto a level, forested plateau. Wander westward to another steepish climb. This will put you on the ridge that journeys northwest all the way to the false summit of the mountain. Be sure you have the ability to gauge landmarks and find your way back through the forested plateau to the fourth class scramble. All other land surrounding this one spot is cliff, and the potential for getting up there and not being able to find a way down does exist.

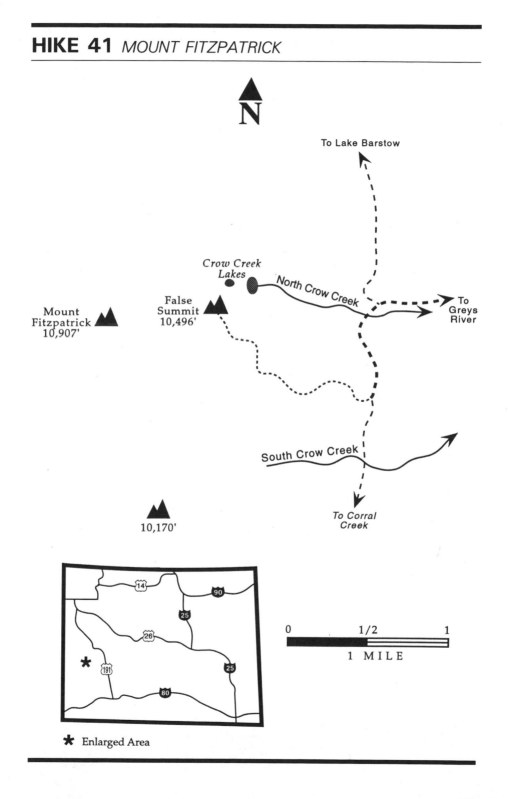

Cross-country ridge hiking up Mount Fitzpatrick.

Along this main ridge, which consists of steep stair stepping and scree slope walking, you'll have to decide if you're dizzy from the elevation or from the awesome views spreading out before you. Crow Creek drainage and the Wyoming Range to the west create spectacular vistas. Along this ridge .6 mile, a rocky cliff obstructs the way. This is a fifth class climb and not recommended as a course. By veering left and staying beneath the base of the rocks, you'll soon find a climbable break in the cliffs that again places you on the ridge. Tiny Crow Creek Lakes are now about 1,000 feet straight down and to the north. You also realize that the view of Mount Fitzpatrick from the Crow Creek Trail reveals but a fourth of the mountain. It's another half mile scree-slope plod to the false summit of the peak.

To keep this adventure in the realm of a hiker's guide, the first summit is as far as I go. One view of the knife edges and intense rockslide slopes of the ridge to the real summit explains why. But the vistas from this point—the Wyoming Range, the Gros Ventres, even the Tetons are visible—and the exhilarating feeling of accomplishment leave you feeling like you're in the Himalayas.

Common sense precautions of appropriate weather gear, being in shape and acclimatized to altitude, and making sure every step is a safe step apply in triple strength on these adventuresome peak explorations.

The Wyoming Range

Wyoming Territory was created in 1868, and this long and wild eastern segment of the Overthrust Belt—originally called the Bear River Range—was renamed after the newfound land. The Wyoming Range towers between the Green River to the east and the Greys River to the west, and is an absolute treasure of lightly traveled hiking opportunities and pure mountain splendor.

From the Bryan Flat Ranger Station twenty miles south of Jackson, to the Snider Basin Ranger Station twenty-five miles west of Big Piney, a barely-known, seventy-mile-long Wyoming Range National Recreation Trail traverses the entire length of the Wyoming Range. The trail is the pride of the Big Piney Ranger District and offers a vast variety of terrain, scenery and challenge for the hiker. Wide and green alpine meadows give way to 10,000-foot knife-like ridges. Wildlife abounds, especially in the many east and west drainages. Many hiking loops are possible along the trail. The Big Piney district ranger notes that their trail crew is in the process of upgrading the Wyoming Range National Recreation Trail, but that some portions are still in a primitive state and not easy to discern. He recommends that hikers purchase topographical maps before venturing into the range. Further information is available from the Big Piney Ranger District, P.O. Box 218, Big Piney, WY, 83113, (307) 276-3375.

HIKE 42 *BOX CANYON CREEK AND PASS*

General description: An unforgettable day hike into and out of a unique "box" of a mountain canyon.
General location: Approximately fifty-two miles east and south of Alpine Junction along the Greys River Road, in the central section of the Wyoming Range.
Maps: Bridger-Teton National Forest Big Piney, Greys River and Kemmerer Ranger Districts map and/or USGS Box Canyon Creek and Mount Schidler quads.
Special attractions: Steep canyon walls surrounding a rushing creek, impressive waterfalls, stunning views.
For more information: Greys River Ranger District, 125 Washington, P.O. Box 339, Afton, WY, 83110, (307) 886-3166, and Big Piney District, Highway 189, P.O. Box 218, Big Piney, WY, 83113, (307) 276-3375.
Finding the trailhead: Three miles from the Idaho border and on U.S. Highway 89, the only paved road in the tiny tourist town of Alpine that journeys east is the Greys River Road. Although the pavement ends after a mile, this sixty-three-mile artery of uncontrolled dust opens endless doors to

HIKE 42 *BOX CANYON CREEK AND PASS*

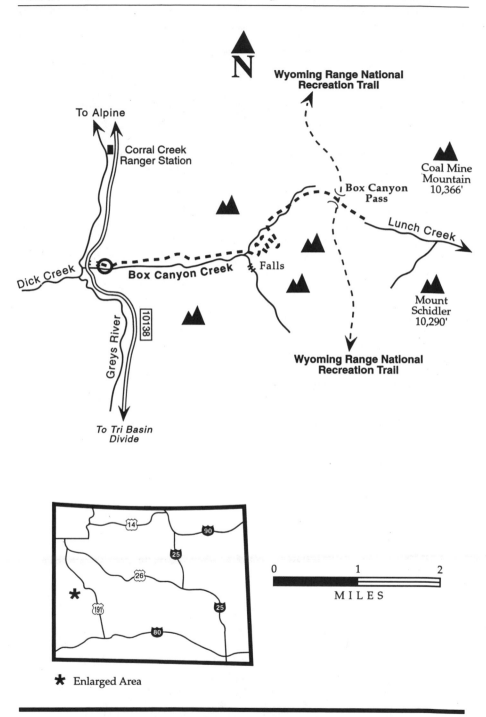

N

Wyoming Range National
Recreation Trail

To Alpine

Corral Creek
Ranger Station

Coal Mine
Mountain
10,366'

Box Canyon
Pass

Lunch Creek

Dick Creek

Box Canyon Creek

Falls

Mount
Schidler
10,290'

Greys River

10138

To Tri Basin
Divide

Wyoming Range National
Recreation Trail

14

90

25

26

25

191

80

★ Enlarged Area

0   1   2

MILES

both the Salt River and Wyoming ranges. Almost all the creeks intersecting this road are labeled with brown signs noting their names. Drive 51.5 miles along this road, enjoying every mile of its changing beauty, and you see a sign "Box Creek Trail." (Dick Creek is directly west of this creek and also labeled.) A two track road turns east at the Box Creek sign and in .2 mile it deadends at a campfire ring.

The hike: I've always been attracted to any landscape with the name "box" attached to it.

A not-so-recent forest fire, a salvaging clearcut and a bulldozer's attempt at land reclamation make the trailhead both unappealing and hard to locate. Do not skirt the creek bank up stream in this first distance. Do cut up the hillside just to the north of the creek. Place yourself atop this little hill and above the stream and then head up canyon. After .3 mile the fire and clearcut end while blaze marks and a viable trail reveal themselves.

An exciting feeling of adventure permeates this canyon. Adventure because the trail is not the most used and the Greys River Ranger District is behind on their maintainance, because the fire wiped out the south side of the creek yet spared the north (trailed) side, and because this absolute wall of a mountain begins to loom ahead, a wall you know must somehow be surmounted to exit the canyon.

After about a mile, in a large and open meadow, the trail disappears. Here you need to head slightly north or uphill, toward the middle of a massive rock slide. About seventy-five yards distance above the creek, the trail cuts directly across the rock slide slope.

After an easy wander beneath amazing cliff structures of stratified rock, another hard-to-follow section manifests. Here you see the impressive Box Creek Falls to the south. The trail now crosses the main stream and veers away (to the left) from the falls to follow the north branch of the creek. Shake hands with the 1,000-foot wall that has predominated this entire trip. I can't begin to describe the views that accompany one up this very steep one-mile section of the hike. The trail does level out though, and by continuing eastward you discover that the crest of the Wyoming Range does not resemble the steep and rocky face the last four miles have presented. Huge and open meadows and gently rolling alpine hills now rule the landscape. Lunch Creek Meadows is a perfect alpine setting to take such a break.

It's easy to spend a leisurely day atop this pass. Several mountaintops are within easy hiking distance, and trails wander off in all four directions. You are situated in the essential heart of the Wyoming Range. Camping is possible in these meadows, as the nearby streams begin their liquid flow not too far down the slopes.

HIKE 43 *CLIFF CREEK PASS*

General description: An overnight or three-day camping trip into lofty highlands with multiple opportunities to explore various intersecting trails.

General location: Approximately twenty-five miles west of Alpine, in the northern section of the Wyoming Range.

Maps: Bridger-Teton National Forest Big Piney, Greys River and Kemmerer Ranger Districts map and/or USGS Pickle Pass and Hoback Peak quads.

Special attractions: A horsepacker's trail few hikers ever experience. Alpine meadows and ridgetops amid panoramic vistas.

For more information: Greys River Ranger District, 125 Washington, P.O. Box 339, Afton, WY, 83110, (307) 886-3166.

Finding the trailhead: From the town of Alpine, the one paved road journeying east is the Greys River Road (pavement ends where the national forest begins, one mile later). At 7.8 miles along this nice gravel road, the well marked Little Greys Road intersects. Follow this road northeast for 12.5 miles to the Telephone Pass Trail sign and here turn right or south. Two miles later, in a small parking area, a sign notes the Cliff Creek trailhead.

The hike: The Greys River was not named for the dense gray sedimentary rocks that constitute much of the surrounding mountains. John Grey, a fur trapper, stabbed a fellow trapper and trader who insulted his daughter. This act somehow placed his name into the chronicles of topography. The clear and playful branch named the Little Greys River is a popular unimproved camping area for RVs and auto campers. But few venture to the road's end and enjoy the adventurous headwaters of this unique little stream.

Except during hunting season, this sweet trail is basically deserted. The first 1.5 miles offer a hefty climb into the forested hills far above the river. An unsigned intersection greets you after this distance, the right fork being the way to Cliff Creek Pass. Then the trail does what Wyoming trails love to do. It loses almost all of that hard-earned elevation gain in a steep descent. But in the next couple of miles you'll regain that height and more. The trail never really skirts the river but stays high on the slopes, so if fishing the Little Greys is your bent, you'll have to cut south through the thick forest to its shores . The first nice camping meadows appear about 3.5 miles into the hike. Now the ascents and descents become more gentle, and the forest opens into inviting views of the high mountains ahead. In July, the hillsides were literal blankets of multi-colored flowers.

After five miles of hiking, the trail crosses the Little Greys River, which is now a small stream. Beyond this crossing lie the massive and lush Roosevelt Meadows. Here the trail plays a vanishing game, but keep heading to the east. It's a bit confusing, because the Wyoming Range National Recreation Trail intersects just before the Cliff Creek Trail veers to the north and ascends the open alpine slopes to the east of the Little Greys River. Meanwhile, nothing is signed, and most of these trails are faded or overgrown. The trick is to look carefully to the north and see the Cliff Creek Trail reappear as it climbs some steep slopes toward the pass. Three miles of almost unbelievable, vast and open alpine beauty carry you to another confusing sector, the pass area itself. You actually have to descend a bit to be atop Cliff Creek Pass and where the

N

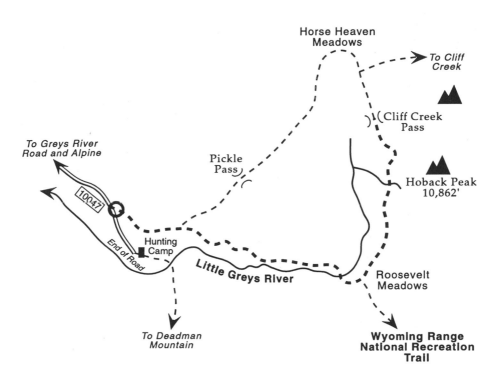

Horse Heaven
Meadows

To Cliff
Creek

Cliff Creek
Pass

To Greys River
Road and Alpine

Pickle
Pass

10047

Hoback Peak
10,862'

End of Road

Hunting
Camp

Little Greys River

Roosevelt
Meadows

To Deadman
Mountain

**Wyoming Range
National Recreation
Trail**

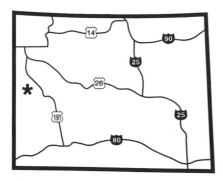

14

90

25

26

191

25

80

0   1.5   3

MILES

★ Enlarged Area

waters part. The camping opportunities from Roosevelt Meadows to the pass area are unlimited.

The maps show a trail making a loop through what's called Horse Heaven Meadows, along a high and broad ridge to a pass named Pickle Pass. Supposedly a trail descends from Pickle Pass and intersects the Cliff Creek Pass trail at about 1.5 miles' distance. I couldn't find it. But if you've an adventuresome spirit and have a sense that allows such wandering, the views are exceptionally grand and trying to complete the loop is a worthwhile journey.

WESTERN WYOMING
The Gros Ventre Range

The Gros Ventre Range may be a bit lower in elevation and not as sharply defined as its neighbors the Tetons, but this colorful, glacier-carved upheaval of stratified rock is no less magnificent and certainly a delightfully unique area to hike.

The Gros Ventre (GROW-vont) Indians were a Blackfoot sub-clan (some references swear they were Nez Perce) who frequented the area. The word means "big bellies" in reference to their always being hungry. The associated Gros Ventre Wilderness contains 87,000 acres of some of the most diverse lands contained in one classified area. These mountains can be a collage of rock colors. Snowcapped peaks in one setting can hide the polychrome badlands soil and rubble cliffs of another. Wildlife is abundant and quite varied, and you may very well witness a large elk herd and catch sight of a grizzly bear track.

The following trail descriptions open and explore the rugged southern section of the wilderness. The entire wilderness area has twenty peaks over 10,000 feet, with several of these exceeding the 11,000-foot mark.

HIKE 44   GRANITE HIGHLINE TRAIL

General description: A rugged, variable-length day hike or a couple-day jaunt and mountainside traverse hike featuring access to several high peaks.
General location: Approximately thirty-five miles east and slightly south of Jackson in the southwestern sector of the Gros Ventre Wilderness.
Maps: Bridger-Teton National Forest Jackson and Buffalo Ranger Districts map and/or USGS Granite Falls, Bull Creek and Turquoise Lake quads. Cache Creek quad is optional.
Special attractions: Superior timberline country traversed by a suitably adventurous trail. Wonderful views, especially south toward the Wyoming Range. And a hot springs is located near the beginning (or end) of the hike.
For more information: Jackson Ranger District, 140 E. Broadway, P.O. Box 1689, Jackson, WY, 83001.
Finding the trailhead: Thirteen miles south of Jackson on U.S. Highways 191, 89, and 26 lies a major highway intersection named Hoback Junction. Here Highways 189 and 191 trace the Hoback River westward toward

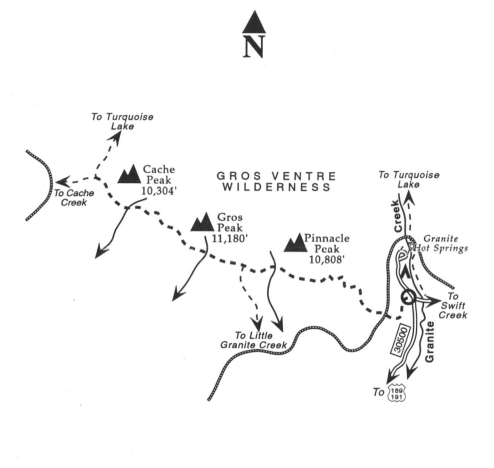

To Turquoise Lake

To Cache Creek

Cache Peak 10,304'

GROS VENTRE WILDERNESS

To Turquoise Lake

Creek

Granite Hot Springs

Gros Peak 11,180'

Pinnacle Peak 10,808'

To Swift Creek

To Little Granite Creek

30500

Granite

To 189 191

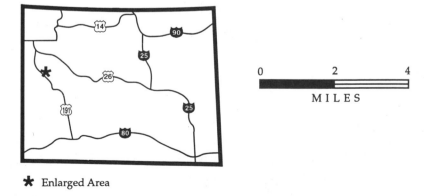

14

90

25

26

25

191

80

★ Enlarged Area

0   2   4

MILES

Bondurant and Pinedale. Twelve miles west of Hoback junction, a large sign notes the Granite Recreation Area, and a gravel Granite Creek Road or Forest Service Road 30500 cuts north for ten miles to end at the Granite Hot Springs pool and picnic area. This is a Forest Service-owned hot springs that is leased and operated by a private concessionaire. A large pool structure, up to eight-feet deep, captures some of the least sulpherous hot water pouring out of the hillside. Pool use fees are $4 for adults and $3 for kids, and the pool is open from 10 a.m. to 7 p.m.

Two miles before these springs, at the Swift Creek Road intersection (hike 45), a sign on the west side of the main road notes the Granite Highline Trail. There is no parking right by the trailhead. The best parking occurs if you turn right or east on the Swift Creek Road and park in the large meadow west and south of the nearby concrete bridge that crosses Granite Creek. One mile north of this trailhead, on the main Granite Creek Road, a Forest Service fee campground forms another nearby place to park and camp overnight.

The hike: I can only offer an introduction to this wonderful trail. An early-season snowstorm caught me off guard and chased everything without a natural fur coat off the mountain. But it's a marvelous adventure into absolutely unique country. Hunting season is about the only time other people use the trail.

If one survives the first very steep 1.5 mile uphill forest hiking, one then enters into a fascinating high country world. The trail more or less levels out and cuts a path into various open alpine meadows. The trees thin out as the pathway traverses these mighty mountainsides near or above timberline. What the hiker experiences are vast miles of alpine colored

Endless open terrain on the Granite Highline Trail.

meadows—flowers in the summer, autumn reds and yellows in the early fall. Awesome views expand toward the Hoback Valley to the south while simultaneous vistas of the seemingly endless slopes of 11,000-foot peaks rise to the north.

The level trail dips into the various gullies and ravines and swings out to the many ridges, and every step affords incomparable views, both near and far.

The land is quite dry, waterwise, for four miles where a first small creek trickles down as part of the headwaters of Little Granite Creek. The surrounding area offers some excellent camping spots which can serve as base camp for further explorations westward or for a climb to the summit of impressive Pinnacle Peak. Westward and beyond this mark, the country can become quite confusing. Both the Forest Service and the USGS topo maps show a confused braiding of trails throughout this area. The maps grossly understate the situation. The soil of this country is so delicate that any larger pack train of horses taking off cross-country can create a new trail. Hunting trails wander in every direction, and many of them appear more mainstream than the official trail. Hiking becomes a matter of moving in a westward traversing course and choosing by inner guidance the trail that "feels" right. (A topo map really gives the intuition a boost.)

If you just make it to the first creek crossing at four miles, you will have experienced an exceptionally splendid hike. The hunters I questioned as we were racing off the mountain in a blizzard declared two things: the country and views only get better the farther west one travels, and nothing is signed. So good topographic maps are essential for exploring this area.

Also know that even though it's named "Granite," the mountain slopes are composed of silts and clays that transform into soft slime when wet. Most of the plant life in those beautiful meadows reach waist-high heights, so a rain storm will also really soak anyone hiking through the area.

The entire trail covers fourteen miles to Cache Creek. From there another seventeen-mile hiking loop down Granite Creek will place you at the hot springs pool. The author plans on hiking (earlier in the year) the entire loop for a future edition of this book.

HIKE 45 *SWIFT CREEK TO SHOAL LAKE*

General description: A three-day hike into the high alpine country of the Gros Ventre Wilderness. An excellent loop hike.

General location: Approximately thirty-five miles southeast of Jackson off U.S. Highways 189 and 191.

Maps: Bridger-Teton National Forest Jackson and Buffalo Ranger Districts map and/or USGS Granite Falls and Crystal Peak quads.

Special attractions: A seldom-used trail leading to flower-studded meadows that offer panoramic vistas of the majestic Tetons.

For more information: Jackson Ranger District, 140 E. Broadway, P.O. Box 1689, Jackson, WY, 83001, (307) 739-5400.

Finding the trailhead: Follow U.S. Highway 189 south of Jackson for twenty-five miles. Turn northeast into the Granite Recreation Area and drive approximately nine miles to the Swift Creek Trail Sign. Turn right at this sign, cross Granite Creek and park near the sign marking the Swift Creek trailhead.

HIKE 45 *SWIFT CREEK TO SHOAL LAKE*

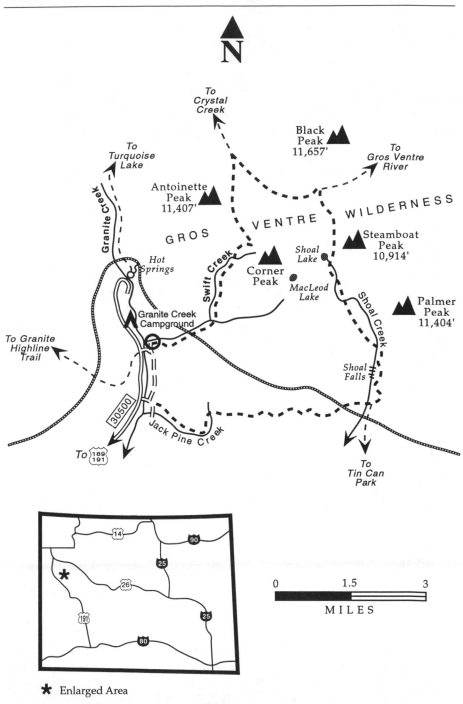

N

To Crystal Creek

Black Peak 11,657'

To Gros Ventre River

To Turquoise Lake

Antoinette Peak 11,407'

G R O S   V E N T R E   W I L D E R N E S S

Steamboat Peak 10,914'

Granite Creek

Hot Springs

Swift Creek

Corner Peak

Shoal Lake

MacLeod Lake

Palmer Peak 11,404'

Granite Creek Campground

Shoal Creek

To Granite Highline Trail

Shoal Falls

30500

Jack Pine Creek

To 189 191

To Tin Can Park

14

90

25

26

191

25

80

★

0   1.5   3

M I L E S

★ Enlarged Area

The hike: The first few tenths of a mile are two-track road hiking. Leaving the Granite Recreation Area, the trail begins its steep ascent through forests, never far from earshot of the cold rushing waters of Swift Creek. There is no scarcity of water on the trail, and level campsites, while not plentiful, are not hard to locate.

Eventually the trail leaves the creek, beginning its ascent toward the talus and boulder fields flanking 11,407-foot Antoinette Peak. Don't be fooled by appearance into thinking Antoinette Peak is an easy scramble. Careful route finding by experienced mountaineers is recommended on this peak.

The trail bears eastward from the base of Antoinette Peak and winds through flower-studded alpine meadows offering vistas of the snow-capped Tetons and the Wyoming Range. Antoinette Peak, Palmer Peak, Triangle Peak and Doubletop Peak form a graceful line of gentle mountains that define the spine of the Gros Ventre.

The trail drops to Shoal Lake and continues to Shoal Falls in a criss-crossing route across Shoal Creek. Shoal Falls is a five-minute walk off the main trail and well worth the diversion. The falls area offers some scenic campsites.

The trail continues on for a gentle up and down six miles back to the Granite Recreation Area. Beaver dams, ponds and waterfowl are plentiful on this home stretch.—*Laurie Muth*

The Mount Leidy Highlands

A marvelous and fairly vast section of critical grizzly bear habitat and major elk migration and calving ground country lies directly north of the Gros Ventre Wilderness. The Mount Leidy Highlands, surrounded by more notable Grand Teton, Yellowstone and Gros Ventre areas, is a forgotten and unknown piece of unclassified wilderness. Actually, the Forest Service is well aware of its presence, and continues to recommend extensive road building, logging and gas and oil exploration in the area. The Jackson Hole area residents, whose entire economy depends on wildlife habitat and undisected peaks and forests, are actively protesting the development in this unique mosaic of forest, aspen, grassland and alpine meadow land. I caught it at a rare time when no one else was around. It proved to be the most peace-engendering country in all of Wyoming.

HIKE 46 *SLATE CREEK TO MOUNT LEIDY*

General description: An exceptionally peaceful and leisurely overnighter or dayhike into the gentle forests and creek drainages of a little-used mountain area.

General location: Approximately thirty miles east and north of Jackson, north of the Gros Ventre River in the southern section of the Mount Leidy Highlands.

Maps: Bridger-Teton National Forest Jackson and Buffalo Ranger Districts map and/or USGS Mount Leidy quad.

Special attractions: Fine family hiking through huge meadowed bowls beneath pretty mountainous country.

For more information: Jackson Ranger District, 140 E. Broadway, P.O. Box 1689, Jackson, WY, 83001, (307) 739-5400.

Finding the trailhead: On U.S. Highways 26, 89 and 191, seven miles north of Jackson and two miles north of the Grand Teton National Park southern boundary, a well-signed Gros Ventre Junction sends a paved road eastward toward Kelly. Driving the seven miles to Kelly and another mile along the road as it swings northward puts you at the junction of the paved Gros Ventre Road. Follow this road east, into the Bridger-Teton National Forest for 13.5 miles (1.2 miles past Crystal Creek Campground). Here the graveled road forks, and you want to go left or toward Slate Creek, as a sign indicates. Then, .1 mile after this fork, Forest Service road 30380 jogs to the left or north. Follow this dirt two-track .6 mile, take the fork to the right or east, drive past the hunting camp and park on the banks overlooking the Gros Ventre River.

The unmarked trailhead begins with a thirty-yard ford of this large river. In late August, the clear waters were never over mid-calf depth.

Should you wish to enter this country in mid-June when the river waters resemble Cataract Canyon, an alternative entrance route exists 4.9 miles after the Gros Ventre Road pavement ends. A short distance before the Red Hills Campground the road crosses the Gros Ventre River via a major bridge. On the west side of this bridge, a jeep road follows the north shore of the river for three miles to this same ford.

The hike: Northwest Wyoming became known through a series of explorations and surveys conducted by government and private enterprises. Three of the more renowned and revealing USGS expeditions were led in the 1870s by Dr. Ferdinand Hayden, who studied the geology and zoology of the area while mapping many of its peaks and drainages. 10,317-foot Leidy Mountain and the Leidy Highlands were named for Professor Joseph Leidy, an anatomist on the Hayden Surveys. Like that unknown researcher, these mountains claim little notoriety but are indispensible to the ecology of the area.

Hike western and northwest Wyoming long enough and you're going to yearn to break free of lodgepole forests. The open sage and meadow country of the Leidy Highland foothills offers a welcome tract of free and easy country to explore. Once across the Gros Ventre River and a few hundred yards up the trail, you'll notice two things. First, an old sign directs you northward onto the Slate Creek Trail. And second, lack of protection has turned this area into an ATV playground. The trail becomes a wide tract that accomodates but does not restrict these mega-wheeled creatures. I can only say that this particular area constitutes some of the most unique and calmly beautiful landscape in Wyoming, and the threat of machines is not enough reason to not hike, explore and enjoy it. Early in the morning on weekdays usually places you alone in the unoffending country. It's worth the effort to explore.

For 1.5 miles the trail traverses rolling, open hills, ridges and valleys that offer endless opportunities for cross-country hiking access. Views of the Gros Ventre Mountains to the south are incomparable. Then the path descends to Slate Creek and in to a massive meadowed valley. Three creek fords and another 1.5 miles of glorious scenery place you in a vast bowl encompassing many square miles of open grasslands. To journey toward Mount Leidy, follow the Carmichael Creek Fork to the left or northwest. A topo map will be handy here, as nothing is signed. This massive basin is used by hikers, horse packers, elk, cattle and ATVs, and a lot of trails wander in a lot of directions.

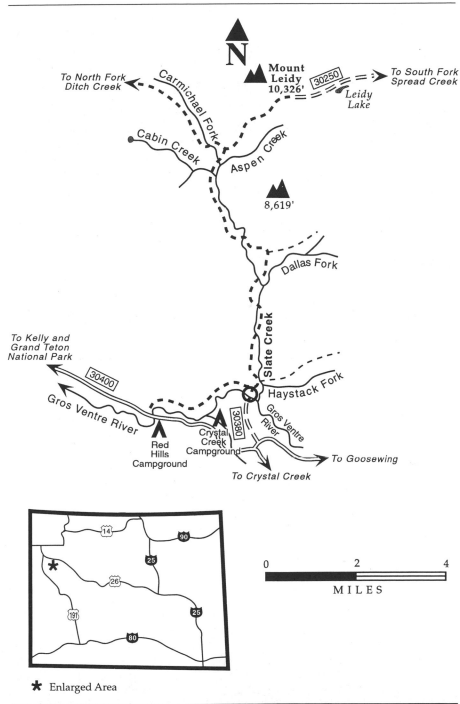

N

Mount
Leidy
10,326'

To North Fork
Ditch Creek

Carmichael Fork

Cabin Creek

Aspen Creek

30250

To South Fork
Spread Creek

Leidy
Lake

8,619'

Dallas Fork

Slate Creek

To Kelly and
Grand Teton
National Park

30400

Gros Ventre River

Haystack Fork

Gros Ventre River

Red
Hills
Campground

Crystal
Creek
Campground

30380

To Goosewing

To Crystal Creek

14   90

★

25

26

191   25

80

★ Enlarged Area

0   2   4

M I L E S

The broad, open and reclusive Mount Leidy Highlands

One mile later the official trail crosses Carmichael Creek and heads westward into the forests. Here the ATV signs are left behind, and after another mile's distance the trail breaks into a second, vast and meadowed bowl, this one sitting beneath the gentle slopes of Mount Leidy. Such a peaceful setting exists only in fairy tales. Hike another mile to Cabin Creek and enjoy the enchantment of this gentle land. When setting up a camp in this area, one feels like one is accepting a natural invitation to peaceful living.

Three tenths of a mile beyond Cabin Creek the trail again crosses Carmichael Creek and forks. To the east you journey toward Mount Leidy and onto the Leidy Lake Road. To the west you can follow Carmichael Creek into several other drainages that help create this unique country.

For a first time backpacking experience, for gentle family hiking, this is the place. Never have I felt a country seemingly extend such an open welcome to hikers.

HIKE 47 RED HILLS/LAVENDER HILLS

General description: A couple-hour to half-day, little-known hike that places you into unusual and picturesque views of the Tetons and Gros Ventres.

General location: Approximately twenty-five miles east and north of Jackson, north of the Gros Ventre River and the Gros Ventre Mountains.

Maps: Bridger-Teton National Forest Jackson and Buffalo Ranger Districts map and/or USGS Mount Leidy and Grizzly Lake quads.

Special attractions: Some of the oddest and most striking land formations in Wyoming. A two-mile trail that yields thousand mile views.

For more information: Jackson Ranger District, 140 E. Broadway, P.O. Box 1689, Jackson, WY, 83001, (307) 739-5400.

Finding the trailhead: Driving directions are the same as found in the Mount Leidy trip, HIKE 46. After you leave the pavement on the Gros Ventre Road, drive another 4.2 miles, just past the large "Red Hill Ranch" sign on the southern side of the road. Land to the south is private ranch property, but those towering, red, crumbly, striated and foreboding-looking hills to the north are Forest Service property and open to exploration. Unmarked and unnoticeable from the road, a good trail exists, its beginning being but a hundred yards east and across the road from that Red Hill Ranch gateway. If you miss the starting point and drive to the bridge crossing the Gros Ventre River, backtrack .5 mile until you see the first larger canyon cutting northeast into those red hills. There is room for parking on the south edges of the road.

Entrancing hiking in the Red Hills.

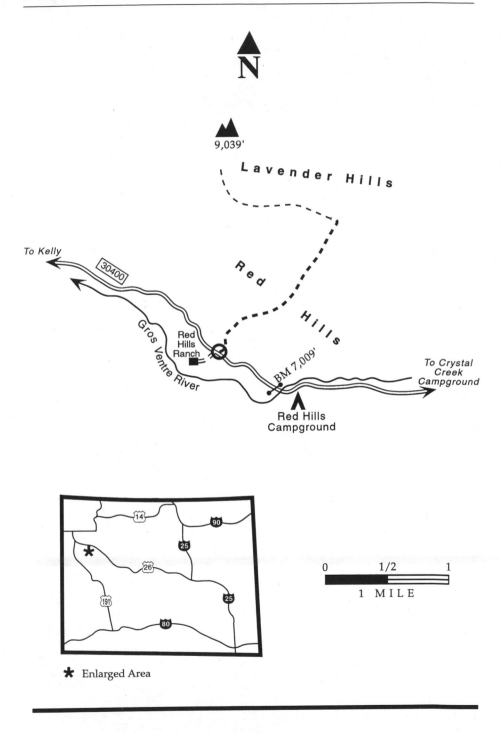

The hike: Outward appearances leave one thinking this is a colorful but desolate and barren landscape. Hiking just a short distance reveals more life and beauty amid these slopes than can be imagined.

The first 1.5 miles climb a good, but steep, grade to an open ridgetop. Count on gasping out what little breath you have left over the views here. To the north sits the kaleidoscopic backbone of these Red Hills, the striated Lavender Hills.

This ridgetop feels climactic in itself, but if you travel westward and climb hills twice again as steep for another .7 mile to a second, higher ridgetop, you encounter what is perhaps the earth's most secluded and glorious view of the Tetons. Here those mighty mountains rise above the red-colored cliffs and slopes of the Red Hills in the foreground. A faint, hard-to-follow trail does lead to this second ridgetop. If you cut a bit to the left or south after you lose the trail above the first ridgetop, you see signs of it barely touching the steep land.

As with most quirky Wyoming landscapes, this area would be hot and hard hiking on a July afternoon. It seems meant for early or late season and/or early morning or late afternoon hiking. Bring water. A second unmarked trail also probes the Red Hills .8 mile to the east. But this is the longer and more spectacular of the two.

NORTHWESTERN WYOMING

The northwest corner of Wyoming owns 10,000 square miles of mountainous country (six different mountain ranges) and a deliciously large portion of it is classified as wilderness or National Park. Rarest of modern-day occurances, an entire ecosystem, the Yellowstone, viably survives in this country.

If the 1984 Wyoming delegation's Wilderness Bill had included the 100,000 acres of important winter range for big game that is found on the eastern drainages outside the Absoraka and Washakie Wildernesses, these incredible biosystems would be self-contained. But even with this example of a classic wilderness proposal that protects glaciers and rock and high mountain pinnacles and opens lower meadows and forests to development, there still remains a lot of land for a lifetime of hiking.

This extensive land—save for the Tetons whose peaks are of an entirely different volcanic time period—is of Tertiary volcanic origin. Yellowstone is a still-active representation of this activity; the Washakie and Absoraka Ranges are the visible results of ancient lava surges and volcanic ash debris build-ups. It's interesting to note that destructive volcanic eruptions and explosions have occured in this Yellowstone country for the last several million years at about 600,000-year intervals. Even more interesting is the fact that the last major blow up happened 600,000 years ago.

Just a reminder. Northwest Wyoming forms the apex of bear and big game habitat. If you are really aware and really cautious, you've more chance of seeing an Ursi or two here than anywhere.

The Washakie Range

The Washakie Mountains, location of the Teton Wilderness, border but do not constitute any of the Washakie Wilderness. The Washakie Wilderness peacefully lies in the southern half of the Absaroka Mountains.

In the 1930's, a Wyoming geologist discovered that buried beneath the southwestern sector of the Absaroka Range lie a second series of mountains of completely different geologic origin. Their resemblance to the Absarokas stems from the bottom range—the Washakies—being covered by the geologic formation materials of the southern Absarokas.

The Teton Wilderness, an unspoiled 585,468-acre parcel of forested and alpine beauty, borders the southern boundary of Yellowstone National Park and the eastern border of Grand Teton National Park and preserves valuable habitat for the kind of large mammals that require elbow room for existance. Nearly every large and indiginous mammal still survives in this part of the country. Headwaters for both the Yellowstone and the Snake Rivers lie with the Teton Wilderness boundries. The Bridger-Teton Forest Buffalo Ranger District located east of Moran administers this area.

HIKE 48 *PILGRIM CREEK/WILDCAT PEAK*

General description: A three-to five-day backpack into exceptionally wild country and traversing everything from creek bottoms to open ridge tops.
General location: Approximately eleven miles north of Moran Junction (Moran is thirty-three miles north of Jackson), in the western section of the Teton Wilderness.
Maps: Bridger-Teton National Forest Jackson and Buffalo Ranger District maps, and/or USGS Two Ocean Lake and Huckleberry Mountain quads.
Special attractions: Perhaps the most difficult and wildest hike presented in this book. Abundant wildlife in country unknown to backpackers. Loop trips are possible.
For more information: Buffalo Ranger District, Blackrock Ranger Station, P.O. Box 278, Moran, Wyoming, 83103, (307) 543-2386.
Finding the trailhead: On U.S. Highway 89 and 287, inside Grand Teton National Park, two miles south of Colter Bay Village or 3.5 miles north of Jackson Lake Junction, the well-signed and graveled Pilgrim Creek Road splits off the paved highway and journeys northeast for 2.5 miles. The trailhead at the end of this road is unsigned, but a visible trail beyond the buck-and-pole fence heads directly north. Plan on arriving at this location with a few hours of daylight left. The Park Service classifies this as a "day use only" area, and you'll need to hike .5 mile to reach Forest Service land where camping is legal. (Believe me, the rangers drive by late at night and early in the morning and enforce this regulation.)

The hike: Every hiking guide needs to present one trail and area like this. Wilderness lives here in large, untouched proportions, and sometimes that kind of wilderness doesn't necessarily welcome strangers into its heart. In

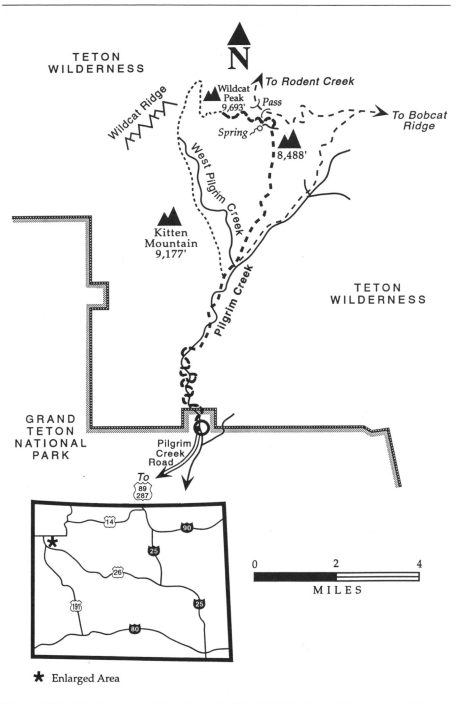

fact, it seems to derive pleasure in testing one's abilities, resolve and patience to the maximum. Even the personnel at the Blackrock Ranger District, the overseers of this area, call it their primitive area within a wilderness and basically know little about what's back there.

The first three miles, although level walking, finds the trail crossing the creek—the creek you can't jump but have to wade, even in late August—fifteen times. When not splashing in the river, you're often slipping over a muddy path that weaves an unthinking route through willowed jungles that surround the creek. Finally the trail leaves the water course via a steep hillside, and for .5 mile it allows you a level walk before again descending to the water and willows.

Now you're in a massive and most striking valley. It's huge beyond comparison and, due to the prelude required to reach it, feels like an especially hidden, secret, and wild place. It's a trick to keep going when fresh bear tracks imprint the trail as you vanish into neck-high, view-strangling willows. For 2.5 miles the trail wanders through this valley, its willows and gentle forests, its bogs and creek crossings. When you reach the first creek you can cross without wading, travel .3 mile farther, east and into the forest. Here the trail forks, and an old sign, the only landmark in this land, points north to Wildcat Peak and east to Bobcat Ridge.

The wilderness experience of this land continues. The steeply climbing trail toward Wildcat Peak always feels like it's but a year away from being overgrown and forgotten. You can always just barely find it as it passes through alternating forests and meadows.

A sharp elevation gain over the course of 3.5 miles brings you to a divide. Where once a sign existed, all that remains now is a bare post. The Rodent Creek drainage stretches to the north. Maps show a trail heading west toward Wildcat Peak, but the first hundred yards west and into the forest are walked on faith. The trail does reappear, only to struggle against downed timber and spot fire scars that are working to obliterate it. Not quite a mile later it vanishes again, and the last .5 mile to Wildcat Peak and ridge is a rugged, steep cross-country climb.

Atop this promontory, the glorious views of the Tetons and the lakes nestled in their shadows take away what little breath one has remaining.

All maps show a loop trail descending from Wildcat Ridge and down the West Fork of Pilgrim Creek. They lie. There once upon a time was a trail, but it is now a five-mile wild cross-country adventure to descend that way. With the many forest fire burns in that area, that trek is only going to become more adventuresome over the years.

This is a hike for the more experienced lovers of original wilderness. That statement also means the lovers know and respect such an area for its potential. Accidents back in this country would not afford an easy rescue.

HIKE 49 *BOX CREEK TRAIL*

General description: A five-mile dayhike (one way) or fifteen-mile two-to three-day backpack on a trail that offers great access to the many miles of exploration available in the heart of the Teton Wilderness.

General location: Forty miles north and west of Jackson in the south-central Teton Wilderness.

Maps: Bridger-Teton National Forest Buffalo and Jackson Ranger District map and USGS Joy Peak, Two Ocean Pass and Gravel Mountain quads.

Special attractions: Awesome after-affects of the Teton Tornado. A generally isolated, unpopulated and pretty hike through vast forests and meadows.

For more information: Buffalo Ranger District, Blackrock Ranger Station, P.O. Box 278, Moran, Wyoming 83103. (307) 543-2386.

Finding the trailhead: You can reach the Box Creek trailhead by driving approximately 3.5 miles east of Moran Junction on U.S. Highway 26 and 287. Here a well signed Buffalo Fork Road, Forest Service Road 30050, jogs to the northeast and toward Turpin Meadows. Follow this graded and graveled road approximately 9.5 miles eastward to the well-signed Box Creek/Enos Lake trailhead sign. Two miles farther the road pauses at Turpin Meadows, from which two other trailheads venture into the Teton Wilderness.

The hike: In 1987 a tornado ripped through the Box Creek area toppling trees, leaving trees stacked ten to fifteen high in places and leaving a 14,000-acre swath of destruction in its path. A tornado had never been recorded at such a high elevation.

Since the blowdown, Forest Service, American Hiking Society, Sierra Club, and Student Conservation crews have worked to reopen the closed trails using only crosscut saws and other primitive tools. In the summer of 1991 the final three miles of the Box Trail Trail were cleared, making it once again accessible to foot and horse travel.

The beginning two miles of this easy-to-follow trail form a fairly strenuous uphill climb. The trail then levels out as it traces the western flanks of Gravel Ridge. Be sure to carry some water for these first five miles. A dry year can leave Lava Creek as the first sure source of water.

Here you intersect the Lava Creek Trail, well signed and jogging to the west. It too offers Teton Tornado views. The Enos Lake Trail continues northeast for approximately four miles to a pretty and large lake resting in a thick forested setting. The forest here offers many camping opportunities. From here you can venture any number of directions deeper into the wilderness and toward Yellowstone. A suggested loop hike would be to return to Turpin Meadows via the Clear Creek Trail. A two-mile road walk back to the Box Creek trailhead would form the ending of such a loop trip.

As you travel through the blowdown area, consider the changes that have occured. Wilderness provides an opportunity to see natural forces at work to observe how plants and animals adapt to these changes. The Teton Wilderness is also home to the grizzly bear. Stop in at the Blackrock Ranger Station for information on the special rules that apply to hiking bear country.—*Rebecca Talbott*

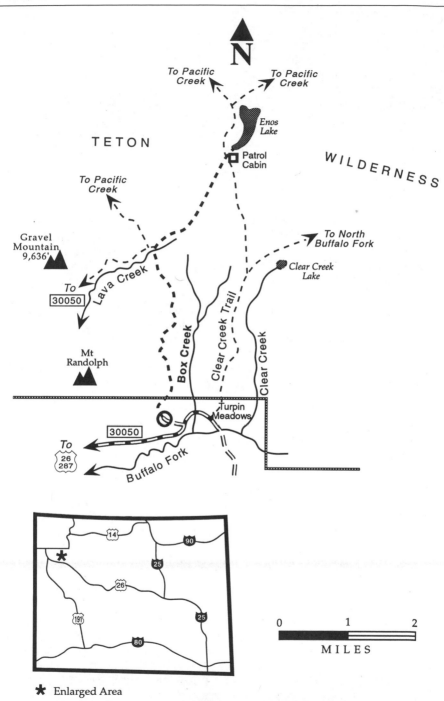

N

To Pacific Creek

To Pacific Creek

Enos Lake

Patrol Cabin

T E T O N

W I L D E R N E S S

To Pacific Creek

Gravel Mountain 9,636'

To North Buffalo Fork

Clear Creek Lake

To 30050

Lava Creek

Mt Randolph

Box Creek

Clear Creek Trail

Clear Creek

30050

Turpin Meadows

To 26 287

Buffalo Fork

14

90

25

26

191

25

80

0   1   2

M I L E S

* Enlarged Area

The Absaroka Range

The Crow Indians in Wyoming and Montana country were sometimes referred to as the Absarokas, a name meaning "people of the great winged bird." Three different pronunciations accompany this word, the local favorite being Ab-SOR-kees. The proper diction of Ab-sar-O-kas holds a second place, while lazy-speech Ab-ZORKS occasionally slips into the conversation.

Tremendous piles of volcanic ash and lava layered themselves onto this country. The high ridges and mountaintops display a plateau-like crest, and this crest reveals a vast and horizontal covering of lava. Massive forces of erosion sculpted the flat-lying rock layers into extremely steep slopes and spectacular pinnacles. The multi-colored and banded cliffs rise to 11,000- and 12,000-foot elevations and often form the beginnings of astonishingly large and level, above-timberline grassy meadows. Lakes are few in this erosion-prone country, while narrow canyons and large creek drainages charge through the crumbly rock with a beautiful vengence.

Little is written about the range and its wildernesses because it is, compared to other areas, little explored. It is an area where a hiker can still discover a remnant tepee ring or an old pile of stones that may have been the poor dwelling of an ancient Sheepeater tribe member called Tukuarika. It's an even more exciting land because here an explorer can anytime leave the trail, snoop into a small side canyon or range across the broad and rolling alpine upland, and feel as if he is the first and only person to walk this section.

HIKE 50 *JADE LAKES*

General description: A short and easy hike to two exceptionally pretty high-country lakes.
General location: Approximately twenty-six miles northwest of Dubois in the northwestern corner of the Shoshone National Forest.
Maps: Shoshone National Forest north half map and/or USGS Togwotee Pass and Dundee Meadows quads.
Special attractions: Beautiful lakes set beneath towering stratified cliffs. Count on fair fishing.
For more information: Wind River Ranger District, Masonic Bldg., P.O. Box 186, Dubois, WY, 82513, (307) 455-2466.
Finding the trailhead: Approximately twenty-seven miles west of Dubois on U.S. Highway 287 and 26, or 7.8 miles east of the Togwotee (To-GUH-tee) Pass crest, the well-signed Brooks Lake road jogs north. This graveled main road is easy to follow the 5.2 miles to the Brooks Lake Campground. Just before the Brooks Lake Lodge, turn north at the campground sign but don't enter the camping area. Stay west and drive the short distance to the signed trailhead near the southern shores of Brooks Lake.

The hike: Highway 287 west of Dubois climbs into an absolutely enticing section of southern Absaroka high country. As one drives the road, one notices that these somewhat wild and unusual stratified layers of volcanic cliff keep

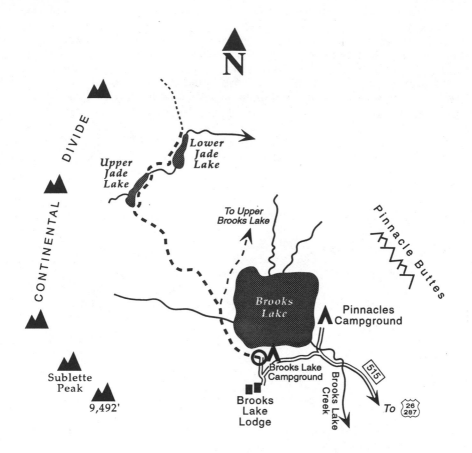

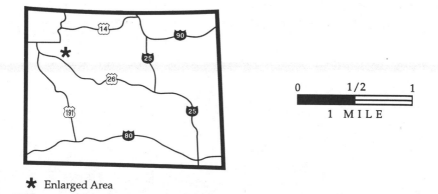

* Enlarged Area

0   1/2   1

1 MILE

bobbing into greater and greater view. Upper and Lower Jade Lakes offer an easy two and a half mile (one-way) hike that places you both directly under the desired cliffs and beside emerald lakes that reflect the majesty of the surrounding country. Jade is the official stone of the state of Wyoming.

The first .5 mile follows the Brooks Lake/Cub Pass trail (HIKE 51). Here a sign points northwestward to Jade Lakes, and you can see five or more eroded, parallel trails cutting up a hillside. Follow one of these trails up the steep slopes for .5 mile. Then the walk mellows out for the final 1.5 miles as the trail—now coalesced to a single path—wanders through a gentle and more open forest.

The tiny, stagnant pond at 1.5 miles, although green in color, is not one of the Jade Lakes. Continue along the trail for another .5 mile and descend into a depression holding the beautiful, greenish and deep waters of Upper Jade Lake. Here those layered blue-grayish, brownish and white cliffs tower over and reflect off the lake's waters. Excellent camping is found near the lake's southwestern shore and at its northern shore by the creek outlet.

Lower Jade Lake lies a steepish downhill .5 mile farther along the trail. It forms the big cousin of Upper Jade, but doesn't carry the reflection or offer many camping opportunities. Both lakes receive excellent fishing reports.

At the extreme northwest corner of the lower lake, a horse/hunting trail cuts to the north. It appears to be an ancient Forest Service trail that they are trying to forget, and my advice is help the Forest Service along and don't follow it. I did, and it was a fun adventure until several miles later when I lost the path along with my sense of direction. Twelve hours later I staggered back to Brooks Lake, having somehow traversed the untrailed Clear Creek Drainage of the Teton Wilderness, an entirely different forest and drainage away. It was a most humbling lesson on how even an experienced hiker can easily get confused and turn a simple hike into a lost-and-found situation.

Absaroka beauty at Upper Jake Lake.

HIKE 51 *UPPER BROOKS LAKE/BEAR CUB PASS*

General description: An easy, level and open hike to a scenic alpine lake. Bear Cub Pass provides an access to the pretty southeastern sector of the Teton Wilderness.

General location: Approximately twenty-seven miles northwest of Dubois in the northwestern corner of the Shoshone National Forest.

Maps: Shoshone National Forest north half map and/or USGS Togwotee Pass and Dundee Meadows quads.

Special attractions: A gentle trail surrounded by spectacular stratified cliffs; great fishing in lovely lake settings.

For more information: Wind River Ranger District, Masonic Bldg., P.O. Box 186, Dubois, WY, 82513, (307) 455-2466.

Finding the trailhead: The same as Jade Lakes (HIKE 50)

The hike: The Jade Lakes Trail (HIKE 50) introduced you to the forested settings of the Togwotee area. The Upper Brooks Lake Trail affords a completely different experience of this spectacular country. Its 3.5 miles (one way) contain some of the most relaxing meadow walking imaginable. Brooks Lake and Creek were named after Bryant B. Brooks, the cowboy governor of Wyoming from 1905 to 1911.

All access directions are identical to the Jade Lakes Trail (HIKE 50) access descriptions, up to and including the first .5 mile of hiking. At this intersection journey right or northeast, continuing the trek through the flowered meadows and around the western shores of scenic Lower Brooks Lake. This area is exceptionally picturesque and photographic, thanks to the multi-layered volcanic cliffs reflecting off the lake waters.

A small climb at the north end of the lake constitutes one of the few uphill slopes on this hike. Above this hill, the trail follows a mini ridge top that runs between two mini valleys that sit below the multi-colored and striated volcanic cliffs that rule the area. After a couple of miles of short-grass meadow walking, the trail fords Brooks Creek from west to east and climbs a short distance into the forest. Here it intersects the Bonnieville Pass Trail, the long-journey access to the secretive Dunoir area. (The Shoshone Forest Service map depicts this trail intersection as being close to Lower Brooks Lake, when actually it's nearer to Upper Brooks Lake.)

After .5 mile of vast and open willowed-meadow walking, Upper Brooks Lake comes into spectacular view. The lake sits in a gentle high-country environment. Camping spots exist all around the lake, but easiest access to them comes via following the trail almost to Bear Cub Pass and then hiking around the northern shores of the lake.

Bear Cub Pass isn't much more than a wooded hilltop that divides the Shoshone National Forest from the Teton Wilderness. But it does serve as an excellent access to this Bridger-Teton wildland. Beyond the pass the trail drops for two miles and into the Cub Creek drainage, a very pretty, private and spectacular piece of open country.

Brooks Lake Trail forms an ideal hike for families or for anyone wanting a leisurely hike that holds as much scenery as possible.

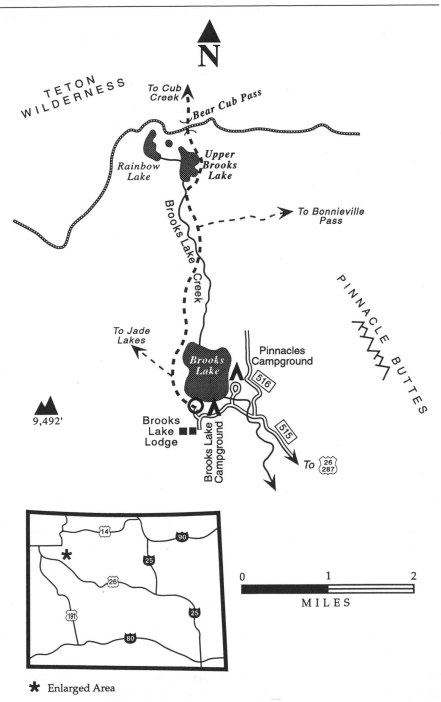

N

TETON WILDERNESS

To Cub Creek

Bear Cub Pass

Rainbow Lake

Upper Brooks Lake

Brooks Lake Creek

To Bonnieville Pass

To Jade Lakes

Brooks Lake

Pinnacles Campground

516

9,492'

Brooks Lake Lodge

Brooks Lake Campground

515

To 26 287

PINNACLE BUTTES

14

90

25

26

191

25

80

* Enlarged Area

0   1   2

MILES

The Washakie Wilderness

Wyoming claims several firsts in the field of national treasures. The first National Park, the first National Monument, and here the nation's first National Forest was established when The Yellowstone Park Timberland Reserve of 1891 became the Shoshone National Forest in 1902. The northern half of the Shoshone National Forest hosts a wonderful abundance of wildlife, including deer—both white-tailed and mule—elk, bighorn sheep, antelope, mountain goat, mountain lion, coyotes, moose, and black and grizzly bears. Watch for numerous eagles, both golden and bald, circling the skys. There is a move to reintroduce the wolf into its historic Yellowstone ecosystem range, although it is facing strong opposition from hunters, livestock owners and some legislators.

Chief Washakie of the Shoshone Indians sports the second most common geographic feature name in Wyoming. He has eleven place names, behind Jim Bridger who has twenty-two. Washakie was sometimes called the best Indian ally the whites ever had. A noted warrior, he nevertheless tirelessly pursued peaceful settlements with the intruders. In 1900 he was buried with full military honors by the United States Army, the only Indian (at that time) ever so honored. It seems fitting that so large and peaceful a wilderness be named after so broad-visioned and peaceful a man.

HIKE 52 FRONTIER CREEK

General description: A two-to three-day, fairly easy backpack into a sheltered canyon surrounded by exceptional cliffs and scenery.
General location: Approximately thirty miles north of Dubois, in the south-central section of the Washakie Wilderness.
Maps: Shoshone National Forest north half map and/or USGS Snow Lake and Emerald Lake quads.
Special attractions: Ancient petrified forest remnants are still visible in this drainage. The scenery is spectacular.
For more information: Wind River Ranger District, Masonic Bldg., P.O. Box 186, Dubois, WY, 82513, (307) 455-2466.
Finding the trailhead: From downtown Dubois, turn north and leave town on paved Horse Creek Road. The road isn't well marked. It begins just west of the one bridge on the main street of Dubois, directly across from Welty's General Store. The pavement ends after five miles, and Forest Service road 285 begins in another five miles. For the next twenty miles this road is your guide into the ever-increasing beauty of the southern Absarokas. Double Cabin Campground is your goal, so follow any intersection signs pointing to it. Don't drive into the campground but continue north for a few hundred yards to the large wilderness trailhead sign sitting in a meadow. The "parking lot" is that meadow, south of the sign.

The hike: When a more recent Yellowstone volcanic eruption added yet another layer of ash on top of this land, the large forests in the southern Absarokas were instantaneously buried under thick and powdery rock debris.

HIKE 52 *FRONTIER CREEK*

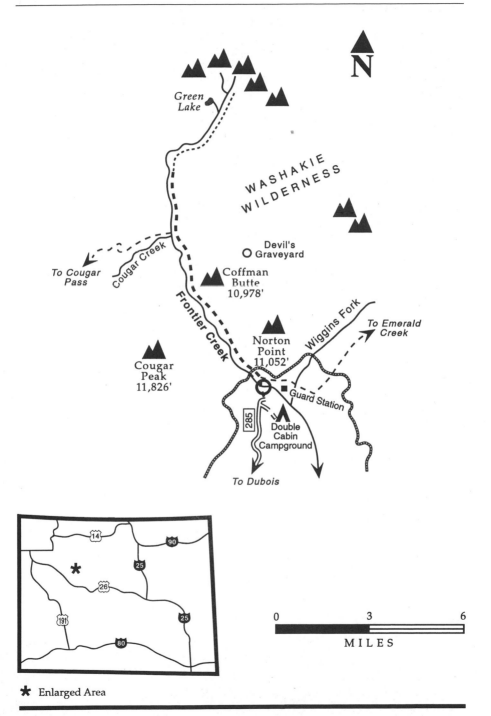

N

Green Lake

WASHAKIE WILDERNESS

To Cougar Pass

Cougar Creek

Devil's Graveyard

Coffman Butte 10,978'

Frontier Creek

Norton Point 11,052'

Wiggins Fork

To Emerald Creek

Cougar Peak 11,826'

Guard Station

285

Double Cabin Campground

To Dubois

0 3 6

MILES

★ Enlarged Area

14   90   25   26   191   25   80

Time and pressure mineralized the encased wood. Water and erosion then excavated the large drainages named Wiggins and Frontier creeks. Huge petrified stumps adorn the higher cliffs surrounding the waterways. Smaller pieces of the mineralized wood lie in the riverbed. Every summer, after high runoff, new samples of this colorful rock are unearthed.

In the past, the petrified wood has been carried out by visitors and by commercial entrepreneurs. Entire rock trees have been dynamited and toted out of the wilderness via mule pack train. While a petrified wood fire place may form an impressive addition to someone's ranch house, it doesn't do a thing for future generations who will hike this wild country and not sample its uniqueness. Leave the wood where you find it. It's the law, and it's the proper course of action.

The Frontier Creek trail sign was down, but the trail begins directly north of the wilderness sign. It's an easy path to make out as it journeys northward across the meadow and toward Frontier Creek Canyon. After .5 mile, the trail crosses Frontier Creek. This can be a cold, swift and slippery-rocked wade. It can also be a July phenomenon of lower water in the morning and hard-to-cross, raging snow melt in the afternoon.

The first 6.5 miles of this trail traverse an easier, mostly level terrain through forested lands. Lodgepole owns the land at first, but by the time you reach the Cougar Pass intersection at 6.7 miles, fir and spruce have claimed control. But the forest doesn't dominate the hike. These somber, gray, conglomerate volcanic cliffs on both sides of the canyon rule the scenery. From four miles onward, several nice camping meadows appear.

One suggestion for a trip is to camp above or below the Cougar Pass Trail intersection (the meadow at this intersection is closed to camping) and day hike to Cougar Pass one day and upper Frontier Creek the next.

Older maps show a trail exiting the main trail to the east and climbing to what's labeled Devil's Graveyard. This supposedly is a hidden alpine bench where a field of flat stones lie perpendicular to the ground and form a sort of natural tombstone cemetery. In four attempts over the years to locate this spot, I never have found the right trail or the graveyard, but some amazing campfire ghost stories are generated around this anomaly.

Above the Cougar Creek Trail intersection, the Frontier Creek Trail continues upstream for a bit more than two miles. Then it drops to the creek and ends. Here is where you want to scan the cliffs to the west. Large stumps of petrified wood, some of them more than eight feet in diameter, occasionally dot the gray rock. Here also you can witness in the cliffs the hundreds of feet of volcanic debris that at on time covered this land.

HIKE 53 *WIGGINS FORK TO EMERALD LAKE*

General description: A several day, quite long, moderately difficult hike into a more wild Absaroka volcanic canyon that ends in an enchanting alpine lake setting.

General location: Approximately thirty miles north of Dubois, in the south-central section of the Washakie Wilderness.

Maps: Shoshone National Forest north half map and/or USGS Snow Lake and Emerald Lake quads.

Special attractions: Petrified wood, lovely creek and woodland settings climaxing in a rubble-rock mountain setting that surrounds a gem of a lake.

For more information: Wind River Ranger District, Masonic Bldg., P.O. Box 186, Dubois, WY, 82513, (307) 455-2466.

Finding the trailhead: Follow trail access directions out of Dubois as found in HIKE 52, the Frontier Creek hike.

The hike: The long and winding Wiggins Fork/Emerald Creek trail accesses some mighty wild Washakie country. Jack Wiggins, a nearby homesteader, enjoyed the country so much that when he packed surveyors into its boundaries in 1900 he gave them a beef quarter to name the creek after him.

At the wilderness trailhead, a sign points westward to the Wiggins Fork Trail. Be sure and bring a pair of tennis shoes and a walking stick on this trip, as there are several river crossings and not a one of them is especially easy.

Immediately you wade Frontier Creek. After following the trail .5 mile around the north side of the Forest Service guard station, you wade the many channels of Wiggins Creek to the west side of the riverbed. Look across the channel to the southwest for the fencepost marker indicating where the trail continues. After walking less than .5 mile in the wrong direction, i.e., southward and away from Wiggins Canyon, you'll intersect the Indian Point Trail. In these open meadows, at a signed intersection, the Wiggins Fork Trail begins its northwest journey.

The next 4.5 miles of trail contain two river crossings, a 1,250-acre man-caused fire that razed the land in 1952, extraordinary views of the the towering and jagged volcanic cliffs that surround Wiggins Fork, and lots of wonderful and fairly easy forest hiking. A bit more than five miles after beginning, the trail crosses Wiggins Fork. Here the Emerald Creek Trail continues northward and the Wiggins Fork Trail branches to the west.

Don't let the first mile of this new Emerald Creek Trail fool you. With its gentle walking, excellent campsites, and vibrant scenery, the trail portends easy hiking. But you must cross the large creek to the west after a mile, back to the east after another .8 mile, across a large side waterway—Burwell Creek—in .3 mile, and back to the west side of the river in another .2 mile. Trying to stay on one side of the river to avoid wading doesn't work. The trail's antics serve the purpose of avoiding steep cliffs that drop into the waters. After each crossing, the country seems to acquire a more wild and remote feel to it.

The next 2.5 miles are dry and travel through a thickly wooded north-facing hillside. After a final creek crossing to the north—which may or may not

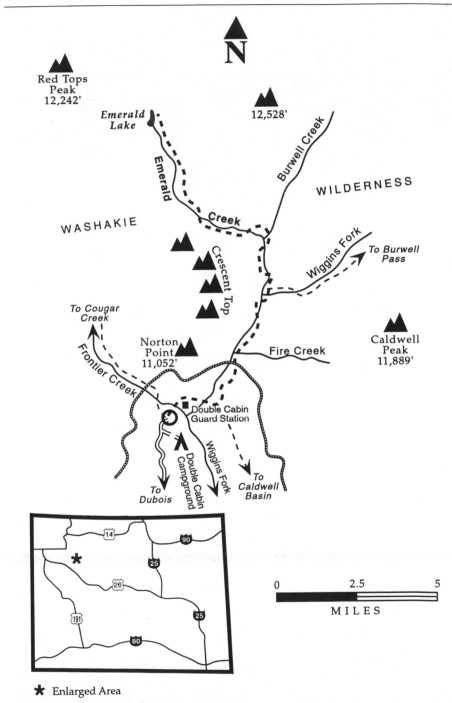

N

Red Tops
Peak
12,242'

12,528'

Emerald
Lake

Burwell Creek

WILDERNESS

Emerald

Creek

WASHAKIE

Wiggins Fork

To Burwell
Pass

Crescent Top

To Cougar
Creek

Caldwell
Peak
11,889'

Norton
Point
11,052'

Fire Creek

Frontier Creek

Double Cabin
Guard Station

Double Cabin Campground

Wiggins Fork

To
Dubois

To
Caldwell
Basin

14

90

25

26

25

191

80

0   2.5   5

MILES

★ Enlarged Area

Looking into the Emerald Creek drainage.

be a wade, depending on your jumping abilities—the trail becomes fairly rugged walking as it begins to gain elevation. This 1.5-mile-trail sported the most unique limber pine forest.

About 11.5 miles from trail beginning, the forest starts to thin, interspersed now with alpine meadows. High and impressive peaks surround the country. The final mile to the lake leaves the hiker in totally open country and picking one's way up long and taxing slopes. The trail vanishes in the grass, but by remaining on the eastern side of the now small creek and mucking out the steep climb, you reach the jewel of the trip, Emerald Lake. The flowered-grassland, cliff-encompassed setting of this long and shallow lake surpasses any words a guidebook author can find. It's about fourteen miles from trail beginning to lake end.

A word needs to be said about potential trail changes in this country. These mountains are steep and extremely friable. A single major rainstorm or a heavy winter runoff can modify the land by creating new gullies that the trail suddenly disappears into. Also, the creek bottom that this trail so frequently crosses is wide, and every year the water changes course and wipes some of the trail out. You may have to continually search for signs of where the trail again enters into the forest across the riverbed.

Be also aware that this is prime grizzly habitat. I beheld the biggest claw and paw print I've ever seen in this drainage.

HIKE 54 *EAST FORK WIND RIVER*

General description: A multi-day backpack into gentle, vast, open and rolling alpine high country.

General location: Approximately forty miles north and east of Dubois, in the southeastern section of the Washakie Wilderness.

Maps: Shoshone National Forest north half map and/or East Fork Basin and Dunrud Peak quads. Add Castle Rock and Wiggins Peak quads if planning on making this a loop trip that joins Bear Creek.

Special attractions: Country that exemplifies the massive openness and beauty of the above-timberline, gently rolling mountaintops of the eastern Absarokas. Great moose and elk habitat.

For more information: Wind River Ranger District, Masonic Bldg., P.O. Box 186, Dubois, WY, 82513, (307) 455-2466.

Finding the trailhead: Exit Dubois and drive east on U.S. Highway 287 and 26 for 10.8 miles. A tiny, green East Fork road sign and a huge 'Thunderhead Ranch Registered Simmentals' sign direct you north onto a good gravel road. This is one long and scenic byway. Marboro cigarettes filmed several of their picturesque commercials in this area. If you thought the country looked impressive on TV, you ought to experience it without herds of horses being chased by white-hatted cowboys with little puffs of carcinogenic smoke trailing behind them.

After ten miles of gravel-road driving, a major fork occurs. Follow the main road to the east. After fifteen and a half miles the road descends into a huge valley. Pass under the Bitter Root Ranch sign, but 1.2 miles later DON'T drive down to the Bitter Root Ranch as the sign points and DO turn left at this fork and head north, up a long hill. You'll pass through a Wyoming Game and Fish Department elk fence, enter the Shoshone National Forest and via road 500 ascend to the top of a pass. The road's fork at this point is unsigned. Left or west journeys toward Bear Creek while straight or north descends into the East Fork Drainage. NOTE: if a major rainstorm catches you beyond this pass, the hill will require four-wheel drive to reclimb. 2.7 miles beyond the pass, the main road ends at a Washakie Wilderness/East Fork Trailhead sign.

The hike: The Absaroka Mountains and the Washakie Wilderness sport many faces. HIKES 52 and 53, Frontier and Emerald creeks, reveal a rougher, wilder, more spectacular aspect of these vast mountains. The East Fork of the Wind River reveals a completely different sort of wilderness personality. Here the mountaintops reach 11,000- and 12,000-foot elevations in peaceful and graceful swoops. Tundra-like meadows create favorable habitat for an abundance of wildflowers and wildlife. Except during hunting season, the area knows little use.

The country this trail passes through in its gradual ascent into the vast timberline and above timberline meadows defies words. After 1.3 miles of gentle hiking and great views overlooking the wide East Fork River drainage, you come to the Tepee Creek Trail intersection. The sign here notes that it's five miles to Bear Creek. What it doesn't say is that in that five miles you go from an 8,600-foot elevation to an 11,500-foot elevation and back down again.

One west-side-to-east-side river crossing exists almost four miles up the trail.

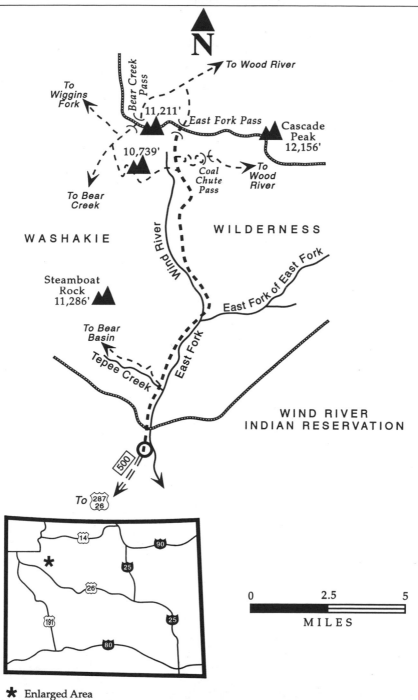

This is usually an easy wade until August when it becomes a hard jump. From here the trail gradually climbs and the trees thin as the country opens into expansive and rolling alpine meadows. Approximately 7.5 miles up the drainage, the Nine Mile Trail jogs to the west and into some alluring mountains. This trail is not high on the maintenance priorities of the district and can be hard to follow at times. Look for rock cairns directing the way.

The joy of the East Fork Trail is the access it affords to many alpine passes. 1.5 beyond Nine Mile Trail, the Coal Chute Pass Trail banks steeply off to the east. If you continue northward on the main trail, a mile of steep climbing places you a top East Fork Pass and overlooking a grand view of the Wood River Valley. Several loop routes will take you around to the headwaters of the Bear Creek drainage. All of this country rolls atop the world in a vast and gentle alpine prairie. Highly recommended is a hike up the East Fork, a circle around any of the trails leading into upper Bear Creek, a journey down Bear Creek and crossing back to the East Fork via steep Tepee Creek and Pass.

The only cautionary note for this trail is that you carry a good topography map on the journey. The trail often disappears in the alpine meadows. It's then nice to be able to determine the route from the map.

HIKE 55 *JACK CREEK*

General description: A two- or three-day, quite difficult and quite wild trip following a little-known and even less-traveled creek drainage.

General location: Approximately thirty miles directly west of Meeteetse, just outside the northwestern border of the Washakie Wilderness. Meeteetse is twenty-five miles south of Cody.

Maps: Shoshone National Forest north half map and/or USGS Phelps Mountain, Francs Peak and Irish Rock quads.

Special attractions: Wonderful journeys across rolling hills of open alpine meadows. Very few people use this trail. It culminates in a wide valley beneath an 11,000-foot peak.

For more information: Greybull Ranger District, 2044 State Street, P.O. Box 158, Meeteetse, WY, 82433.

Finding the trailhead: Twenty-five miles south of Cody, or fifty-two miles north of Thermopolis, on Wyoming Highway 120, sits the most scenic town in the world, Meeteetse. The name translates into a literal meaning of "measured distance near and far." In the middle of town, Wyoming Highway 290 heads due west and remains paved for 11.6 miles. At pavement's end turn right and head for Pitchfork. Drive this road .2 mile and turn left and onto the Pitchfork Ranch Road. Don't go right and across the bridge at this intersection.

Too many intersections exist along the next eighteen miles to describe. Simply follow one rule: always follow the signs that say Jack Creek. All the road intersections are well signed. The last five or six miles is a narrow, one-lane gravel road where you hope you don't meet an oncoming horse trailer. Follow the signs left and through the campground, uphill to the Jack Creek trailhead.

The hike: In response to my queries, the Greybull district ranger wrote the following. "The Greybull District offers opportunities for the hiker who is interested in solitude, scenery, wildlife and who does not necessarily need to rely on well marked trails to navigate in the wilderness." She also mentioned that the trails cross streams and rivers a number of times, and that high water conditions, usually in existance until after July Fourth, can make these crossings dangerous if not impossible. When she noted that hikers often travel ten days and have limited or no contact with other people, I knew I had to explore this area.

Jack Creek is a swiftly tumbling tributary in a large and long drainage. The trail climbs steeply above the creek's eastern hillsides and for more than a mile cuts through the meadows that surround the canyon's lower end. By 1.6 miles and the first creek crossing (on a large log spanning the waters), the forest has crept into and claimed the hillsides and stream bottom. In fact, because the creek channel is such a timbered or rocky maze, the trail generally stays high, dropping to the creek only when it crosses it two more times. These crossings are fun wades.

Lots of steep climbing and lots of short switchbacks dominate the first 3.5 miles of trail. But then you find out what all the work is for. The trail enters the most unique feature of the Absaroka Mountains and Washakie Wilderness, the vast, rolling plains of high alpine country with miles of views. After about two miles, where the trail crosses meadows and is somewhat hard to follow, look for the green steel fence posts, cairns and tree blazes that mark the trail's path.

At nearly six miles the trail again descends to the creek and joins an old road. According to the map, the road is open to vehicles, but there were no signs of motorized usage on that road. Here you get to choose directions. You can wander for several miles up the road and to the canyon's most beautiful beginnings. You might even climb the northwest ridge of 11,202-foot Jacks Peak. (In early July, it was solid snow and ice.) Or you can follow the road for a few hundred yards, cut uphill to the right or west and intersect the unsigned Haymaker Trail. Two miles of uphill on this trail places you atop a high pass that overlooks the massive, serene, and verdant upper Greybull River Valley. Excellent opportunities exist here to explore the open alpine fields that create the high mountains, including 10,942-foot Irish Rock to the north of Haymaker Pass.

This is not an easy trail. Uphill gains some new definitions when hiking it. And remember when I noted in the bear section at the beginning of the book that if you saw the track of a grizzly bear you would know it. A huge set of such tracks preceded me by about twelve hours over Haymaker Pass. Be aware that this is prime bear country.

At least two Jack Creeks flow in Wyoming. As best I can tell, this particular one was named for an early trapper and not for a villainous desperado.

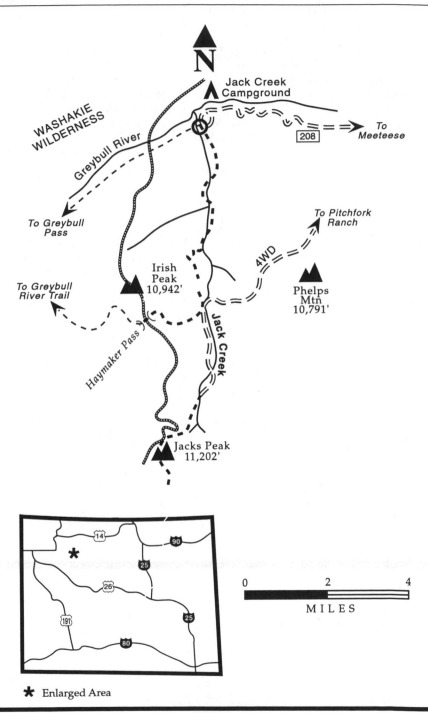

★ Enlarged Area

HIKE 56 *GREYBULL RIVER*

General description: A week-long, or longer, trek into a spectacular and important river drainage in the western section of the Washakie Wilderness.

General location: Approximately thirty miles west of Meeteese.

Maps: Shoshone National Forest Visitor's map (north half) and USGS Phelps Mountain, Irish Rock, Francs Peak and Mount Burwell quads.

Special attractions: This is probably the largest section of untrammeled wilderness in the state. The wandering and long trip possibilities are endless, and it all lies in inexhaustible beauty.

For more information: Greybull Ranger District, 2044 State Street, P.O. Box 158, Meeteetse, WY, 82433.

Finding the trailhead: Follow the long Jack Creek Trailhead road directions (HIKE 55), including the drive through the campground and north to the Jack Creek Trailhead parking area.

The hike: The Greybull Ranger District out of Meeteetse notes that this is their most popular trail. I never saw a soul my entire time there. Perhaps some of the original medicine still lives along the Greybull River. It was named by and remains sacred to Indians because of an albino bull buffalo that once roamed the land.

The Forest Service did a neat thing here in recognizing the difference in leg length between horses and backpackers. At the west end of the parking lot a sign reads "Greybull River high flood water and backpacking trail." The original horse trail starts directly west of the campground with an immediate neck-deep (human) river ford. On this high trail, you too must begin with a ford, but wading Jack Creek is possible. The Greybull River can be big-time water.

This is a delightful and wonder-filled trail. The first .2 mile place you high above the river and into exceptional views of the valley. The horse trail across the river appears to suffer all kinds of up and down gyrations, but for several miles this trail is so gentle you can actually look around while walking. After three miles of traversing diverse and lusher north-slope vegetation, the trail dips down to the river level. Here the horse trail again crosses the river, joining the hiker's path. For two miles it parallels a rather wild and white river that cuts through a thick forest and between variegated cliffs. There really is no camping for the first five miles. A wilderness rule here states "no camping within fifty feet of the trail," and for the five-mile distance, level spots away from the trail are nonexistent.

Just beyond those first good camping sites (at five miles), the trail crosses to the west side of the river. About .8 mile later it crosses back. Be aware that the water at these two fords, especially the second one, is a bit deeper and a lot swifter and much colder than it looks. In fact, around July 1 it was hip-deep, and I'm a long-legged person. Tennis shoes and a hiking stick are necessities. Although the water will have less volume later in the year, an upstream rain or a hot day melting snow could leave you stranded on one side or the other. On the return journey I stayed on the east side of the river, attempting to avoid both crossings. Stay with the trail and fords. That sure path, even with the crossings, takes a lot less time and is easier and safer.

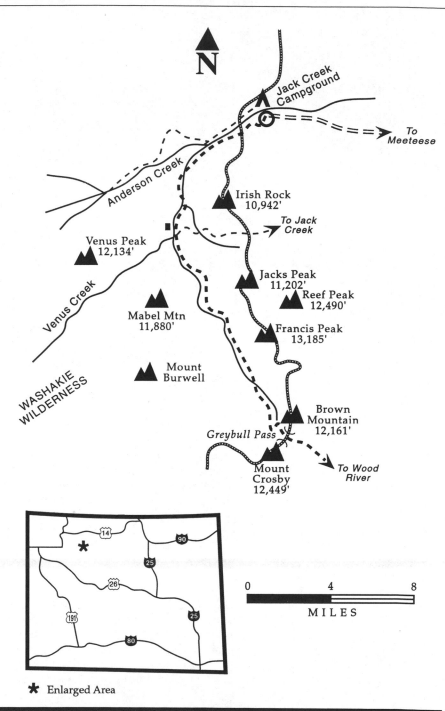

Now the Greybull basin really broadens its scope. The valley is wide and open, and huge peaks line its boundaries. The river braids into several courses through its rocky bottom. At seven miles the trail intersects the Haymaker Creek Trail, and a few tenths later it meets the Venus Creek Fork. In fact, in the more than twenty miles from tràilhead to the top of Greybull Pass, numerous trail intersections occur. Some of these trails are maintained, many are old stock driveways that get listed as trails but are rough to find and follow. Signs may or may not survive in this country. 1991 information from the Greybull Ranger District indicated that the Greybull River, Anderson Creek, Venus Creek and Wiggins Fork trails received the most use and maintenance. (All are listed on the Forest Service visitor map.)

There are numerous possibilities for longer hikes: south toward Dubois and the Wind River Indian Reservation, west via some lengthy journeys into the Teton Wilderness, and east in a circle back toward the Greybull River road. All are doable from this Greybull River Trail.

HIKE 57 *BLACKWATER FIRE MEMORIAL*

General description: A moderate and enjoyable day hike to high mountain vistas and through a fifty-five-year-old forest fire scar.
General location: Approximately forty miles due west of Cody, outside the northern boundaries of the Washakie Wilderness.
Maps: Shoshone National Forest north half map and/or Clayton Mountain, and Chimney Rock quads.
Special attractions: Beautiful views of the North Absaroka wilderness and into Yellowstone. A moving memorial to firefighters who lost their lives at their work.
For more information: Wapiti Ranger District, 203 A Yellowstone Ave., P.O. Box 1840, Cody, WY, 82414, (307) 527-6921.
Finding the trailhead: Driving west from Cody on scenic highway U.S. 14, 16 and 20, travel 24.3 miles through remarkable Shoshone Canyon to the Shoshone National Forest boundary. Add 12.7 miles to this westward trip and you come to a first firefighters' memorial and a large sign noting the Blackwater Creek Ranch. Leave the highway here and travel south across an older steel bridge, across another wooden bridge spanning Blackwater Creek, through a pole gate and to a large sign south of some corrals marking the trailhead. Actually, the trail is open to vehicles for another two miles beyond this sign, but this is four-wheel-drive stuff, and even they are going to be unhappy if they meet an opposing-direction vehicle on this narrow path. At the road/trail's end, beside the waters of Blackwater Creek, lives a sweet little camping spot. This camp area makes a great headquarters for a hike up to the memorial one day and another hike to the Blackwater Natural Bridge (HIKE 58) the next.

The hike: In 1937, between August 20th and 24th, an intense fire consumed much more than the 1,254 acres of forest it blackened. A sudden gale-force wind on August 21 whipped the fire into a roaring inferno. Fifteen men died and thirty-nine more were injured as the blaze raced up the mountainside

N

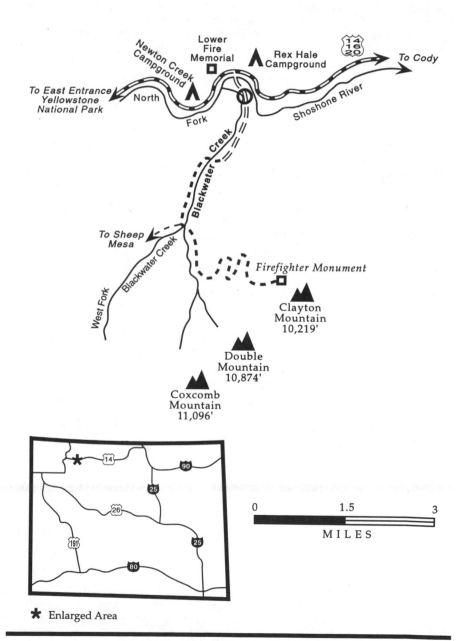

Blackwater Fire Memorial overlooking Yellowstone country.

on which they were working. A stone and brass memorial now stands high on the northern slopes of 10,000-foot Clayton Mountain, honoring these men.

From the camp, your first dozen steps wade Blackwater Creek. Then it's a gentle journey through an intricate forest that contains every conifer imaginable, including juniper and Colorado blue spruce. Just over a mile later the trail forks. Someone has shredded most of the signs on this trail, but journeying left or southeast and across the Blackwater Creek's east fork (a rock hop at this point) sends you moderately upward for a couple miles and to the fire's beginnings.

After hiking so many areas in this sector of Wyoming that were crisped by the 1988 fires, it's refreshing to touch a forest where the new-growth trees are thirty feet high and reveal first-hand that the land does heal itself. For a couple of miles the trail switchbacks up a steeper hill and to a ridgetop. The views of high peaks to the south and of the valley below spreading northwest toward Yellowstone become more magnificent with every step of elevation gain.

Four miles after that first crossing of Blackwater Creek you come upon the main memorial. It's a beautiful work of rock art that overlooks the entire valley. From here you can easily trace the broad path of the fire, see the rocky gully in which the men tried to escape its heat, and read their names on the brass covering. "They gave their last full measure of devotion," is part of the epitaph, and it's natural to be emotionally overwhelmed in this meditative setting.

A trail does continue beyond the memorial and to the top of Clayton Mountain. But in 1991 the Forest Service had closed the trail above the memorial due to washouts and bear activity. With budget cutbacks and continued bear activity, it's probable they will let that part of the trail fade out.

The trail has a few steep grades, but its an amazingly rockless path and quite easy to walk. Bring some water, as the gullies of Clayton Mountain are a bit stingy in that regard.

HIKE 58 BLACKWATER NATURAL BRIDGE TRAIL

General description: A long and arduous hike to exquisite alpine meadows and great views of a massive, spectacular natural rock arch.

General location: Approximately forty miles due west of Cody, outside the northern boundaries of the Washakie Wilderness.

Maps: Shoshone National Forest north half map and/or Clayton Mountain, Chimney Rock and Sheep Mesa quads.

Special attractions: Hard hiking with final rewards of thrilling buttes and alpine meadows second to none. A quite large, ridgetop natural rock bridge further culminates this hike.

For more information: Wapiti Ranger District, 203 A Yellowstone Ave., Cody, WY, 82414, (307) 527-6921.

The hike: It's always amazing how neighboring trails so often lead to totally different hiking and scenic experiences. This trail presents a lot of rugged and uphill work, but the many rewards at trail's end more than compensate for the efforts.

Directions for the beginnings of this natural bridge trail are the same as found in HIKE 57, the Blackwater Fire Memorial Trail, up to the first fork in the trail 1.1 miles after crossing Blackwater Creek. Here a half-broken sign points you westward toward the west fork of Blackwater Creek. A couple of hunting/horse trails also intersect at this point, so be sure and stick with the main trail that follows the west shores of the creek. This is also a good place to tank up with water, for the next couple of miles are steep, rocky and rugged hiking with the trail staying high above the creek waters.

Washakie Wilderness country is composed of extremely friable soils, and many of the small side canyons and ravines intersecting the trails tend to be washed out creating irregular and broken hiking. For almost five uphill miles the trail traverses a rock-strewn landscape beneath fir, lodgepole and finally spruce forests. Then, as it crosses to the east side of the creek, the real uphill switchbacks begin. After .75 mile of pure huff and puff, the trail breaks into gorgeous alpine meadows. Straightfaced cliffs of striated volcanic rock surround the high fields. As the trail continues to climb, the meadows become more glorious and the forests are reduced to sporadic and isolated clumps of trees. Six arduous miles after the first creek crossing, the trail disappears, the trees simply stop, and a vast tundra-like valley stretches before you.

These luxuriant meadows afford wonderful camping. Several horse camps exists here, but more than enough room exists for the few users this area feels. The meadows are waterless, but a steady and crystal-pure creek flows about .25 mile to the east.

Now the adventure begins. All that uphill hiking has simply been gearing you for the finale. Standing where the trees end and facing south, you see the vast and open high country and the surrounding cliff faces. There are views

HIKE 58 *BLACKWATER NATURAL BRIDGE*

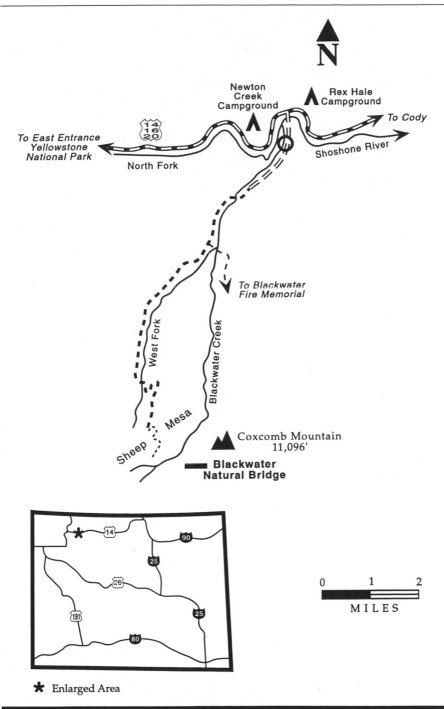

Climbing Sheep Mesa toward Blackwater Natural Bridge.

of the natural bridge from atop Sheep Mesa and the cliffs to the east. Look at these cliffs, to the south and a bit to the east, and you'll see one grassy area leading to the top of the mesa. A sort-of trail leading to that one break in the rock structure is also visible. The climb through that grassy break is steep—not quite fourth class scrambling, but close enough, and should only be attempted by those with some mountaineering experience. The effort puts you atop a seventy-five-yard-wide ridge and into an incredible view of the large natural bridge and the surrounding mountainous world. Remember that the bridge is at least a mile away even as it appears so large before you.

Anyone atop Sheep Mesa is quite vulnerable to adverse weather. And bring water with you to the top. .

The North Absaroka Wilderness, the Beartooth Mountains, and the Clover Mist Fire

An integral part of the Greater Yellowstone Ecosystem, situated along the northeastern boundary of Yellowstone National Park, is the 350,488-acre North Absaroka wilderness. Although the wilderness is touched by 217 miles of maintained trails, much of the wild country lacks any trail access. The land's character is that of rugged volcanic mountains disected by numerous creeks, and its vastness is relatively inaccessible. Renowned for its wildlife populations, the wilderness is considered essential habitat to the survival of the grizzly bear. According to the Clarks Fork district ranger of the Shoshone National Forest, hikers tend to leave the North Absaroka Wilderness to horse packers. She notes: "The area is quite rugged and there are numerous stream crossings and almost no lakes. In addition, a limited number of campsites tends to create problems of specific-area overuse."

1988 was the year that added a new thermal feature to the Yellowstone area. Fire! Lightning storms in late June and early July touched off a series of blazes that burned approximately 1.5-million acres of forest land. That equals an area larger than the State of Delaware.

The largest of the eight major fires in Greater Yellowstone—the Clover-Mist fire—burned huge portions of the North Absaroka Wilderness and the Shoshone National Forest. "Black Saturday" or August 20th, when sixty-mile-per-hour wind gusts fanned the Clover-Mist and other fires into raging infernos, left massive portions of the wilderness and its surrounding areas blackened. Intensely burned landscapes are fascinating to behold, but trails in the North Absaroka Wilderness will be included in a future updated and expanded edition of this book. By then rehabilitation of the area, which includes trail reconstruction, helicopter hillside reseeding, timber salvage operations, should be farther along. If a trail in this area beckons you before that time, write or call the Clarks Fork District Ranger, 1002 Road 11, Powell, WY, 82435, (307) 754-7207, for current information.

North and slightly east of the North Absaroka Wilderness, bordering and extending into Montana, lie the Beartooth Mountains. These rugged and high mountains are part 75-million-year-old sea bed, part twenty million year old volcanic lava, ash and dust, part ancient granite, part glacial sculpting and all beautiful. U.S. Highway 212 dips into the high Wyoming lake country of the Beartooth Mountains over Beartooth Pass on its way north to Red Lodge, Montana. The 10,947-foot pass looks out upon the Beartooth Plateau, the highest contiguous stretch of land in North America. This breath-taking area is filled with peaks, with huge granite boulder formations strewn throughout, and with wildflowers. Animal life is abundant and the area is rich in Native American history.

HIKE 59 *BEARTOOTH HIGH LAKES WILDERNESS STUDY AREA*

General description: A good day hike loop beginning and returning to Beartooth Lake. This trip is best done as a two or three day wander.

General Location: Approximately seventy-four miles north and east of Cody, 37.5 miles southwest of Red Lodge, Montana, and twenty-seven miles east of Cooke City, Montana.

Maps: Shoshone National Forest north half map and USGS Beartooth Butte quad.

Special attractions: Easy trail hiking with gentle grades, beautiful lakes, and high alpine openness filled with wildflowers.

For more information: Clarks Fork Ranger District, 1002 Road 11, Powell, WY, 82435, (307) 745-7202.

Finding the trailhead: Begin at Beartooth Lake Campground, located approximately twelve miles west of Beartooth Pass along U.S. Highway 212. Parking is provided at a well-marked trailhead.

The hike: Apply liberal amounts of mosquito repellent and bring along an old pair of sneakers for the trip through the boggy inlet area along the east side of Beartooth Lake. About 200 yards beyond the information sign, you will wade Little Beartooth Creek and begin a gentle arc to the left around the lake. The next .5 mile is wet and willowy, with Crane Creek and Beartooth Creek crossings along the way. At the north end of the lake, continue bearing left as you approach the lower slopes of Beartooth Butte. Here the

Beauty Lake with Beartooth Butte on right horizon. JERRY SWAFFORD PHOTO.

trail begins a gentle grade upward to the right (north) along Beartooth Creek through a two-mile-long open meadow filled with wildflowers. If you brought your wildflower book, you may identify thirty to forty different species in this area. The trail flanks the terraced east slope of Beartooth Butte, 10,514 feet high, looming above to the left.

Near the ridgetop, watch for a sign indicating the Island Lake Trail to the right. This is the Upper Highline Trail. The path is indistinct for a few hundred yards, so watch for cairns marking the route. The trail picks its way across the headwaters of Beartooth Creek through subalpine fir, whitebark pine and massive boulder formations. After a pleasant walk through this parklike area, the summit is reached, and you look down over a beautiful horseshoe-shaped lake nestled in an open alpine basin. This is the first in a chain of five lakes that lie along a lush open valley that descends to the right (east). To the north are the higher mountains in Montana, with Lonesome Mountain to the northeast. The trail runs southeast along this little valley.

Camping sites along these five alpine lakes are limitless, but remember to camp 200 feet from lakes and 100 feet from streams.

An ideal plan would be to stay here one or two nights and explore the area in all directions. The terrain is gentle and open, so cross-country wandering is in order. A topo map is advised.

Proceeding east, the trail stays along the south side until it crosses the inlet of Claw Lake, the lowermost in the lake chain. From here it travels along the north side of the lake for another .75 mile, then descends down steep switchbacks toward Beauty Lake. Another .25 mile and the trail drops off another a steep ridge to the inlet stream of Beauty Lake. Along the southeast edge of this lake are the trail sign and trail back toward Beartooth Lake. If you are returning to Beartooth Lake, take the trail south along the east side of Beauty Lake. From here it is a pleasant downhill meander for a couple of miles to the trail intersection that leads back to the parking area.

If you are continuing to Island Lake, approximately three miles ahead, stay on the Upper Highline Trail you have been traveling. Climb the 200 foot grade out of Beauty Lake and proceed toward Flake Lake. The trail passes between two unnamed ponds. Watch for the waterfall on the far side of the lake.

After leaving this meadow, the trail drops over another steep area toward Night Lake. Night Lake flows into Island Lake, and the trail continues along the western shore. This area is well traveled by day hikers and anglers. Continue south until the outlet stream of Island Lake is encountered. This crossing is tricky in early season, so find a stout stick for balance. The trail now cuts to the left around the bottom of the lake toward the campground and parking area.

By highway, Island Lake Campground is 3.2 miles from Beartooth Campground, so you have to beg, borrow or buy transportation back to your vehicle. Be of good cheer however, for the Top of the World Store is 1.2 miles west on Highway 212, if you find yourself walking and in need of junk food and pop.—*Jerry and Maryette Swafford*

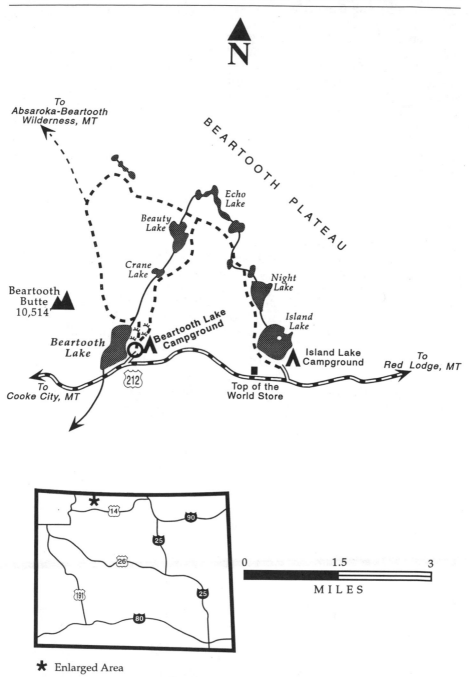

HIKE 60 BEARTOOTH LOOP NATIONAL RECREATION TRAIL

General description: A two-day trip dropping gently from a high alpine ridge to deep canyon meadows then looping back along several lakes to Highway 212 seven miles west of the departure point. Can also be done as a long loop hike back to the starting point.

General location: Approximately seventy-four miles north and east of Cody, twenty-eight miles southwest of Red Lodge, Montana, and forty-one miles east of Cooke City, Montana.

Maps: Shoshone National Forest north half map and USGS Deep Lake quad.

Special attractions: High alpine fields dropping gradually down into forest meadows, forty to fifty species of wildflowers, pristine lakes, good fishing.

For more information: Clarks Fork Ranger District, 1002 Road 11, Powell, WY, 82435, (307) 754-7207.

Finding the trailhead: From Island Lake Campground (HIKE 59) drive 9.5 miles east along U.S. Highway 212 to the Gardner Lake Overlook, which lies in a saddle atop Beartooth Pass. Watch for the rest area and drive exactly two miles farther northeast. This trailhead is also twenty-eight miles from Red Lodge, Montana.

The hike: There is a large signboard marking the trailhead, and the trail takes off down to the left of the sign. The ending pickup point is on Highway 212 at the upper end of Long Lake, three miles east of Island Lake, where a sign marks the end of the Beartooth Loop Trail.

The trail descends downward along the open alpine hillside toward the east side of Gardner Lake. After passing this small open lake, you must cross its outlet stream on rocks. The trail now bears to the right of the valley and approaches the north end of Tibbs Butte. At .75 mile you'll encounter some trail intersection signs, left leading to Sawtooth Camp and right to Losekamp Lake. If your only transportation is at the Gardner Lake trailhead, you will return to this point from Losekamp Lake and retrace your steps back to the parking area.

Sawtooth Camp Trail goes downward into the green, tree-scattered valley and crosses the stream a couple of times before the canyon begins to narrow. This is Little Rock Creek Canyon. The trail crosses the stream again and skirts the left side of this pretty little valley for another two miles. At about one mile sit two signs, one pointing east to the Highline Trail and the other indicating the trail you are on, the Sliderock Trail. 200 feet further another sign announces the Lower Highline Trail to the left.

One more time the trail encounters Little Rock Creek, which is now somewhat wider and deeper but can still be crossed without getting the feet wet. Then a short upward grade to the right or west forces the trail away from the creek. The trail tops a small rise and then begins its descent through pine and fir forest, finally dropping steeply into a large and open meadow replete with flowers. The trail crosses this boggy and wet meadow toward the west (right) and re-enters the pine forest. About 100 yards into the trees is a sign indicating Camp Sawtooth to the left and Dollar Lake trailhead ahead. Camp Sawtooth, less than .5 mile to the south, is a parklike area that has been used

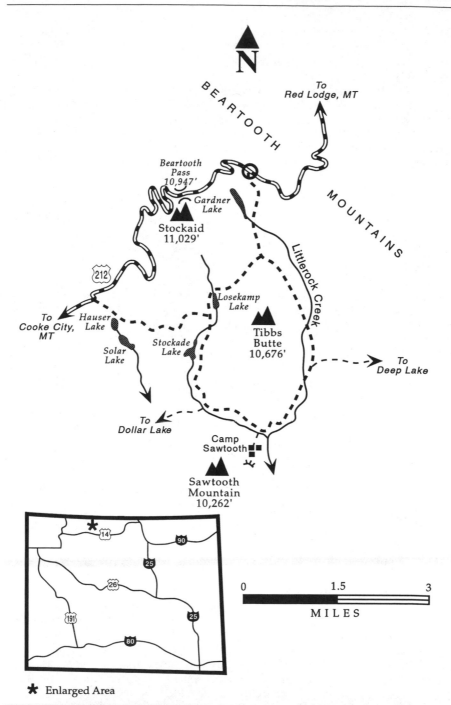

N

BEARTOOTH

To
Red Lodge, MT

MOUNTAINS

Beartooth
Pass
10,947'

Gardner
Lake

Stockaid
11,029'

212

Littlerock Creek

Losekamp
Lake

To
Cooke City,
MT

Hauser
Lake

Tibbs
Butte
10,676'

Solar
Lake

Stockade
Lake

To
Deep Lake

To
Dollar Lake

Camp
Sawtooth

Sawtooth
Mountain
10,262'

14

90

25

26

191

25

80

0   1.5   3

MILES

★ Enlarged Area

Atop Beartooth Pass looking north. JERRY SWAFFORD PHOTO.

as a destination campsite by hunters and campers for at least fifty years. It's a pleasant and clean place to stay. As with all boggy meadow areas, however, mosquitoes are abundant.

Continuing the main loop toward Dollar Lake, the trail meanders through shaded and open forests for another mile and a quarter, paralleling long and open meadows. Here a Forest Service sign points to Stockade Lake Trail angling to the right. Stockade Lake is 1.75 miles and Losekamp Lake is two miles on this trail. For the next mile the trail climbs gradually through open forest. Tibbs Butte can be seen beyond the ridge to the east. Stockade Lake is an enchantingly beautiful area with plentiful flat campsites and waters teeming with trout, a choice place to spend a day or two.

Losekamp Lake is .75 mile to the north. Near the lower end of this lake is the trail fork that cuts back southwest toward Hauser Lake. If you plan to return to Gardner Lake trailhead, you need to take the northeast trail over the north slope of Tibbs Butte (called Tibbs Pass, elevation 10,060 feet). The return to the Gardner Lake Trail is slightly over 1.5 miles and climbs steeply.

If exiting via Hauser Lake to Highway 212, turn left at the Losekamp Lake Junction and proceed southwest. This well-used trail cuts around the bottom of a cliff, along a meadow then into the trees. After .5 mile a sign lets you know that Hauser Lake trailhead is three miles farther. Climb upward to the ridge crest and into subalpine meadows. Here the country is rolling and easy, filled with scattered trees, open grass/flower fields, massive boulders and small lakes. The Absaroka Mountains can be seen to the west, Sawtooth Mountain is south, and the steep cliffs to the southeast mark Deep Lake.

From lovely Hauser Lake the trail ascends upward along the right side of a small draw to a ridge. Follow the cairns across the open ridge to Highway 212 and to the sign marking the Beartooth Loop National Recreation Trail.—*Jerry and Maryette Swafford*

HIKE 61 *CLARKS FORK OF THE YELLOWSTONE RIVER*

General description: A long, rugged and exceptionally scenic trail above and along the southern fringes of a major mountain river. This trail and area can easily consume four or more days of good hiking and never cease to amaze you.

General location: Approximately fifty-five miles north and west of Cody, along the southern boundary of the Beartooth Mountains.

Maps: Shoshone National Forest north half map and/or USGS Muddy Creek, Hunter Peak, Windy Mountain, Dillworth Bench and Bald Peak quads.

Special attractions: Some of the wildest, most spectacularly scenic country imaginable. Unique microenvironments and exceptional hiking.

For more information: Clarks Fork Ranger District, 1002 Road 11, Powell, WY, 82435, (307) 754-7207.

Finding the trailhead: Clarks Fork Trailhead begins five miles south of U.S. highway 212 on Wyoming highway 296. Near mile marker five, on the west side of the road, lies Shoshone National Forest's Hunter Peak Campground. Opposite this is a trailhead sign noting Clarks Fork, and Forest Service Road 167 takes you east for .3 mile of a mile to the trailhead. Another approach, on what must be the most breathtaking highway in America, is to access state highway 296 sixteen miles north of Cody and drive the switchbacks and high cliffs and nearly fifty miles of this Chief Joseph Scenic Highway, again to Mile Marker 5 and the Hunter Peak Campground and Clarks Fork trailhead signs.

The hike: The Clark Fork River is named in honor of Captain William Clark, explorer and co-leader of the Lewis and Clark Expedition in the early 1800's. This wonderful trail explores the wild country around and beside a recently designated wild and scenic river. The journey here can be as long and as exciting a hike as you care to make it. A long day or overnight trip will bring you to some incredibly scenic river canyon vistas. Three days of packing will let you stroll beside the timeless flow and see the many changing faces of the pristine river. Four or five long days, a stomach grabbing ford of the river and a shuttle vehicle at Dead Indian Campground will allow you to follow the entire course of one of the wildest and most picturesque hikes in Wyoming.

Eight miles of hiking are required to reach the river's shores. But what absolute beauty this first distance offers. The trail is mostly gentle, following a benchland above the river. Many small and a few huge creeks tumble down from the high Beartooths, providing good water near the many fine camping spots.

At 3.5 miles the trail climbs steeply north for a half mile to place you on a higher bench where hawks fly and the views become magnificent. After 5.5 miles, the dark, ominous and towering cliffs of the Clarks Fork Canyon come into view. Although the trail shies from and hangs above these walls, do take a short cross-country journey south through the meadows to view this awesome, gaping hole of a river canyon. The trail fades for a bit in a vast meadow setting at six miles. The trick here is to stay high and a bit to the north. Rock cairns do dot the meadow and will lead you east to the forest and the trail's reappearance.

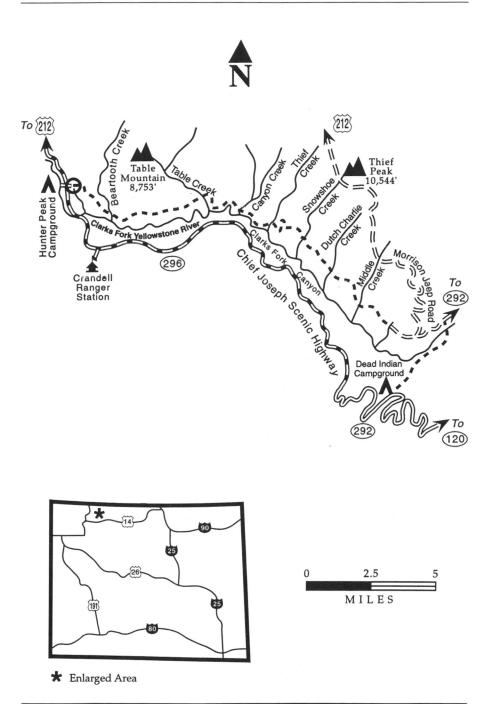

Enlarged Area

0   2.5   5
MILES

Table Creek in late June was a wade, and after this crossing, the trail angles into a sharp descent to the canyon floor. Tall forests now hide the mighty cliffs, and walking is leisurely along the flat river bottom. One mile later, Canyon Creek forms a big wade, and one mile beyond that the trail decides that two miles of river bottom is all you get. Near Thief Creek it leaves the river's shores and steeply ascends the mountainside. A mile of huffing and puffing bring you to another bench, and the next eight miles of hiking is a somewhat rough up-and-down, in-and-out traverse until you intersect the Morrison Jeep Road.

This is wild and free country. You can hike as far as you desire and then return to the Clarks Fork Trailhead, or with another vehicle parked either on the Morrison jeep road or on Wyoming highway 292 (which begins approximately nine miles from the trail/jeep road intersection), you can engage on a one way expedition through the country .

You should be aware that very few hikers know about or use this trail. Lots of horse packers do. Also, sadly, it is a trail open to ATV's. I only met a few, and they did not infringe on the wild and awesomely beautiful aura of this landscape. Also, you will most likely meet some of the many cattle of the area. Even so, this trip remains as one of the best true wilderness adventures outside of classified wilderness that Wyoming offers.

The Jedediah Smith Wilderness

Less renowned than the National Park, but certainly no less dramatic or awe-inspiring, the western slope of the mighty Tetons allows for an exciting portrait of these awesome mountains. More densely carpeted forests and lush meadows here blanket the mountains' lower slopes, mainly due to the fifty inches of yearly rainfall—the wettest spot in Wyoming—that moistens this country. High-elevation glaciated basins and their accompanying lakes afford splendid hiking opportunities.

Jedediah Smith was a fur trapper and contemporary of Jim Bridger and Tom Fitzpatrick—two other mountainman names in Wyoming wilderness. This 116,535-acre wilderness area preserves the western Tetons.

Access to the Jedediah Smith Wilderness is possible by either a long-distance hike from Grand Teton National Park over any of the many passes that top the range, or by driving the rowdy road into very western Wyoming from eastern Idaho. Although the following trails describe accesses from Idaho and a round trip that returns to the original trailhead, an excellent option would be for one party to park in Idaho/western Wyoming and a second in the Grand Teton Park. Both parties could hike so as to cross paths on a spectacular mountain pass and then continue, each to the other's vehicle.

The wilderness and recreation coordinator from the Teton Basin Ranger District of the Targhee Forest does not encourage trips into Alaska Basin, due to the heavy use the area incurs. No fires are allowed in this area. She also encourages all hikers to acquire a free Winegar Hole and Jedediah Smith Wilderness Areas map, which details use regulations. Permits are required to hike and camp in Grand Teton National Park even when entering from western approaches. These permits are available from both the Park and from the Teton Basin Ranger District in Driggs. (See the Grand Teton National Park section for complete permit details.) Earthwalk Press's Grand Teton National Park recreation map offers a wonderful topographic and trail overview of the Jedediah Smith Wilderness and of the following hikes.

HIKE 62 *ALASKA BASIN*

General description: A moderately rugged three- to four-day trip into paramount glacial basin country.

General location: Approximately eleven miles west of Driggs, Idaho, in the southern portion of the Jedediah Smith Wilderness.

Maps: Targhee National Forest Island Park, Ashton, Teton Basin and Palisades Districts map, and/or USGS Granite Basin, Mount Bannon and Grand Teton quads.

Special attractions: Unparalleled views of the back sides of the Tetons, glorious lake reflections, challenging country.

For more information: Teton Basin Ranger District, P.O. Box 777, Driggs, ID, 83422, (208) 354-2431.

Finding the trailhead: Idaho state highway 33 takes you to Driggs. Near the southern end of town, with the Valley Bank on one steet corner, Little Avenue jogs westward toward Alta, Wyoming. This soon becomes the Targhee Road, and you want to follow it's pavement toward the Grand Targhee Resort four miles into Wyoming and another 2.25 miles to the Alta cemetery. Here, to the right or south, a graveled and signed road (FS road 009) leads to the Teton Campground. Follow this road as far as it goes (5.1 miles), past the first parking lot and to the South Teton Creek trailhead.

The hike: In this particular case I confess to being strongly attracted to an area even though the wilderness ranger advised avoidance and warned of heavy use.

It's good that this is such a well-used trail, because the meadows in the first 2.5-gentle-but-uphill miles are so lush with chest- to head-high plant foliage, the path would soon be swallowed without it. Continuing up the gentler South Teton Trail instead of opting for Devils Stairs at this first intersection, the trail now gains a lot of elevation but is so skillfully switchbacked that the hike never seems too difficult. Another 2.5 miles finds the trail weaving through these amazing and huge benches and platforms of polished granite lying flat on the ground. Another couple miles and a few steeper switchbacks place you in the beginnings of Alaska Basin. The trees have thinned to subalpine fir and the rich, multicolored flowers grow but a few inches high.

I list this as a three- or four-day backpack but recommend allowing more time. There is so much to see and so many directions to wander in this area. I highly advise hiking the trail to Hurricane Pass. Sunset Lake west and below this mountainous area is an ideal camping spot, and the two miles of fairly steep hiking to the top of the 10,500-foot pass affords you every view imaginable. The backsides of the three mighty Teton Peaks tower into the sky and over the rocky canyons below.

A great and scenic loop back to the parking lot is possible by following the Teton Crest Trail around the head of South Teton Canyon and then turning onto the Teton Shelf Trail toward Devils Stairs. This second trail gently slopes

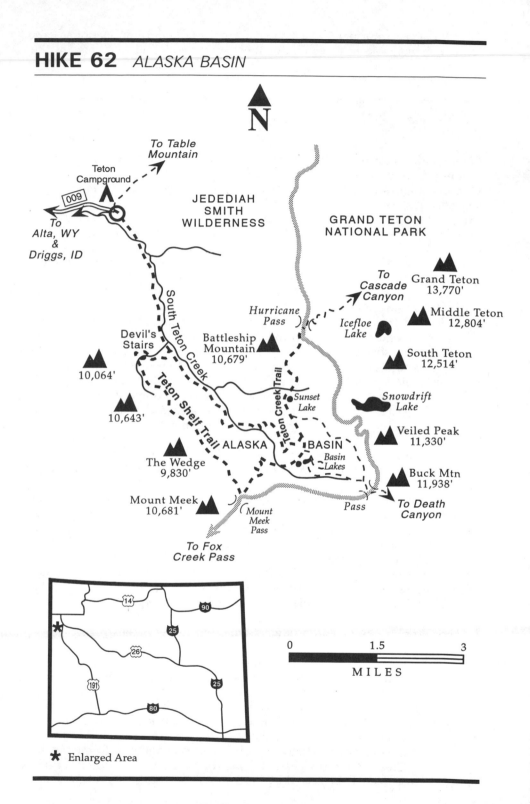

downward along a broad alpine bench for 3.5 miles, tracing a pathway directly beneath a huge and towering wall of stratified cliff.

Devils Stairs are not for those who suffer from acrophobia. The trail is plenty wide but also knows some exposure, and its 1.5-mile distance will work your knees to the maximum.

A few notes of caution: Alaska Basin area is notorious for its powerful thunderstorms, and there isn't a lot of shelter in the open alpine country. Also, Hurricane Pass didn't acquire its name from gently wafting breezes. Be prepared for extreme weather up there.

The trails are easy to follow, and all trail intersections are well-marked. Camping exists the entire lenth of the hike. There are a lot of people, but the country is so huge it can handle them.

HIKE 63 *TABLE MOUNTAIN*

General description: An exceptional day hike that gradually travels uphill for four miles and gets quite steep for the last two miles.

General location: Approximately ten miles east of Driggs, Idaho, in the southern portion of the Jedediah Smith Wilderness.

Maps: Targhee National Forest Island Park, Ashton, Teton Basin and Palisades Districts map, and/or USGS Granite Basin and Mount Bannon quads.

Special attractions: A beautiful canyon hike to an upper basin, followed by high alpine ridgetop vistas.

For more information: Teton Basin Ranger District, P.O. Box 777, Driggs, ID, 83422, (208) 354-2431.

Finding the trailhead: The North Teton Creek Trailhead may be reached by following the same road directions from Driggs, Idaho that are found in HIKE 62, the Alaska Basin hike. One half mile from the end of Forest Service Road 009, at the east end of the campground, find the trailhead signs and parking area for the Table Mountain hike.

The hike: In 1872, photographer William H. Jackson decided he wanted the perfect picture of the Grand Teton from the west. He, an assistant and Molly the mule, loaded with ancient photographic equipment and processing glass photo plates, climbed piles of untrailed rocks for nine days to the summit of Table Mountain. Here Mr. Jackson did get his picture.

Bring a jacket or windbreaker and a lunch, and allow ten to twelve hours for this hike. The first .5-mile section of the hike climbs a switchbacked canyonside to join the North Fork of Teton Creek. The trail then flattens out and follows the creek through lovely meadows and flower fields within a scattered forest. The Boy Scouts call this first section 'Huckleberry Canyon' because of the abundance of huckleberries, but the huge serviceberries are even better. The trail grades gradually upward for another two miles before becoming somewhat steeper and rougher in places. It crosses the creek several times, but good foot bridges make this pleasant.

As it nears the upper end of the canyon, after about four miles, the trail crosses the creek for the last time to the right and begins angling upward along the south side of the canyon. There is a gentle swing to the right for .5 mile (all uphill) into the large and beautiful upper canyon basin. From here the

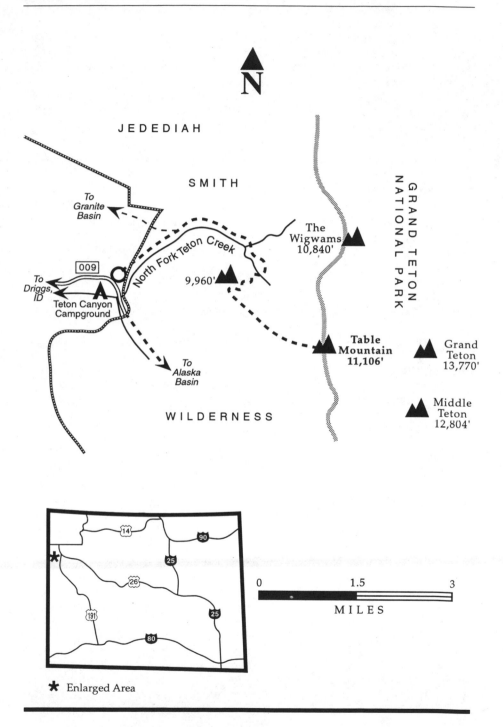

N

JEDEDIAH

SMITH

To
Granite
Basin

North Fork Teton Creek

The
Wigwams
10,840'

009

To
Driggs,
ID

Teton Canyon
Campground

9,960'

GRAND TETON NATIONAL PARK

Table
Mountain
11,106'

Grand
Teton
13,770'

To
Alaska
Basin

WILDERNESS

Middle
Teton
12,804'

14

90

25

26

25

191

80

0   1.5   3

MILES

★ Enlarged Area

Looking toward Table Mountain from the head of the North Fork Teton Creek Canyon.
PHOTO BY JERRY SWAFFORD

goal, Table Mountain, can be seen looming above to the east. Continue bearing upward to the right and approach the south wall of the basin. Watch for the switchbacks going up the face to the south. Below the switchbacks, the trail leaves the last of the water springs, so fill a water jug and drop in a iodine pill.

Now the work begins. The trail climbs out of this beautiful open basin filled with wildflowers and terraces to ascend the ridge above. After switchbacking up to the ridge, the world opens up in all directions. Table Mountain looks like a mesa stretching to the east, and the top of the Grand Teton stands behind it. The trail skirts the south canyon rim and looks down into a subalpine basin to the north. This is a pleasant walk along a rocky and high alpine ridge through scattered scrub whitebark pine. Enjoy the vast views to the south and west.

The final approach to Table Mountain is rocky and steep, with some rock scrambling required to reach the summit. Snowfields are late leaving this area, and there are usually wet areas into August, so watch the footing. As the 11,106-foot summit is reached, you quickly see why you came. The view is simply awesome. Below to the east is a yawning maw, nothing but 2,000 feet of air and a knee-buckling view. The majestic Tetons stand directly in front of you; straight ahead is the Grand Teton reaching 13,770 feet into the sky. One does not walk out here on the first visit; one crawls.

This is one of the most heavily hiked trails in the area. The Boy Scouts from Treasure Mountain Scout Camp hike this trail in mid-week, usually on Wednesdays, and the rest of the week is almost as busy. The best time to take this hike is in September.—*Jerry and Maryette Swafford*

HIKE 64   *HOMINY PEAK/JACKASS PASS/ SOUTH BOONE CREEK LOOP*

General description: A little-known, two- or three-day loop trip that travels along high, timbered ridges.
General location: Twenty-five miles due east of Ashton, Idaho, in the Jedediah Smith Wilderness and the northern portion of Grand Teton National Park.
Maps: Targhee National Forest Island Park, Ashton, Teton Basin and Palisades Districts map and/or USGS Hominy Peak and Survey Peak quads.
Special attractions: Solitude among high virgin-forest ridges, impressive vistas and open mountain meadows.
For more information: Ashton Ranger District, P.O. Box 858, Ashton, ID, 83420, (208) 652-7442.
Finding the trailhead: The road to this hike begins in Ashton, Idaho. Drive west of town on Main Street to the cemetery just beyond the city limits and turn right (south) on Highway 32. In one mile the highway curves to the right. DO NOT take the curve but continue straight ahead a hundred yards to intersect a paved county road, Fremont County Road 261. A sign here announces Squirrel Meadows due west. Turn left here. The pavement ends at 9.3 miles, Targhee National Forest is entered in 12.1 miles, and dusty Forest Service road 264 begins at 23.2 miles. At this point a sign indicates Jackass Meadows is five miles south. Turn right onto road 264 and drive 3.2 miles to the Hominy Creek Trailhead sign (drive past the South Boone Creek trailhead and campground). A narrow but passable dirt road continues .6 mile to the east (left) up a hill and into the forest to the well-signed Hominy Peak trailhead parking area.

The hike: Begin the trek steadily upward and eastward through the pine forest. The first three to four miles is a bit of a grind, but then the hardest work is over. Jedediah Smith Wilderness is entered at one mile. At about two miles, look to the right for large open meadows in a low saddle. Tiny water channels are cut deeply into the meadows here and there and provide the only water on this ridge in late summer. One must listen for the tinkle of the water rivulets in the deep grass.

A steep grade climbs out of this saddle as the trail ascends the south slope of Hominy Peak. However, no "peak" can be seen. As the trail levels again after the grade, look for a small sign on the trail's left announcing the presence of Hominy Peak, elevation 8,362 feet. Hominy Peak is a sagebrush-, grass-

Overlooking the head of South Boone Creek Canyon. JERRY SWAFFORD PHOTO.

and flower-covered hump in the ridge. From this altitude the view to the west looks back across the Snake River plain toward the mountains a hundred miles away.

The trail continues east along this high ridge through beautiful meadows and scattered timber. Soon the view to the south looks down into Conant Basin and Hidden Lake, a little over two miles away. One mile east of Hominy Peak the trail passes beside more lovely meadows and then begins another steep climb up the final ridge to Jackass Pass. After this climb the trail tops a timbered ridge and drops into a little open valley where another trail—the Teton Crest Trail—intersects and signs mark Jackass Pass, elevation 8,280 feet.

At this point the nearest water in late summer is Berry Creek, two miles east and into Grand Teton National Park. The trail to Berry Creek drops gently through a forested canyon, loops back toward the north, then climbs back out of this drainage to reconnect with the South Boone Creek Trail. This route adds over four miles to the trip.

If you have water and wish to miss the Berry Creek loop, take the Teton Crest Trail north from Jackass Pass. In about a mile the trail circles above the cliffs and rocky bluffs overlooking the South Boone Creek drainage. The view here is impressive and expansive. This forms a pleasant walk around the canyon's head along the west slopes of Survey Peak. (Survey Peak, like Hominy Peak, is not a "peak" but a grass/flower/tree-covered mountain.

The trail now wanders west and after 2.5 miles it begins its descent—and a very roundabout way—through beautiful high meadows and rolling subalpine fields. The trail intersects South Boone Trail, and a sign notes that it's 6.4 miles back to the Jackass Road. Where the trail snakes back to the south on a large and open meadowed ridge, watch for trail signs indicating a side trail into Middle Boone Creek. Continue bearing left (due south). A few

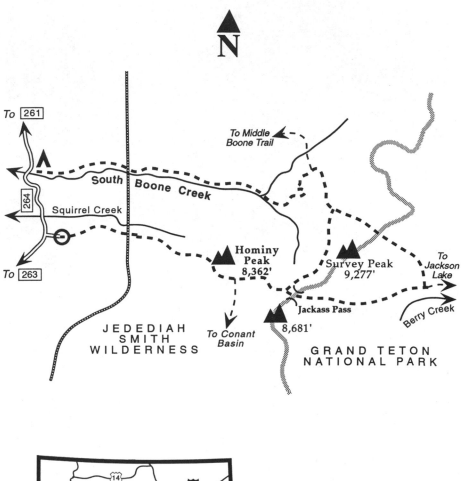

To 261

South Boone Creek

264

Squirrel Creek

To 263

To Middle Boone Trail

Hominy Peak 8,362'

Survey Peak 9,277'

To Jackson Lake

Jackass Pass 8,681'

Berry Creek

To Conant Basin

JEDEDIAH SMITH WILDERNESS

GRAND TETON NATIONAL PARK

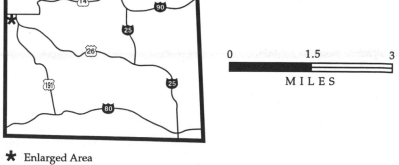

14

90

25

26

191

25

80

* Enlarged Area

0   1.5   3

MILES

more rolling meanders and the trail drops steeply into South Boone Creek Canyon. This steep, twisting, switch-backing section explains why this route is not recommended as the route into the area.

South Boone Creek flows in the bottom of a heavily-forested canyon, and its cold water is welcome. From here the trail follows the creek west back to the road, but for no apparent reason the trail designer chose to provide more climbing while descending the canyon. Uphill grades take the trail hundreds of feet above the creek in places, but it does eventually rejoin the canyon floor and exit at Jackass Road. At the trailhead campground drop the packs, soak your feet in the creek, then amble the 2.2 miles back up the road (south) to your car.—*Jerry and Maryette Swafford*

The Teton Range—
Grand Teton National Park

Perhaps someday a group of ardent and determined climbers will tote enough rocks to the top of the Grand Teton to increase its elevation the thirty-five feet needed for it to exceed Gannett Peak and become Wyoming's highest mountain. After all, they argue, the Tetons are the most startling, showy and famous core of rocky faces in the state. With no foothills to hinder the spectacular 1.5 miles of towering rock walls that rise above the valley floor, why shouldn't the Grand own the State's "number one" classification?

The Precambrian granite core of the Tetons formed from molten rock that was buried at least four miles below the earth's surface. This future mountain range mostly escaped the wild faulting and thrusting efforts of the Laramie Revolution that shaped the other ranges surrounding the Jackson Hole area. As Yellowstone volcanoes covered northwest Wyoming with lava and ash, the Tetons remained a small bubble on the surface of the earth. Ten million years ago that changed. In a very short succession of years the Tetons climbed to towering heights while the earth's crust covering the Jackson Hole area sank. Erosion, plus three major Ice Age glaciers honed the sharp faces of the range. Today's thrilling view of these mountains provide what older Park Service pamphlets labeled "the scenic climax of Wyoming."

Grand Teton National Park encompasses most of the eastern side of this mighty range. The western banks of the mountains are occupied by the Jedediah Smith Wilderness. Yellowstone became the world's first National Park in 1872 after two years of effort. Fifty some years of unbelievable political conflicts finally produced an enlarged Grand Teton National Park in 1950.

An impressive trail system of more than 200 miles accesses many of the peaks and drainages and all of the vistas in the National Park. Grand Teton's backcountry rules are a bit different than Yellowstone's:

• Instead of designated camping sites (with a few exceptions), the Teton Park is divided into camping zones. With a permit, one can stay almost anywhere within a camping zone.

• Grand Teton allows hikers to reserve backcountry camping permits. Up to thirty percent of the available permits may be reserved between January 1 and June 1. Know your final itinerary (including dates, what zones you want to camp in each night, the number of people in your party, a second alternative and a telephone number) and submit the request in writing to Permits Office, Grand Teton National Park, P.O. Box 170, Moose, WY, 83012. Information on the camping zones may also be obtained from this address.

• Other non-fee camping permits may be obtained in person at the Moose or Colter Bay Visitor Centers or the Jenny Lake Ranger Station. The backcountry camping limit is a total of ten nights parkwide.

• No fires are allowed anywhere in the backcountry. Campstoves are the requirement.

Often an ice axe requirement is in effect in the park until mid-July. Many of the trails begin at over 6,800 feet and climb from there, so snow is slow to leave the various divides and passes. Check with the rangers for up-to-date information.

HIKE 65 *HERMITAGE POINT TRAIL*

General description: A leisurely day hike and stroll beneath the towering Teton Mountains and by the reflective shores of Jackson Lake.

General location: Directly south of Colter Bay Village, in the center of Grand Teton National Park.

Maps: Earthwalk Press has a recreation map of the Grand Teton National Park that is great. It's available at all visitor centers. Also USGS Colter Bay, Two Ocean Lake and Jenny Lake quads. (Topographic maps are not needed for this hike.)

Special attractions: Lake-reflected views of the Tetons that can never grow old. High probabilities of wildlife viewing.

For more information: Grand Teton National Park, P.O. Drawer 170, Moose, WY, 83012.

Finding the trailhead: Colter Bay Village is the main information and lodging center on the shores of huge Jackson Lake. It is well signed and easy to access from U.S. Highways 287 and 89 approximately thirteen miles north of Moran Junction. Drive as far west as possible to the visitor's center. Here follow the curve of the road south, drive this direction past the marina and to the southern end of the parking lot. The Hermitage Point trailhead sign is quite visible, with the foot trail beginning to the west and a few paces up a gravel maintenance road.

The hike: Here's an easy and special trail that places you directly into that post card scenery and away from the crowded overviews where everyone else stops. You do have to hike .5 mile to get beyond the noise of motor boats entering and exiting the marina.

This is an almost nine-mile multi-loop trail that takes you in and out of views of the northern Tetons dramatically rising above forest and lake waters. Many different sub-loops are possible, so the journey can be as long and varied as you wish. But once you begin, so phenomenal are the views that the next mile is too alluring not to hike. All intersections are well signed, but carrying a trail map gives you perspective on where you are and knowledge of what it is you're viewing.

Heron Pond, 1.5 miles from the trail's beginning, captures half the Teton Range in its reflection. If you're lucky, you'll see the white pelicans, the osprey,

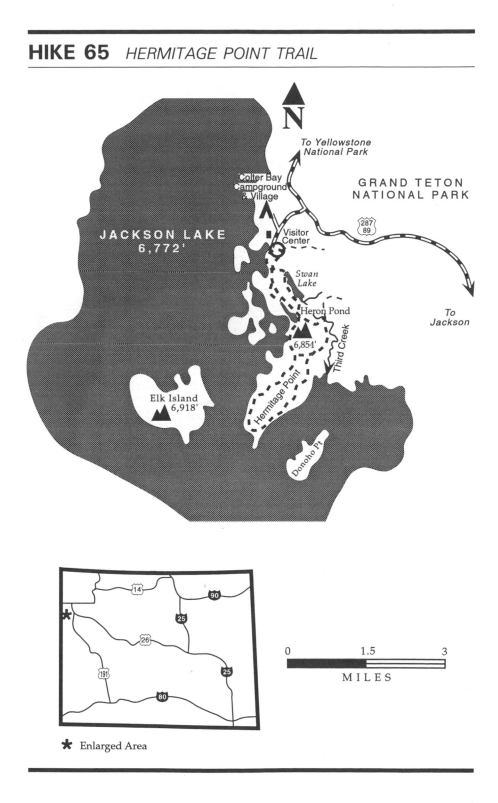

Teton reflections along the Hermitage Point Trail.

the kingfishers and the herons all fishing the lake for supper.

The entire trail is mostly level lodgepole forest hiking. But incredible vistas suddenly pop into view and another half a roll of film disappears. The tip of this point of land has some treeless stretches that place no impediments to the mountain panoramas. It's easy to return hike along different trail segments. Do journey by Swan Lake and view the moose grazing in the water, the endless varieties of waterfowl and forest birds, and the swan family.

This trail presents many opportunities to contact international hikers and walkers. I met friendly folks from several different countries. Be aware that the only water on this trip is lake water, so carry a container or two of your own fresh liquid.

HIKE 66 PAINTBRUSH CANYON TRAIL TO PAINTBRUSH DIVIDE

General description: A steep and rugged nine-mile (one way) journey into the spectacular, rocky innards of the Teton Range.

General location: Approximately twenty-five miles north of Jackson, in the center of Grand Teton National Park.

Maps: USGS Grand Teton National Park system map. Also, USGS Jenny Lake and Mount Moran quads. The Bridger-Teton National Forest map affords a fair contoured overview of Grand Teton National Park. The best hiking map for the Park and surrounding area is Earthwalk Press's Grand Teton National Park Recreation Map, available at all Park gift shops and ranger stations.

190

Special attractions: Cliffs, canyons, mountain peaks.

For more information: Grand Teton National Park, P.O. Box 170, Moose, WY, 83012.

Finding the trailhead: Fifteen miles north of Jackson on U.S. Highways 26, 89 and 191, Moose Junction sends a road westward to the entrance station and park headquarters and visitor center. Twelve miles north along this Teton Park Road places you at the signed North Jenny Lake Junction. This same junction is 9.1 miles from the Jackson Lake Junction, farther north in the park. Another 2.8 miles westward and you intersect the String Lake road. It's but a .5-mile drive along this paved road to the String Lake Picnic Area whose northern end holds the Leigh Lake Trailhead and beginning of this hike. NOTE: In 1991, intense construction was reshaping the road routes between South and North Jenny Lake Junctions. When completed, mileages and final directions may be slightly different than presented here. But a national park is always well signed; String Lake Picnic Area and the Leigh Lake Trailhead remain the goal for this hike.

The hike: Aptly-named String Lake is but a wide and calm spot between Jenny and Leigh lakes. The trail circumvents its gentle eastern shores for .8 mile before crossing a bridge and entering the woodlands to the west. Seven tenths of a mile farther the Paintbrush Trail intersects, jogging to the right or north. A fair amount of elevation needs to be gained in the next couple of miles before the trail enters the mouth of Paintbrush Canyon. The hardest part of this sector of trail, at least in late August, is escaping the prolific huckleberry bushes along the way.

Enter the high-walled Paintbrush Canyon and you pass into a wilder kind of country. The many creeks go crazy in steep cascades; the colorful rocks twist up to phenomenal heights; even the forests grow in spastic patterns as the contours allow.

Overlooking Paintbrush Canyon and the Snake River Valley from Paintbrush Divide.

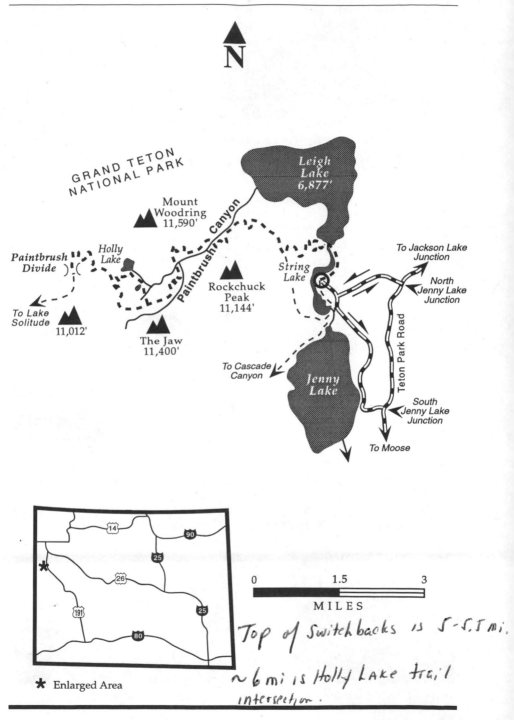

N

GRAND TETON
NATIONAL PARK

Leigh
Lake
6,877'

Mount
Woodring
11,590'

Paintbrush Canyon

Holly
Lake

Paintbrush
Divide

String
Lake

To Jackson Lake
Junction

North
Jenny Lake
Junction

Rockchuck
Peak
11,144'

To Lake
Solitude

11,012'

The Jaw
11,400'

To Cascade
Canyon

Jenny
Lake

Teton Park Road

South
Jenny Lake
Junction

To Moose

★ Enlarged Area

0   1.5   3
MILES

Top of Switchbacks is 5-5.5 mi.

*~6 mi is Holly Lake trail
intersection.*

If you're walking this trail as a day hike, try to get to the top of the awesome switchbacks between five and 5.5 miles. Views into the lakelands and prairies directly below are astounding.

Beyond six miles and the Holly Lake trail intersection, the trail departs from the trees and arcs along the feet of a 1,000-foot-high crescent of tortured peaks and cliffs. For two miles the trail steeply climbs through a perfect combining of primal granite and gentle alpine meadow splendor. The last .5 mile leaves all connotations of gentle behind as the trail switchbacks up talus slopes to barren, windswept, 10,700-foot-high Paintbrush Divide. Paintbrush Divide is one of the areas in the park where an ice axe mandate is in effect, usually through mid-July. Indeed, even in later August a fair-sized and more vertical than horizontal snow field covered the trail and required careful kick-steps to cross.

Paintbrush Canyon hosts two camping zones, one just above the mouth of the canyon and one above Holly Lake. A hiker can camp at either of these locations and ascend the divide as a dayhike.

HIKE 67 *CASCADE CANYON TRAIL TO LAKE SOLITUDE*

General description: A long but not too severe hike of fifteen to twenty round trip miles into the most noted rock-grandeur of the Teton high country.

General location: Approximately twenty-five miles north of Jackson, in the center of Grand Teton National Park.

Maps: USGS Grand Teton National Park system map. Also, USGS Jenny Lake and Mount Moran quads. The best hiking map for the park and surrounding area is Earthwalk Press's Grand Teton National Park Recreation Map, available at all park gift shops and ranger stations.

Special attractions: Steep canyon walls, and cascading creek.

For more information: Grand Teton National Park, P.O. Box 170, Moose, WY, 83012.

Finding the trailhead: Approximately eight miles north of the Moose Entrance Station or thirteen miles south of Jacks on Lake Junction on the Teton Park Road, a South Jenny Lake Junction sign directs you westward to a campground and ranger station. Drive to a huge parking lot and follow the signs and the paved paths directing you to the boat dock and the Cascade Canyon trailhead.

The trail begins as you cross a ramp that spans an arm of the lake waters by the boat dock. There is a motorboat shuttle across Jenny Lake that eliminates the 2.2-mile walk around the lake's southern shores. Since it knocks off over four miles of the round trip journey, most hikers opt for this fun ride. The boats arrive and depart at twenty minute intervals, beginning at 8 a.m. Be aware that the last return trip happens at 6 p.m. Miss it and you'll add a couple miles to your hike ending.

The hike: This is the most popular, most-hiked trail in Grand Teton National Park. Whether you hike around or ride across Jenny Lake, the uphill slopes and the amazing scenery begin immediately beyond the western shores. .7 mile above the boat dock, a short, well-marked trail places you before Hidden

N

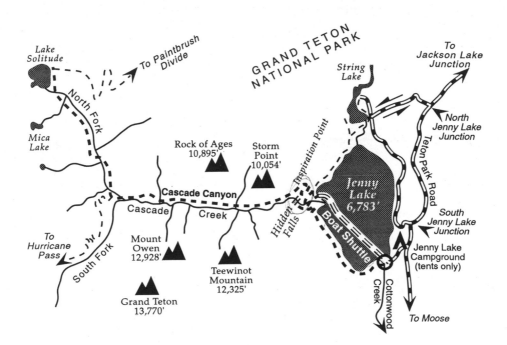

Lake
Solitude

To Paintbrush
Divide

GRAND TETON
NATIONAL PARK

String
Lake

To
Jackson Lake
Junction

North Fork

Mica
Lake

Rock of Ages
10,895'

Storm
Point
10,054'

Inspiration Point

North
Jenny Lake
Junction

Teton Park Road

Cascade Canyon

Jenny
Lake
6,783'

Cascade   Creek

Hidden
Falls

Boat Shuttle

South
Jenny Lake
Junction

To
Hurricane
Pass

South Fork

Mount
Owen
12,928'

Teewinot
Mountain
12,325'

Jenny Lake
Campground
(tents only)

Grand Teton
13,770'

Cottonwood Creek

To Moose

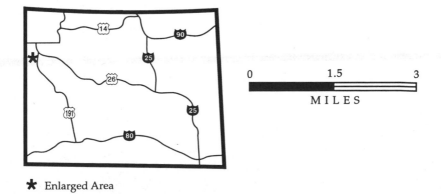

14

90

25

26

191

25

80

★ Enlarged Area

0   1.5   3

MILES

A Cascade Canyon view of the Grand Teton

Falls, a powerful cascade of white water that gives meaning to the name of the canyon. A half mile of steep switchbacks places you atop Inspiration Point, another aptly named outcropping that overlooks Jenny Lake and the Snake River Valley to the east and sits beneath pinnacled Teewinot Mountain, 12,325 feet, to the west. It's at this point, and at the canyon mouth .7 mile farther, that more than half the number of people—the sight seers—end their journey.

The next three miles distance offers what everyone should sometime experience. The trail is gentle and easy to follow so viewing is facilitated. The north faces of Teewinot Mountain, Mount Owen (12,928) and the mighty Grand Teton (13,770) form an impressive and nearly continuous southern wall. The Rock Of Ages is also no slouch. 2-3,000 feet directly below these sheer summits treads the hiker. Above a constantly changing setting of open meadow and tall forest, these mighty rock heads peer over and down at the viewer. As the sun moves across the sky, shadows change the stoney faces into new forms.

3.8 miles above Inspiration Point, Cascade Canyon splits into north and south forks. Five miles of ever-upward climbing to the south places you atop scenic Hurricane Pass (HIKE 62). The trip northward to Lake Solitude is somewhat shorter and gentler. About three miles of scattered sub-alpine forest and glorious meadow hiking puts you beside this quiessent pond living beneath a high cirque of rocky mountains. Here wonderful and more distant views of the mighty mountains you've hiked directly beneath come into play. This area (below Lake Solitude) contains the one overnight camping permit zone on this hike.

If time and ambition are yours, try following the trail from Lake Solitude up to Paintbrush Divide (HIKE 66). This amazing three miles in three huge switchbacks is an easier ascent to the pass than from Paintbrush Canyon.

(Easier is a relative concept. This trail still climbs steeply and steadily, and at a high elevation.)

Many people hike the Cascade Caynon and Paintbrush Canyon trails (HIKES 66 and 67) as a loop. These two amazing and completely different canyons sitting side by side form a remarkable trip. Such a journey is best accomplished by beginning at the String Lake or Leigh Lake trailheads (see HIKE 66) and hiking the northwestern shores of Jenny Lake at the beginning (if up Cascade and down Paintbrush) or at the end (if up Paintbrush and down Cascade). The Park Service quotes this as a 19.2 mile loop hike, but my pedometer and I both think they underrate it by a few miles.

Yellowstone National Park

Yellowstone is the country's oldest National Park and the largest (outside of Alaska), nearly sixty miles in width and length. It's 2.2-million acres is three times larger than the state of Rhode Island. Elevations range from 5,000 to 11,000 feet, and numerous biospheres and ecosystems create habitat for an incredible variety of flora and fauna. The steaming geysers and bubbling thermal mud pots, the many lakes and mighty river canyons, the multicolored, extraordinary examples of Nature's forces at play almost overwhelm the visitor who attempts to grasp the Yellowstone landscape in one setting. One of the earliest explorers of the Yellowstone area, General W.E. Strong, wrote about the area in his diary: "Grand, glorious, and magnificent was the scene as we looked upon it from Washburn's summit. No pen can write it—no language describe it."

The Park maintains over a thousand miles of hiking trails. More variety and beauty awaits the explorer here than one can possibly imagine. Obviously, the "Hiker's Guide to Wyoming" can serve as but an introduction to this immense area. Making an acquaintance with Yellowstone can easily become one of the most rewarding experiences of your life.

The park, certainly one of the most popular places in the world, finds itself visited by millions of people. The rules necessary to protect the land and the experience of such a unique land are much more comprehensive here than in the rest of Wyoming.

Following is a brief listing of major regulations associated with hiking the park, but be aware that specially designated areas along with changing conditions and management policies constantly create variations on these rules. Be sure and contact a park ranger before you begin a day hike or an overnight trip.

• Permits are required for some day hikes and all overnight trips. Also, Yellowstone Park has a designated backcountry campsite system. You have to have your trip's daily itinerary planned and be able to tell the person issuing the permit where you wish to camp on what night. The backcountry use permits are free, but understand, they must be obtained in person and are not available more than forty-eight hours in advance of the start of the trip. As with the park's few campgrounds, it's a first come, first served ordeal. I strongly advise you to have a couple of alternative trips and several alternative campsites in mind. A map showing all the trails and designated campsites is posted at the following locations (this is the summer schedule):

Mammoth Ranger Station/Visitor Center, Canyon Ranger Station/Visitor Center, Grant Village Visitor, Center South Entrance Ranger Station, Belcher Ranger Station, Old Faithful Ranger Station

- Use permits are available from these locations seven days a week between 8 a.m. and 4:30 p.m.
- Open fires are permitted only in established fire rings at certain designated backcountry sites.
- Firearms (including bows and arrows) and pets are prohibited in the backcountry.
- The feeding, touching, teasing, frightening or intentional disturbing of wildlife may grant you an appearance before a U.S. Magistrate. So may destroying or removing any plant, rock, animal, mineral, cultural or archeological resource of the park. This includes throwing or rolling rocks into the thermal features.
- Unlike many national parks, Yellowstone does require a valid park fishing permit. State licenses and regulations do not apply here. The permit is acquirable from the above locations.
- They also require all the common-sense rules of backcountry no-impact camping espoused in the ethics chapter.

Entrance fees jumped a bit in 1988. It now costs $10 for a vehicle or $4 for each visitor entering by bus, bike or foot for a seven day pass to both Yellowstone and Grand Teton parks. There is an annual calendar year pass to these parks available for $15. The Golden Eagle Passport at $25 allows access to every National Park in the nation.

1988 added another dimension to Yellowstone's enchantment. Over 800,000 acres of the park was touched by the natural cycle of fire. Nearly every trail now takes you into examples of canopy and mixed burns. The long-range reality of the fire is that new habitat diversity has been created and that the Yellowstone ecosystem is rejuvenating itself nicely because of this.

HIKE 68 *AGATE CREEK TRAIL*

General description: A long day hike, mostly atop an open alpine ridge in uncluttered country.

General location: Approximately two miles east of Tower Junction, on the Northeast Entrance Road in Yellowstone National Park.

Maps: There are several trail maps of the park available at the visitor's centers, including Earthwalk Press's Hiking Map and Guide. Also USGS Tower Junction quad and USGS Yellowstone 1:125,000 vicinity map.

Special attractions: Abundant wildlife and glorious views. Probably one of the least known and traveled trails in the park.

For more information: Park Superintendent, Yellowstone National Park, P.O. Box 168, WY, 82190, (307) 344-7381.

Finding the trailhead: 2.1 miles east of Tower Junction, or about twenty-seven miles west of the northeast entrance on the Northeast Entrance Road, sits a wide spot in the road that holds an interpretive sign explaining glaciers and glacial moraines. Across the road is a sign, "Trail Head," with an arrow pointing south. This is actually the west trailhead of the Specimen Ridge Trail.

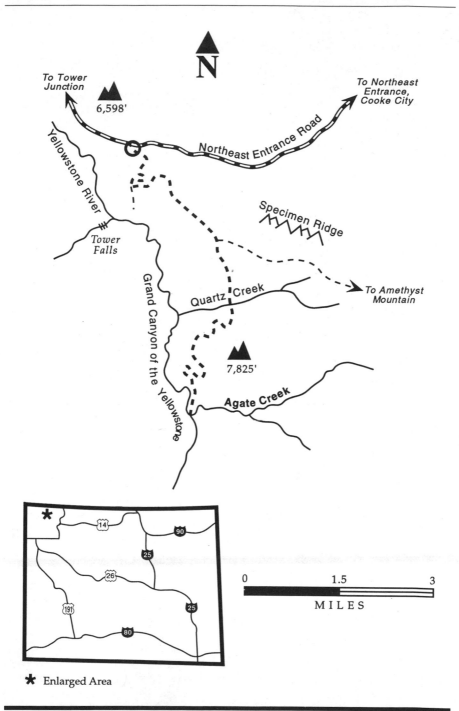

The hike: The north-central portion of Yellowstone doesn't house the thermal springs, mud pots and fabled gyser features for which the park is renowned. Its countenance is that of high and open country, land that was created by glacial moraines. It's meadows and valleys are home to the many wonderful varieties of wildlife that inhabit the park. And this section of Yellowstone seems the least traveled and crowded by human visitors.

Agate Creek trail almost has to be hiked as a day hike. It's final destination, pretty Agate Creek as it merges with the Yellowstone River, borders a special bear management area that is closed to humans from March 10 through November 10. But one backcountry campsite exists near the river bottom, and that site is closed Memorial Day through mid July and whenever bear activity is probable. This makes for a fifteen-mile round trip, but the country is enchanting every step of the way.

A few tenths of a mile along the Specimen Ridge Trail places you at the "official" trailhead and registration box. The first mile of this trail slopes moderately upward, through open meadows and sections of forest to a ridgetop that affords an ineffable view of the Grand Canyon of the Yellowstone River. It's a fun place to be. Across the river and in the distance you can view hundreds of tourists bumping into each other as they congregate at a road-side overview while here you are, alone, higher, and with a much better outlook on the scenery. After a steep climb for .5 mile to the east, the trail tops out on the beginnings of Specimen Ridge. Here begins an incredible walking experience. The alpine tundra country is so vast, so open, you feel you're always in the middle of this endless expanse of huge space. Panoramas of distant peaks accompany every step.

After another mile there is a signed intersection; follow the arrow pointing right or south to Agate Creek. The next 2.5 miles is high country walking at its level best. After crossing the only water on this ridge, Quartz Creek, I encountered a herd of 250 elk cows and calves, and reveled in their cries and wanderings. Past Quartz Creek the trail does fade in and out, but it's easy to guess its route. It hangs over the Grand Canyon of the Yellowstone River, and occasional orange markers trace its route.

The final two miles of the trail drop steeply to the shores of the Yellowstone River. It's a real sliding boot-jammer of a descent that ends in a gravel bar intruding into the river and forming a nice place to have lunch. Fires have done a number to portions of this area, and the hiker can view all kinds of burn patterns. On the hike back, you get to see all the scenery that was behind you as you hiked in.

Watch for bears and elk on this trail, especially as you approach the river. Weather changes should be kept in mind because most of the distance is open and exposed. There are so many elk in the country that they create their own trails. Look for the orange trail markers noting the park trail.

HIKE 69 BLACKTAIL CREEK TRAIL

General description: A popular and enjoyable day hike or easy overnighter affording access to several other one-way hikes and loop trails.

General location: Approximately six miles west of Mammoth Springs in the north-central sector of Yellowstone National Park.

Maps: Several trail maps of the park are available at the visitor's centers, including Earthwalk Press's Hiking Map and Guide. Also USGS Blacktail Deer Creek quad and the USGS Yellowstone 1:125,000 vicinity map.

Special attractions: Continually changing and spectacular scenery, a fairly easy access to the Black Canyon of the Yellowstone River.

For more information: Park Superintendent, Yellowstone National Park, P.O. Box 168, WY, 82190, (307) 344-7381.

Finding the trailhead: The trailhead is well signed, being 11.9 miles east of Tower Junction or 6.1 miles west of Mammoth Springs on the northernmost sector of the Grand Loop Road.

The hike: A pet ploy of mine is to become friendly with people who carry long-time experiences and knowledge of an area and ask them to direct me to a favorite hike of theirs. This interesting day hike is ranger recommended because it traverses some of the lowest elevations in Yellowstone Park. Earlier access and completely different plant ecosystems are two special features of the country this trail touches.

The trail is well traveled, and may not afford the highest of impressions for the first 1.5 miles. Rolling hills with grass prairies so short as to make them appear bald rule the landscape for this distance. But then the conifers began sneaking into the scenery, and after a couple of miles the trail drops into the Blacktail Creek drainage. Here the open forest settings gain an undeniable fascination. Here also the creek sinks deeper and deeper into the earth, creating an impressive valley which turns into a formidable chasm. And all of this is but a prelude to the mighty Black Canyon of the Yellowstone River.

The last mile of the trail drops steeply into a mountainous gorge of dark-colored volcanic rock cliffs. Impressive also is the steel suspension bridge that crosses the mighty river. .2 mile north of this bridge, the Blacktail Creek Trail intersects the Yellowstone River Trail. You've actually crossed into Montana here, and if you happen through at the right time of year, the nearby land bench is flagrant with Bitterroot blossoms, the Montana state flower. The journey from trailhead to trail intersection is four miles, but the scenery undergoes endless transformations along the way.

A joy of this particular trail is the access it gives a person to so many further hiking opportunities. Several backcountry campsites exist along the route and near the Yellowstone River. One can set up camp here and day hike both up and down the river and beneath the towering cliff walls of the canyon. Other options include a couple of one-way hikes: a 12.6-mile hike westward and along the river to Gardiner, Montana, and a 11.3-mile hike east to Hellroaring Creek and the many trails that slice through that country. The only warning advice I received was that this lower elevation country can cook during the heat of the summer.

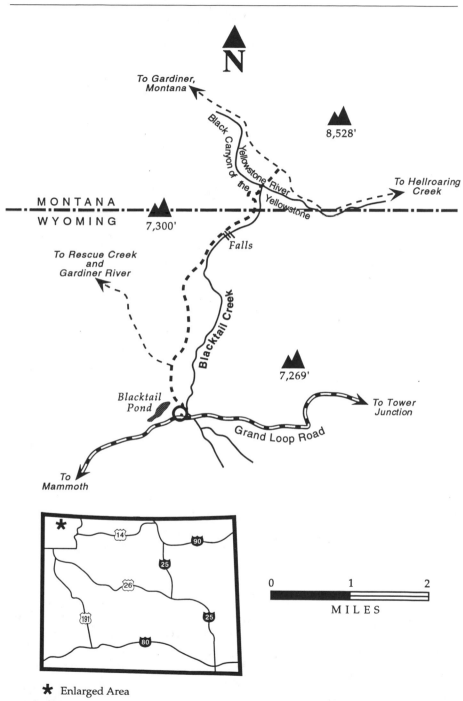

N

To Gardiner,
Montana

8,528'

Black Canyon of the

Yellowstone River

To Hellroaring
Creek

MONTANA

WYOMING

7,300'

Falls

To Rescue Creek
and
Gardiner River

Blacktail Creek

7,269'

Blacktail
Pond

To Tower
Junction

Grand Loop Road

To
Mammoth

14

90

25

26

191

25

80

0   1   2

MILES

★ Enlarged Area

HIKE 70 *BECHLER MEADOWS*

General description: An easy day hike into the exceptionally unique and little-known southwest corner of Yellowstone.

General location: Approximately twenty-four miles east of Ashton, Idaho, in the southwest sector of Yellowstone National Park.

Maps: There are several trail maps of the park available at the visitor's centers. The best and most current is Earthwalk Press's Hiking Map and Guide. Also USGS Bechler Falls and Cave Falls quads. Also the USGS Yellowstone National Park 1:125,000 vicinity map.

Special attractions: Many square miles of hiking through grassy and absolutely flat meadows. Long distant views and wildlife abound.

For more information: Park Superintendent, Yellowstone National Park, P.O. Box 168, WY, 82190, (307) 344-7381.

Finding the trailhead: From the small farming community of Ashton, Idaho, journey east on State Highway 47 for six miles to a highway sign pointing the way toward Cave Falls and Yellowstone National Park. Six miles along this road brings you to pavement end and Forest Service road 582 beginning. This well maintained gravel road travels 11.1 miles to where it is interesected by the well-signed road jogging north and to the Bechler Ranger Station. This more primitive station was originally an army post where soldiers were posted to protect the Yellowstone area before the official National Park Service was created in 1916. The trailhead begins northeast of the station's few buildings.

The hike: When the startling call of trumpeter swans greeted the rosy dawn, I had a feeling this day's hike was going to be unique. G. B. Bechler (pronounced bek-ler), when he mapped this southwest corner of Yellowstone National Park in 1872, must have known the same premonition.

The Bechler area is unique in that it's a forested land where you can hike for miles and miles and never gain or lose more than twenty feet in elevation. The first 3.5 miles of the trail wanders through a grassy lodgepole woodland that never varies its height. One of the few areas unscathed by the 1988 fires, the forest sports trees in all stages and ages of development.

Then the forests end, and for the next two miles you enter and walk through fascinating, undisturbed grassland meadows. Eons ago this meadowed area was a vast lake that silted in and allowed a grassy biosphere to claim it. If a packtrain happens by, you can actually feel the earth undulate from the party's weight and motion. Low and forested hills surround this seemingly endless savannah. Long-range views of the Tetons augment the picture. Swampy areas exist throughout, but the Park Service has spanned them all with various bridge designs.

At 5.5 miles the trail fords the Bechler River. The first week in August this formed a most refreshing, mid-thigh-deep wade a cross a gravel and sandy bottom. A single-person suspension bridge provides a secondary route across the river. In a short distance, the Bechler Meadows Trail ends at an intersection with the Bechler River Trail. From here you can return via the same route or make a loop circle back to the Bechler Ranger Station via this second trail (see HIKE 71).

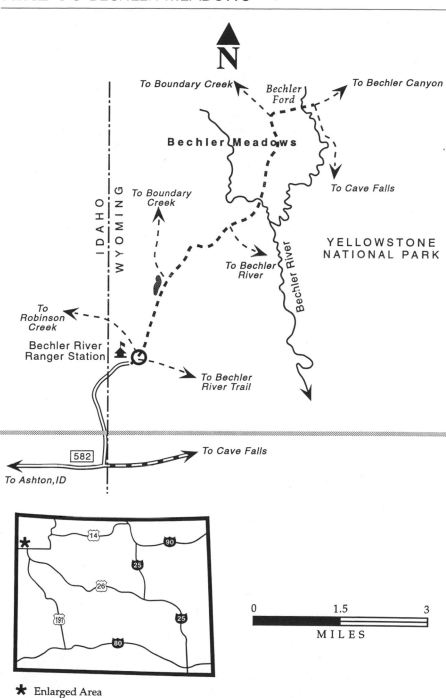

Vast sea of grass in Bechler Meadows.

There is no camping at the Bechler Ranger Station. If you arrive at night, you'll need to camp on the surrounding Targhee National Forest lands or at Cave Falls campground. Also, .1 mile beyond the trailhead is the first of many well-signed trail intersections—the Bechler River Cutoff Trail. Be sure and go left or north at this point to journey to the meadows. A wide variety of loop trips are possible in this area.

HIKE 71 *BECHLER RIVER TRAIL*

General description: A three- to five-day, relatively easy backpacking trip into an incomparable river canyon.

General location: Approximately twenty-seven miles east of Ashton, Idaho, in the southwest sector of Yellowstone National Park.

Maps: Several trail maps of the park are available at the visitor's centers, including Earthwalk Press's Hiking Map and Guide. Also USGS Warm River, Grass Lake, Old Faithful, and Buffalo Lake 15 minute quads. Also the USGS Yellowstone National Park 1:125,000 vicinity map.

Special attractions: The Bechler River in all its aspects.

For more information: Park Superintendent, Yellowstone National Park, P.O. Box 168, WY, 82190, (307) 344-7381.

Finding the trailhead: You'll need to follow the trailhead directions of the Bechler Meadows Trail (HIKE 70) to the Bechler Ranger Station, because you'll need to obtain a backcountry camping permit to hike overnight into the Bechler River Canyon. Then return to Forest Service road 582 and continue

HIKE 71 *BECHLER RIVER TRAIL*

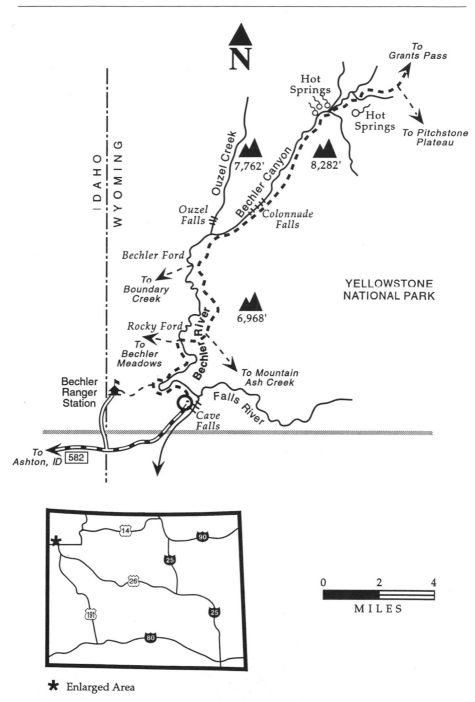

To Grants Pass

Hot Springs

Hot Springs

To Pitchstone Plateau

IDAHO

WYOMING

Ouzel Creek

7,762'

8,282'

Bechler Canyon

Ouzel Falls

Colonnade Falls

Bechler Ford

To Boundary Creek

YELLOWSTONE NATIONAL PARK

Bechler River

6,968'

Rocky Ford

To Bechler Meadows

To Mountain Ash Creek

Bechler Ranger Station

Falls River

Cave Falls

To Ashton, ID 582

14

90

25

26

191

25

80

0   2   4
MILES

★ Enlarged Area

eastward for 3.1 miles on what has suddenly become a paved road. Just beyond spectacular Cave Falls is the road's end and the Bechler River trailhead. It may be advisable to park at the Bechler River Ranger Station, which provides safety from car break-ins, as well as trail information.

The hike: The first .4 mile the trail follows the Falls River, with a series of impressive and thundering cascades. Then the Bechler River takes its own path, and for the next almost twenty miles you and the ever-changing Bechler River are going to make many acquaintances.

The first couple miles of level forested hiking reveal a river rushing in delicate rapids over a rocky-bottomed floor. The next couple of miles of level forested walking show you the quiet, noiseless and completely smooth face of the winding waters. Here, at Rocky Ford you get to taste a thirty-five-yard wade of the crystal-clear river. In August the waters were never over my knees (although it rises to knee/mid-thigh some years), but a walking stick was a necessity because the flat but rocky river bottom was moss-covered and a bit slippery. The next three miles of quite hilly forested walking place you near the Bechler Ford and the intersection of the Bechler Meadows Trail (HIKE 70). Another 1.5 miles of varied country puts you in the mouth of Bechler River Canyon and into yet another phase the many-faced river.

The rocky and forested canyon allows the river a mostly gentle and peaceful passage. But every few miles a series of impressive waterfalls tend to torture the smooth waters, Iris and Colonade Falls can be found 2.5 miles up canyon. Ragged Falls is located five miles farther. Designated campsites dot the canyon in well-measured spaces. Just beyond Three River Junction, the trail climbs out of the canyon, but not without a few more waterfalls saying adieu.

This trail actually continues all the way to the Old Faithful area, making it an excellent two-vehicle or drop-off hike. If you must return to the trailhead, be sure and hike the Bechler Meadows Trail to the Bechler River Cutoff for a unique loop experience.

In 1991, fishing in the Bechler area was catch and release. It will be for years to come.

HIKE 72 *BEULA LAKE*

General description: A short and easy day hike to a serene lake setting amid dense lodgepole forested hills.
General location: Approximately fifteen miles west of the south entrance to Yellowstone National Park, along the southernmost border of the park.
Maps: The Yellowstone National Park hiking maps are available at the visitors centers. The Bridger-Teton National Forest Buffalo and Jackson Ranger Districts visitor map also shows this trail. Also USGS Grassy Lake Reservoir quad.
Special attractions: Quiet, solitude, fair fishing and a unique microenvironment.
For more information: Park Superintendent, Yellowstone National Park, P.O. Box 168, WY, 82190, (307) 344-7381.
Finding the trailhead: Approximately two miles south of Yellowstone National Park's south entrance station, along U.S. Highways 287 and 89, the paved Grassy Lake Road jogs to the west. This is also signed as the road to the Flagg Ranch Campground (not the Flagg Ranch Village, which is .5 mile

Beula Lake.

farther south on the main highway). Follow this wide road west .5 mile to a "T", here turning right or west toward Ashton. The road is paved for a couple of miles as it crosses the Snake River, and then becomes a narrow gravel lane. The last four miles of this ten-mile passage represent some of the roughest two-wheel-drive road in Wyoming. Not quite .3 mile after you exit the John D Rockefeller Jr. Memorial Parkway and enter the Targhee National Forest, at the uppermost end of Grassy Lake Reservoir, a signless parking area to the north that accomodates about three vehicles forms the Beula Lake trailhead.

The hike: You don't meet many of them these days, but Beulas were quite prevalent among Wyoming pioneering women. Several land features in the state have been given the name "Beula", all of them named after settlers' wives.

A tenth of a mile up the trail, a registration sign will let you know you are on the right track. This mellow and peaceful hiking trail is ideal for easy family treks or for when you simply want to wander leisurely through the woodlands with no real exertion. The first .2 mile forces you to climb a slope, but the rest of the trail's three miles affords a gently rolling and amiable walk. As with most trails in Yellowstone, this path offers lessons in forest fire ecology. In fact, for a fair distance the trail itself serves as the barrier between a mixed burn setting and a spared forest.

The lake is surprisingly large and creates a unique watery oasis in a sea of dense lodgepole. Designated campsites dot the lake's western shore. It's a typical downed lodgepole forest walking adventure to circumvent the lake's shores. To make a complete circle, you'll also have to wade a few swamps. Birds and waterfowl, frogs and dragonflies are the denizens of Beula Lake. The atmosphere surrounding the lake's setting is one of almost overwhelming serenity.

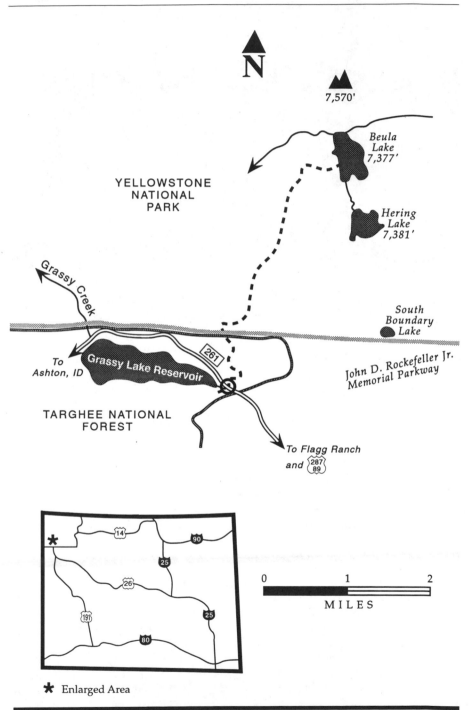

N

7,570'

Beula
Lake
7,377'

YELLOWSTONE
NATIONAL
PARK

Hering
Lake
7,381'

Grassy Creek

South
Boundary
Lake

To
Ashton, ID

Grassy Lake Reservoir

261

John D. Rockefeller Jr.
Memorial Parkway

TARGHEE NATIONAL
FOREST

To Flagg Ranch
and 287 89

14
90
25
26
191
25
80

★ Enlarged Area

Overnight camping does require a permit from the Park Service. Also, catch-and-release fishing is the rule. The lake, shallow and surrounded by brackish wetland, furnishes the only liquid in the area, so be prepared to boil or filter drinking water.

HIKE 73 *AVALANCHE PEAK*

General description: A half-day or longer, exceptionally steep hike into 360-degree vistas of the entire Yellowstone and northern Absaroka regions.

General location: Approximately eight miles west of the East Entrance Station in eastern Yellowstone National Park.

Maps: There are several trail maps of the park available at the visitor's centers. The best and most current is Earthwalk Press's Hiking Map and Guide. Also USGS Sylvan Lake quad and USGS Yellowstone 1:125,000 vicinity map.

Special attractions: One of the best kept secret trails of Yellowstone. Views over Yellowstone Lake and into neighboring states are astounding.

For more information: Park Superintendent, Yellowstone National Park, P.O. Box 168, WY, 82190, (307) 344-7381.

Finding the trailhead: Eight miles west of the Park's East Entrance Station or one mile west of Sylvan Pass, a small picnic area opens up the western shores of tiny Eleanor Lake. The Avalanche Peak Trail—unnoted and unsigned—begins directly north and across the highway from this picnic ground. A trailhead register and information sign occurs a few hundred feet up the trail.

The hike: East central Yellowstone Park forms a special parcel of land. For one, it's one of the few areas in the park that escaped the massive fires of 1988. The landscape remains green and fresh and invigorating. Secondly, the park's eastern border forms the western beginnings of the mighty Absaroka Range. Huge lava flows, some several thousand-feet deep, created the region. Severe winter conditions have turned that rock into cracked and broken rubble piles.

Be prepared. In 2.5 miles you are going to ascend over 2,000 feet elevation. The trail begins with steep uphill climbs and offers nothing but that for its entire length.

At .6 mile there is a tricky, unmarked intersection where a game trail continues northward and a smaller trail jogs to the east. Stay on the northern route as it heads into a grassy micro-meadow. So rapidly does this path ascend the mountain that you'll pass through variegated forests, lodgepole stands, spruce woods, and fascinating limber pine forests all in a mile's distance. At 1.2 miles the trail tops out on a ridge, the forests end, and you'll be standing beneath a vast and beautiful bowl, a semicircle of crumbly, rubbled, towering mountains that show you why this peak is named Avalanche.

Above-timberline hiking now predominates. Views soar over Yellowstone Lake, across to the Tetons to the south and toward the ranges in Idaho looming to the west. The last .3 mile—a high ridgetop walk to the summit—forms the easiest part of the hike. Now you stand amid 360 degrees of every view imaginable.

It's just as captivating, observing the tiny, mountaintop alpine plant species, so delicate yet so hardy.

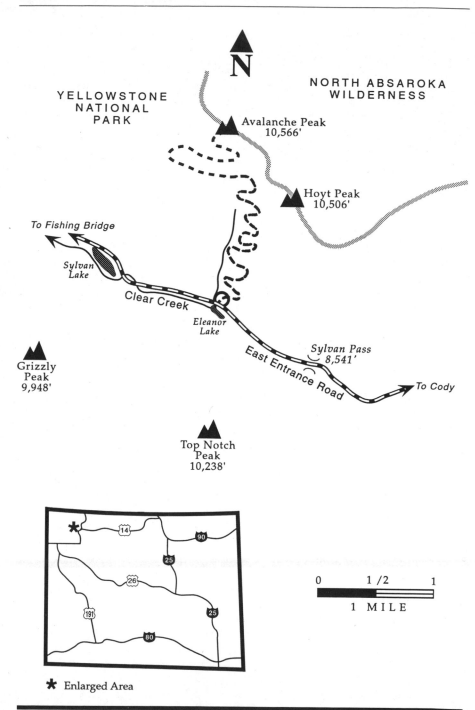

N

YELLOWSTONE
NATIONAL
PARK

NORTH ABSAROKA
WILDERNESS

Avalanche Peak
10,566'

Hoyt Peak
10,506'

To Fishing Bridge

Sylvan
Lake

Clear Creek

Eleanor
Lake

Sylvan Pass
8,541'

East Entrance Road

To Cody

Grizzly
Peak
9,948'

Top Notch
Peak
10,238'

★ Enlarged Area

0   1 / 2   1

1 MILE

This is not a recommended trail for those folks doing their first hike of the year. Some endurance and wind power are necessary. The landscape is steep and rocky, and tennis shoes aren't appropriate. During an average summer there are snowdrifts along the trail into July. The pitched downhill trek has the potential to demonstrate an old mountaineering platitude: "Rolling rocks under Vibram soles are no fun." Leaving early in the morning helps one avoid thunderstorms and other weather considerations. Do carry water and a snack to the top.

HIKE 74 *HEART LAKE*

General description: An easy seven-mile (one way) hike to a large and most beautiful lake.
General location: South of Yellowstone Lake and west of Lewis Lake, in the southcentral section of Yellowstone National Park.
Maps: There are several trail maps of the park available at the visitor's centers. The best and most current is Earthwalk Press's Hiking Map and Guide. Also USGS Mount Sheridan and Heart Lake quads and USGS Yellowstone 1:125, 000 vicinity map. Snake Hot Springs and Mount Hancock quads are optional.
Special attractions: Much of the hike to the lake is downhill. The lake supports loons, otters and occasional elk and bear. Thermal pools and geyser basins add wonderful dimensions to the trip.
For more information: Park Superintendent, Yellowstone National Park, P.O. Box 168, WY, 82190, (307) 344-7381.
Finding the trailhead: The well-signed Heart Lake Trailhead and parking area sits .5 mile north of the northern shores of Lewis Lake. Travel approximately fifteen miles north of the south entrance or approximately nine miles south of West Thumb, both on the South Entrance Road.

The hike: An old, pre-1870 Wyoming hunter, Chat Hunney, had this large Yellowstone lake named after him. Mapping the country soon revealed that the lake carries a sort of heart shape, and the spelling of Chat's last name was slightly altered to accommodate the new information. My history source didn't say whether Mr. Hunney was pleased, displeased or dead when this happened.

The Heart Lake Trail is a well-used, wide, and well-maintained trail with a gradual uphill beginning. After a couple of miles of easy climbing, the hiker can see the lake in a broad valley below. The trail then gradually descends into Witch Creek, which begins as a few steam vents on the hillside. Soon it becomes a small hot-water creek flowing into the lake. The trail roughly follows the creek down though a beautiful meadow and comes out at the Mauger Ranger Station at lakeside.

Rustic Geyser Basin lies across Witch Creek to the south, on the way to the designated campsites for the Heart Lake area. Caution is urged here and at the Geyser Basin Area, as the earth's crust is thin and the water is hot, up to 190 degrees Fahrenheit. The hottest pools are a beautiful deep blue, and the patient hiker can witness Rustic Geyser spout off at no set interval.

The Heart Lake Trail did not escape the fires of 1988. In fact, this area was

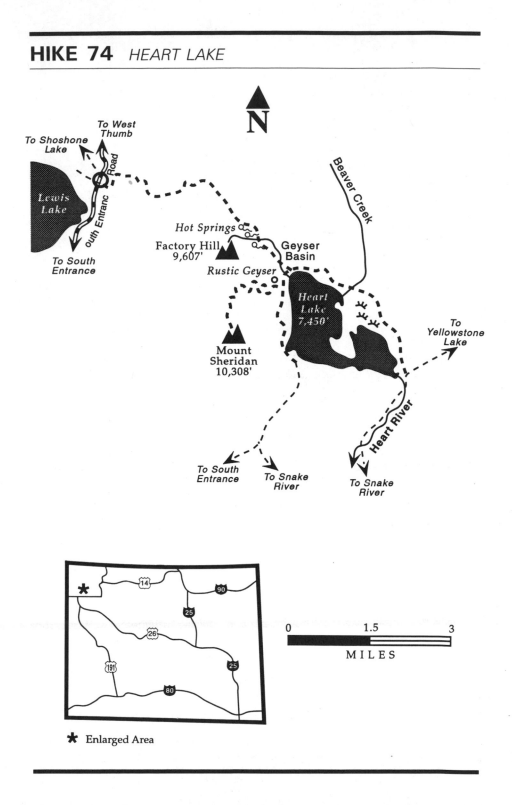

Recent fire ecology is now a part of many Yellowstone trails.

heavily burned, especially on the rise between the trailhead and the lake. Be aware of the potential of falling trees in the years to come.

Mount Sheridan, 10,308 feet, rises above the western end of the lake and offers grand vista for those willing to follow its steep ridge trail for two miles. This trail starts near the first campsite, just south of Rustic Geyser.

The Heart Lake Trail accesses the well-developed and extensive Yellowstone Trail System, and it is possible to continue your hike around the north and east ends of the lake to other campsites. These are located eleven miles from the trail's beginning. Heart River flows from the south end of the lake, joining the Snake River. Here the adventurous hiker can turn southwest or downstream and hike all the way to the South Entrance Ranger Station, or one can jog upstream or southeast and hike to the Snake River headwaters, out of the park and into the bordering Teton Wilderness. Actually, there are several hundred miles of trail options in this country. Consult your maps.—
Mike Gossi

HIKE 75 *PITCHSTONE PLATEAU*

General description: A long but very level and gentle hike into a vast and high elevation grassland plateau.

General location: Approximately thirty miles north of Moran Junction, in the southwestern sector of Yellowstone National Park.

Maps: Several trail maps of the park are available at the visitor's centers. The best and most current is Earthwalk Press's Hiking Map and Guide. Also USGS Lewis Canyon, Lewis Falls, Grassy Lake Reservoir and Shoshone Geyser Basin quads and USGS Yellowstone 1:125,000 vicinity map.

Special attractions: A unique journey into some severe forest fire burn remnants. Beautiful, open land and large, encompassing meadows.

For more information: Park Superintendent, Yellowstone National Park, P.O. Box 168, WY, 82190, (307) 344-7381.

Finding the trailhead: On the South Entrance Road of Yellowstone, about fourteen miles south of West Thumb Junction or eight miles north of the South Entrance, a "trailhead" sign points to the west and a tiny widened spot in the road, one able to accommodate three cars, forms the parking lot for this access to Pitchstone Plateau. It's not a popular or well-traveled trail.

The hike: The word plateau means a level, table like surface of high elevation. The French person who came up with this word had to have somehow visited Pitchstone Plateau in Yellowstone. It forms the living and best example of a "plateau" imaginable. Also noteworthy is the word "pitchstone," meaning "a glassy igneous rock resembling hardened pitch." The lava flows in this area represent the most recent volcanic action in the park, and the rocks scattered over the plateau's surface are black and shiny.

The trail diagonals up the eastern slopes of the plateau side for about .5 mile in a steep beginning. Then the land flattens out and the rest of the eight or so miles to the heart of the plateau has little if any up and down. The first 3.5 miles of this hike wander through some incredibly intense burn remnants of the 1988 forest fires. Eerie and bizzare are two apt adjectives for this part of the hike. It's as if some kind of alien death ray zapped the miles of flat landscape into black non-being. There are zones where nothing lives, including revegetative efforts by grasses and other plants. Almost no wildlife shows itself and no noise exists but an occasional tree falling in the distance. Even the breezes sound awkward because they're wafting through charred fence posts instead of pine boughs. The miles will either enthrall you every step of the way or give you the heebie-jeebies.

After 3.5 miles, the lodgepole and spruce forests show more beetle kill than fire kill. Meadows, some quite large in size intersperse themselves between the forests. 4.5 miles and you encounter what's called the Phantom Fumarole, a colorful and active, bubbling mudpot of gasses and hot water. It may be called "Phantom" because whiffs of its spent-fireworks scent have been noticable for the last mile while no indication of their source is available. CAUTION: Don't approach this thermal wonder. The surrounding ground is a catacomb of vents and recent volcanic activity. If the earth collapsed and you fell into any of these holes, you'd become the cooked phantom of the fumarole.

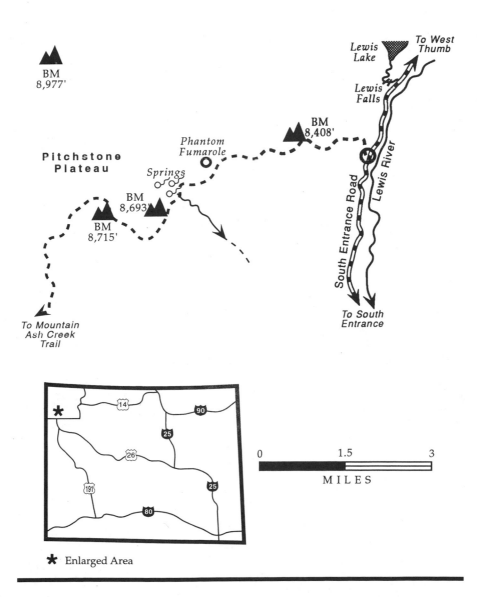

★ Enlarged Area

At 5.5 miles huge plateau meadows begin. This beginning massive meadow contains the first and only water on this trip, a stream emanating from several welcome springs. The one designated campsite happens to be here too. If you're the one who gets the permit and can pack to this area and camp, it makes a great home base from which to explore farther into the plateau.

The next couple of miles weave through the various meadows and forests leading to the endless plateau meadows. Here the trail ceases to exist as a pathway, keeping its continuity as a series of rock cairns stacked at various intervals through the short-grass fields. BE ADVISED: It is imperative that you always be able to return to the last cairn you passed. And don't leave the trail. Tempting as it might be to explore the massive plateau area, the Park Service frowns on it, and if you happened to return and couldn't locate the trail cairns, eight miles of hell-hiking may form your exit trip. If you can't find the next cairn on this trail, look around, but don't lose sight of the last cairn. You do not want to have to find your way back to the trailhead through this timbered and burned country without the benefit of a trail.

Pitchstone Plateau's open vastness culminated my journey. A point-to-point trail option continues southward, intersecting the Mountain Ash Trail. One can follow it all the way to the Bechler area (HIKES 70 and 71), or one can intersect the Grassy Lake Road south of the park (HIKE 72).

Moose are a fairly common sight in the Yellowstone backcountry. CHRIS CAUBLE PHOTO.

APPENDIX I

Federal, state and local land access regulations

One of the trickiest and stickiest aspects of traveling Wyoming is the reality of legal public and private land access. The state is both blessed and cursed with an absolute hodgepodge of mingled federal, state and private lands. Sometimes every other section is owned by a different agency or private party, and thus a different set of rules apply every mile. Understanding a modicum of the state's land laws at least allows you to know what choices are available.

• First, Wyoming law states that it is the public's obligation to know the ownership classification of the land you travel. Put in simple terms, the statement "I didn't know it was private land" will not hold up in trespass court.

• You do have the right to access public lands (i.e. federal and most state owned lands) only when a public road or right-of-way provides an access to that land. Here's a sticky part. If a piece of public land is surrounded by private land and no easement for public access exists across that private land, you have no right to cross those private lands, even for the purpose of reaching public land, unless you first obtain permission from the landowner. The landowner is under no obligation to grant such permission. And here's a tricky part. The law states that all public lands intersected by a public road may be used by the general public free of charge, but sometimes distingushing public roads is a real chore. State and county roads are fairly easy in that regard. But Forest Service and Bureau of Land Management roads, especially if the sign proclaiming the road's status has been removed, may be indistinguishable from private roads. As noted before, it's up to you to know which is which.

Actually, the reality of traveling Wyoming isn't as harsh as the above legal description makes it sound. Most private lands are posted as such, and most public access roads are well marked. In addition, the BLM has the state divided into 56 1:100,000 named quadrates and has compiled a surface management map of each section that details every square inch of land ownership. Ordering information may be obtained from any of the BLM offices listed in the hikes in this guide, or the Wyoming State BLM office at 2512 Warren Ave, P.O. Box 1828, Cheyenne, WY, 82001, (307) 772-2334. Another mitigating factor is that most of Wyoming's private land owners are wonderful people who are not averse to allowing access across their lands. If you can convey half an impression that you won't be harrassing livestock or leaving gates open or wrecking private structures, and if you can locate the owner, most will gladly let you explore or cross their territory.

A special land classification occurs on the Wind River Indian Reservation. This includes the defacto wilderness of the Wind River Roadless area and the slopes of the Owl Creek Mountains. Much of the land is exceptionally unique and wild, but to hike on the reservation requires a tribal permit and may require a hired guide. The 1991 price of the hiking/fishing permit was $35. Contact the Wind River Indian Reservation, P.O. Box 217, Fort Washakie, WY, 82514, (307) 332-7810 for further information.

Cultural Norms

You can count on sharing a number of your hikes with cows, pack horses, and ORV's.

Cattle gave the state it's beginnings. Cattle form a Wyoming way of life more deeply rooted than any other calling. Grazing is allowed in wilderness areas. It always has been. Remember, cows (and cowboys) won't bother you if you don't bother them. The exception to watch for, as with any animal, is placing yourself between a mother cow and her baby calf.

God created the mountains. Then He created cattle. Then He created horses to herd the cattle and more horses to pack over the mountains, at least that seems to be the case. Horse packers and outfitters are another grand and embedded Wyoming tradition. Long before hikers discovered they had legs, horses were carrying people and loads into Wyoming's wilderness areas. They're good people, horse packers. And they are good animals, horses.

The final reality I know God didn't create. But He's stuck with it and so are we. Machines permeate almost every aspect of our lives, and roads take us almost everywhere. Why anyone would want to inject more machines into the last sanctuaries of quiet is beyond comprehension, but off-road vehicles (ORVs), especially motorcycles and those four-wheel ATVs, are now a legal part of much of the mountain trail experience outside classified wilderness. The fact is, more people are claiming their right to earn the scenery via machine. I deleted a few hiking trails that I discovered receive heavy ATV use. A few others in this book are open to motorized use. But the areas are too beautiful not to enjoy hiking them just because a few other folks motor over them. The machines pass in a few minutes and the quiet returns. The people riding them are more often than not friendly. You can minimize contact by hiking ATV open areas on weekdays, before Memorial Day, and after Labor Day.

Maps and Trails

I planned the hikes in this book at home by scanning topography and Forest Service maps of areas. That often proved to be an incredibly inaccurate means of preparation, especially outside of wilderness and roadless areas. Hiking realities showed the USGS topography maps to be unfailingly accurate in one thing, Topography. Many of these maps were compiled in the sixties and seventies. So many more roads have been cut into the land since then. So many trails have been logged or rerouted or have disappeared from forest fires or lack of use since then. The Forest Service maps tell much the same story. Although usually more up-to-date than the topogs, endless inaccuracies and changes leave the trip itself as the final guide, and the map as an aid and beginning. It is probably best to have at least a couple of different maps to use as reference and even better to check with the nearest administering agency before starting out.

The other writers and I searched for a taste of Wyoming's unknown and unusual hiking to include in this book. Off the beaten track in many cases means just that. The track is no longer beaten. Land agencies, the Forest Service and especially the BLM, never have afforded recreation top budgeting and manpower priority. Trail maintenance and signing can fall years behind, and if its a hot fire year, they can be forgotten altogether. Add a rarely traveled trail in an unknown range to this picture, and you inherit the exciting pastime of route-finding added to a glorious hike.

A few of these hikes have trail portions that require a keen eye and trail sense to follow. I've tried to mention the tricky spots in the hike descriptions, but be aware that twenty five years of hiking these kinds of trails puts me at a real advantage. If you lose a trail, go back to the path's last known location and just stop. Look for cairns, which are rock piles of various sizes that mark trails. Look for blaze marks on the trees. The official Forest Service trail blaze is a smaller square atop a larger perpendicular rectangle etched into the bark of a tree. Many times I've located a faint trail by looking for horse hoof prints in the ground. Since most trails, if they disappear, disappear in meadows, scan the distant land for a sign of the path. And finally, use your maps. If they say the trail continues up a ridge or beside a stream, it usually does, and by journeying in that general direction indicated you can relocate the trail.

Actually, *The Hiker's Guide To Wyoming* is the most up-to-date guide available.

Hunting and Fishing

If hiking is your love, and hunting isn't, you may be wisest to not plan your hiking trips to Wyoming during hunting season. Unfortunately, that also happens to be the finest season for hiking. The dates vary every year, but from the beginning of September until about mid November, those hills and woods and prairies can sometimes touch insanity in shear numbers of hunters. Most hunters are courteous and safe sportsmen, but at the very least, wear lots of orange and don't tie a pair of antlers found on the ground to your pack during hunting season.

Good fishing and Wyoming are synonymous. The lakes and streams are productive, fun and rewarding for any angler. And they are regulated. 1991 Wyoming fishing license fees are: $7.50 for a resident; $35.00 for a nonresident; $20.00 for a ten-day tourist fishing license; $15.00 for a five-day tourist fishing license; $5.00 for a one-day tourist fishing license; $3.00 for a resident youth (age 14 to 19) license; $10.00 for a nonresident youth license.

There is also a twenty-four page booklet of area specific regulations. You can write for information to the Wyoming Game and Fish Department, Information Section, 5400 Bishop Blvd., Cheyenne, WY, 82006, or call toll-free 1-800-233-8544.

I really suggest getting a license if you fish. The game and fish personnel are not numerous, but they are ubiquitous. As a wilderness ranger, I saw those red-shirted officers pop up in the darnest places, asking surprised packers for their license.

Yellowstone National Park has separate fishing regulations and requires a special (free) permit. It's available at any ranger station.

APPENDIX II

Map Orientation by *Mike Gossi*

Maps are little more than rough and expensive toilet paper unless you know how to use them. Fortunately, map orientation is easy with a good compass and a couple of rules.

- Rule one: never assume.
- Rule two: carry a GOOD compass.

On the bottom of every USGS topographic map rest a pair of lines showing the magnetic declination. One line notes Grid North. This line, if extended, goes all the way to the official North Pole and Santa's house. The other line shows where the colored end of your compass needle will point and is called Magnetic North. These two norths are not the same and will vary, depending on where you and your compass are located.

If you have a round compass that looks like a watch face with little N, S, E, and W markings and little or nothing else on it, go buy another compass. Good compasses with swiveling 360 degrees of numbered markings and short rulers and direction lines and optional sighting/signal mirrors are much cheaper than search parties.

To orient yourself and your map, first turn the movable degree scale on your compass so that north or 0 degrees aligns with the arrow on your compass body. Laying your map flat and level and with the straight side of your compass body along the map edge, turn the map so that the red end of your compass needle points at the number of degrees your map says the declination is. Your map is now aligned with the world, or oriented.

To determine your position:

Your position is always in reference to everything else. Leaving your map oriented with the world, sight a prominent landmark (such as a peak, lake or large drainage, one you are absolutely certain is the same as one on the map) alongside the edge of your compass body. While sighting the landmark, note the degree numbers the compass needle is pointing to. Now put the compass on the map with the edge of the compass body on the sighted topographical feature and with the needle pointing at the noted degree number. Draw a line along the compass' edge. Your position is on that line. To determine precisely where on that line you reside, make a second and different topographical feature sighting and draw another line. X marks the spot.

To determine a course:

First orient the map and prove or find your position. Now lay the edge of your compass body along the line of your intended course. So that it will not be necessary to pull out the map every time you wish to check your bearing, align the N with the centering arrow on your compass body to your intended course direction and note the degree number the red end of your needle is pointing to. This simple procedure will allow you to check your bearing at any point along the way by making sure the compass' red needle end is still aligned the degrees noted. Then your intended course will be in the N direction. With careful and frequent checks, it is possible to navigate cross-country even in blizzard white-out conditions.

Please, please and please, practice these map and compass techniques before you wander into the field, which is to say, before they are needed. Enjoy and good luck.

APPENDIX III

Some Final Notes

The Forest Service is drafting plans to upgrade the road system around the Medicine Wheel Archeaological Site in the Bighorn National Forest. Many watchdog groups complain that under the guise of faciliting recreation, the ultimate plans are road improvement for future timber sales in this highly scenic and sacred area. Noranda Minerals has submitted an application to began major pit mining operations two miles north of Yellowstone National Park. Three major tributaries of the Yellowstone River and the survival of a crucial component of the Yellowstone grizzly bear population would be affected.

The Wyoming Game and Fish Department, after years of study, has realized that the state's early hunting season is drastically hurting the deer and especially elk populations by eliminating too many rut-crazy male animals when they are most vulnerable to human hunting tactics (bugling). They propose to eliminate the early season, but face overwhelming political opposition from outfitters and legislaters.

The ever-growing list of environmental attacks hitting wild Wyoming goes on and on and on. One needs but fly over the boundary between Yellowstone National Park and neighboring Targhee National Forest, or over the boundary between the North Absaroka Wilderness and Shoshone National Forest in the Clark's Fork area to witness first-hand how vast the tide of development is. The landscape that looks like a sheep-shear gave it a butch haircut is huge; the protected sanctuarys grow smaller and more crowded every year.

Without offering a long listing of the many axes chopping away at natural and beautiful Wyoming, and also without ticking off a long list of organizations trying to parry the blows, I simply and strongly urge you to get involved in protecting the special land you have just hiked. Perhaps one of the best starting places is through a group called the Greater Yellowstone Coalition. Over 80 preservation organizations belong to this single entity whose interest and actions extend from Yellowstone National Park through a radius of several hundred miles into Idaho, Montana and all of northern and western Wyoming. They are working to counter the many threats to the entire ecosystem and can serve as a springboard for meeting other like-minded organizations. Also, most libraries have a Conservation Directory available that lists the many ecologically-oriented groups working for the world. The major national conservations groups usually sport a Wyoming Chapter, and grassroot efforts exist most everywhere in the state. The Greater Yellowstone Coalition's address is 13 South Willson, P.O. Box 1874, Bozeman, MT, 59771, (406) 586-1593.

My final note forms a call. I'd love to know your comments on *The Hiker's Guide to Wyoming.* One doesn't just hike Wyoming trails and country.

The state is so full of verve and life and adventure and laughter and spirit that a portion of these qualities has to seep into the guidebook writing. It's my hope that you not only gained valuable information from this book, but also enjoyed the learning. Also, in the heat of organizing over seventy hikes and completing their many aspects by a deadline, if I said something was "east" when it should have read "west" and didn't catch the mistake in the many following rewrites, do let me know, so it can be corrected for future editions.

Perhaps the hardest thing about authoring a book like this is the knowing that you will be drawing even more folks to the isolated, special and/or secret spots you treasure. Perhaps one of the greatest joys in writing such a book comes from the same knowing. Until shown otherwise, I get to assume that those venturing into my beloved Wyoming as a result of reading this book are the ones who will return care to the land, who perhaps need what peace or beauty or glory a particular area has to offer, who will enjoy the treasure they are beholding.

If you have a special piece of Wyoming you know and care about, let me know. I'd love to hike it. Or, perhaps you'd like to write about it and share its story with others in a future edition of this book. I can be reached by mail through: Guidebook Editor, Falcon Press, P.O. Box 1718, Helena, MT, 59624.